04924743

THE LOST FLEET

BEYOND THE FRONTIER

INVINCIBLE

JACK CAMPBELL

TITAN BOOKS

The Lost Fleet: Beyond the Frontier: Invincible
Print edition ISBN: 9780857689214
E-book edition ISBN: 9780857689221

Published by Titan Books
A division of Titan Publishing Group Ltd
144 Southwark St, London SE1 0UP

First edition: May 2012
10 9 8 7 6 5 4 3 2

This is a work of fiction. Names, characters, places and incidents either are the products of the author's imagination or are used fictitiously, and any resemblance to actual persons, living or dead, business establishments, events, or locales is entirely coincidental. The publisher does not have any control over and does not assume any responsibility for author or third-party websites or their content.

The right of John G. Hemry to be identified as the author of this work has been asserted by him in accordance with the Copyright, Designs and Patents Act of 1988.
Copyright © 2012 by John G. Hemry writing as Jack Campbell.

Cover images © Dreamstime.

Visit our website: **www.titanbooks.com**

What did you think of this book? We love to hear from our readers. Please email us at: readerfeedback@titanemail.com, or write to us at the above address.

To receive advance information, news, competitions, and exclusive offers online, please sign up for the Titan newsletter on our website: www.titanbooks.com

A CIP catalogue record for this title is available from the British Library.

Printed and bound in Great Britain by CPI Group UK Ltd.

To Lieutenant Colonel Robert W. Lamont, USMC (ret.), who
wanted to see the Marines assault a fort; Commander Christopher
J. Lagemann, USN (ret.), who really would have made a darn good
admiral; and Captain Michael A. Durnan, USN (ret.), who (with
varying degrees of success over the years) has tried to keep all of the
rest of us out of trouble.

For S., as always.

THE FIRST FLEET OF THE ALLIANCE
ADMIRAL JOHN GEARY, COMMANDING

Second Battleship Division

Gallant
Indomitable
Glorious
Magnificent

Third Battleship Division

Dreadnaught
Orion
Dependable
Conqueror

Fourth Battleship Division

Warspite
Vengeance
Revenge
Guardian

Fifth Battleship Division

Fearless
Resolution
Redoubtable

Seventh Battleship Division

Colossus
Encroach
Amazon
Spartan

Eighth Battleship Division

Relentless
Reprisal
Superb
Splendid

First Battle Cruiser Division

Inspire
Formidable
Brilliant
Implacable

Second Battle Cruiser Division

Leviathan
Dragon
Steadfast
Valiant

Fourth Battle Cruiser Division

Dauntless (Flagship)
Daring
Victorious
Intemperate

Fifth Battle Cruiser Division

Adroit

Sixth Battle Cruiser Division	Fifth Assault Transport Division
Illustrious	Tsunami
Incredible	Typhoon
Invincible	Mistral
	Haboob

First Auxiliaries Division	Second Auxiliaries Division
Titan	Witch
Tanuki	Jinn
Kupua	Alchemist
Domovoi	Cyclops

Thirty-one heavy cruisers in six divisions

First Heavy Cruiser Division
Third Heavy Cruiser Division
Fourth Heavy Cruiser Division
Fifth Heavy Cruiser Division
Eighth Heavy Cruiser Division
Tenth Heavy Cruiser Division

Fifty-five light cruisers in ten squadrons

First Light Cruiser Squadron
Second Light Cruiser Squadron
Third Light Cruiser Squadron
Fifth Light Cruiser Squadron
Sixth Light Cruiser Squadron
Eighth Light Cruiser Squadron
Ninth Light Cruiser Squadron
Tenth Light Cruiser Squadron
Eleventh Light Cruiser Squadron
Fourteenth Light Cruiser Squadron

One hundred sixty destroyers in eighteen squadrons

First Destroyer Squadron
Second Destroyer Squadron
Third Destroyer Squadron
Fourth Destroyer Squadron
Sixth Destroyer Squadron
Seventh Destroyer Squadron
Ninth Destroyer Squadron
Tenth Destroyer Squadron
Twelfth Destroyer Squadron
Fourteenth Destroyer Squadron
Sixteenth Destroyer Squadron
Seventeenth Destroyer Squadron
Twentieth Destroyer Squadron

Twenty-First Destroyer Squadron
Twenty-Third Destroyer Squadron
Twenty-Seventh Destroyer Squadron
Twenty-Eighth Destroyer Squadron
Thirty-Second Destroyer Squadron

First Fleet Marine Force
Major General Carabali, Commanding

3,000 Marines on assault transports and divided into
detachments on battle cruisers and battleships

1

"When you find yourself going through hell, keep going."

Admiral John Geary didn't shift his gaze from the display, which showed his fleet in chaos as it tried to re-form in the wake of an attack by whatever creatures lived in this star system. "Did you just make that up?"

"No," Captain Tanya Desjani replied. "Some ancient philosopher said it. My father likes to quote him."

Geary nodded, only half of his attention on her words. Desjani's meaning was clear enough, if you defined hell in terms of a fleet far from human-controlled space on a mission to determine the strength and size of a newly discovered intelligent alien species, a fleet that had fought its way out this far only to face another alien species, which seemed even more hostile than the first. Or maybe hell could be defined as getting into a damaged survival pod as your stricken cruiser counted down the last moments before it self-destructed, to be frozen into survival sleep and lost for a century, only to be eventually found with death imminent and revived to discover that in your long absence and apparent death, you had been elevated to the status of legend. For an instant, Geary's mind flashed back to those moments, recalling how it had felt to learn that everyone he had once known was dead, that the war that had started as he froze into sleep was still going a century later, and that the people who had awakened him expected the great Black Jack Geary to save them from what seemed certain defeat.

He had managed to save them then though he saw no connection between the legend of Black Jack and who he actually was. He had managed to win the war with the Syndicate Worlds. And now he had to manage somehow to save this fleet from this trap in an alien-controlled star system very distant from any human help.

But he had done none of that alone. Without the support of this fleet, and of people like Tanya Desjani, he could have done nothing. And those who hadn't died in battle were still with this fleet, still with him.

"Your concern is noted, Captain," Geary said, banishing thoughts of the past to concentrate on the present. "We won't hang around here any longer than we have to." The fleet wasn't at rest right now in any event. They had been accelerating outward as the aliens tried to overtake them, and now that the immediate threats had been destroyed, many ships had altered trajectories and velocities, but both the fleet and the wreckage of the alien attackers were still racing away from the massive alien fortress guarding the jump point at which the human fleet had arrived. Orbiting the distant star and slaved to the jump point, the fortress was almost large enough to qualify as an artificial minor planet.

A squadron of destroyers tore past beneath and to one side of *Dauntless*, close enough to the battle cruiser to trigger collision warning alarms. Desjani's jaw tightened. "Tell those tin cans to keep their distance," she ordered her communications watch. "Admiral, request permission to assist you in getting this fleet back into order."

Well aware that his fleet more closely resembled a swarm of agitated insects than any kind of military force, Geary gave her a sour look. "The maneuvering systems have already produced solutions. It's taking a while to untangle everything and avoid wreckage." Fortunately, the great majority of that wreckage came from the alien attackers. There wasn't anything left of the destroyer *Zaghnal*, though, which had only taken one hit. The warheads on the alien ships were so large they had blown the destroyer into little pieces. *Invincible* had also taken at least one direct hit, inflicting massive damage on the lightly armored battle cruiser. That was the worst news, fortunately. *Orion* had been struck twice by the blasts from near misses while knocking out two alien craft on final approaches against *Titan* and *Tanuki*, but though battered, *Orion* was still reporting combat-ready status. Numerous other warships had suffered lesser degrees of damage from near misses, even the vacuum of space no protection against explosions that massive and that close. "We got off very easy," Geary marveled. "Did you see what *Orion* did during the last part of the fighting?"

"I didn't catch that," Desjani admitted. "I was busy watching *Dreadnaught* almost ram my ship."

"I'll have another talk with my grandniece when time permits." Jane Geary had been reliably steady and dependable, not flashy or prone to high-risk actions. Had been. Now she was flinging her battleship *Dreadnaught* around as if *Dreadnaught* were a battle cruiser. Wishing that new problems didn't develop as fast as he dealt with old problems, Geary called Commander Shen of *Orion.*

Shen's expression never varied all that much, so Geary wasn't surprised to see Shen looking ill-tempered. "How is your ship doing, Captain?" Geary asked. He could call up the information about damage to individual ships on the fleet net as quickly as the damage was assessed and entered, and usually he did so since that was fast and simple. But sometimes he needed information from the people on the scene, information that always contained important impressions and details that couldn't be found in the automated reporting.

"*Orion* can still fight." Shen seemed ready for Geary to challenge that assertion. "Seventy-one casualties; of those, thirty dead and the rest injured, five seriously. Two of those may have to be transferred to one of the assault transports for treatment. *Orion*'s sick bay can handle the rest. Main propulsion unit one is off-line, but repairable. Most of the damage is on the port forward upper quarter. Armor breach, compartment damage ranging from total to minor. We're sealing that area off pending major repair actions. All weapons and sensors in that area are nonoperational, reducing *Orion*'s combat capability by twenty percent for the long term. Numerous systems elsewhere in the ship require repair because of shock transmitted through the hull and structure, but we can handle that."

Coming from *Orion*, such an optimistic assertion was unprecedented in Geary's experience. "I saw *Orion* save *Tanuki* and *Titan*. Those ships probably wouldn't have survived a hit from something that could inflict that much damage on a battleship. You and your crew acted in the finest traditions of the service and have greatly honored your ancestors."

"That's what battleships are supposed to do," Shen replied in a gruff voice. "We bail out the battle cruisers when they get into trouble and can't handle things. Please tell Captain Desjani I said that."

"Are you sure you wouldn't rather tell her yourself?"

"No, sir."

"She's right here."

"Then she already heard it, sir." Shen paused. "Hell of a mess there. I thought we'd lose a lot more ships than we did. Interesting tactics. Is that all, Admiral?"

"No. Keep me informed about the status of your wounded. I can get *Tsunami* over to you if you need her medical assistance. And we need that propulsion unit online again as quickly as possible. If we tangle with the inhabitants of this star system again, *Orion* will need full propulsion capability. Captain Smythe will be sending *Kupua* over to assist in getting that propulsion unit working again."

"Thank you, Admiral," Shen said.

"Thank *you*, Captain." Geary ended the conversation, then looked at Desjani. "You didn't seem bothered by disparaging comments from a battleship captain."

"He earned the right to one comment during that fight," Desjani replied. "Besides, he saved my butt once when we were both serving on the *Pavis*. And he told you how much you'd impressed him, so I'll give him a pass this time on his otherwise-amateurish opinions."

"He told me I'd impressed him?" Geary asked.

"Absolutely. In his own way."

Geary shook his head, looking at the damage being displayed on *Invincible*. "Luck had as much to do with it as anything I did."

"Wrong," Desjani said. "Sir. Look at the combat systems evaluation of the engagement. When our formation scattered, the enemy required from ten to twenty seconds to alter courses and seek out new targets. We weren't lucky. The last-minute disintegration of our formation confused the aliens, just as you intended. Those seconds of hesitation gave us enough time to evade and blow away the enemies who hadn't already been destroyed. The ships that took advantage of that avoided getting hit, except for poor *Zaghnal*. She must have just had bad luck."

"And *Invincible*..." He ordered the combat systems to replay the moments before *Invincible* got hit. The order went out to scatter, maneuvering independently to confuse the attackers. All around *Invincible*, warships altered trajectories, but the battle cruiser didn't change either direction or velocity as seconds crawled by. Five seconds. Ten seconds. At fourteen seconds, *Invincible*'s thrusters started firing but hadn't been able to change the warship's vector before an alien missile ship slammed into contact and detonated. "He froze up. Captain Vente froze up instead of immediately taking action."

"And you're surprised?" Desjani murmured.

"Assuming he's still alive, Vente has had his last command in this fleet," Geary replied, hearing the savage edge to his voice. *Why didn't I relieve him earlier? Why didn't I find a reason? Now who knows how many of* Invincible's *crew are dead because Vente wasn't qualified for his command, and I had good reason to believe he wasn't qualified but didn't act in time. It's my fault as much as Vente's, damn it.*

"It's not your fault," Desjani said.

He stared at her. "How did you——?"

"I know you. Listen. Headquarters assigned him to command of *Invincible*. You had suspicions he wasn't qualified, but you can't relieve a commanding officer purely on suspicions. Otherwise, you might have taken Shen off *Orion* before this. You need *cause* to relieve a commanding officer. It's been that way for a long, long time, and for good reason." Desjani watched him. "Understand?"

"No. It's still my fault. We may have lost *Invincible* because I didn't act in time when I knew I should." As if summoned by his words, an alert flashed on his display. "Message from *Tanuki*, Admiral," the communications watch announced.

"Forward it," Geary ordered, and an instant later the image of Captain Smythe popped up before Geary. Smythe, commanding officer of the auxiliary *Tanuki* and the senior fleet engineer, for once lacked his usual jaunty attitude. "I've personally gone over the damage to *Invincible*, Admiral. I doubt that you'll be pleased to hear that your choices are simple and limited."

"She's hurt that badly?" Geary asked.

Space being as huge as it was, ships were often light-minutes or light-hours apart, leading to incredibly frustrating delays in conversations as messages crawled across millions or billions of kilometers at the speed of light. This time the fleet was close enough together that only a couple of seconds passed before Smythe shrugged in response. "It depends which parts of *Invincible* you're talking about. Many of her weapons are actually in surprisingly good shape. But what really matters is the structural and propulsion damage inflicted by those missile ships. It's severe. *Invincible* can't move herself, and if anyone else tries to tow her, she'll probably crack into a few large pieces. Give me a few months and a fleet dock, and I could get her going again." Even though that couldn't happen, Smythe clearly wished he could fix up the wrecked ship.

"We don't have either the time or the repair facilities," Geary said, his eyes going to the part of his display showing considerable numbers of other alien warships, some of them massive but, fortunately, none of them close. After the fleet's dash away from the orbital fortress guarding the jump point, that menace was now about seven light-minutes distant and getting farther away with every moment. Some of the alien warships were about three light-hours from the human fleet, but the main armada of alien warships had been identified at nearly four light-hours away, near the primary inhabited world in this star system. That armada wouldn't even see the light from the human fleet's arrival for another three hours; and then, even if they immediately accelerated on intercepts with the human force, would require days to get within range unless Geary decided to turn and race toward contact. But *Invincible* couldn't maneuver, making her a sitting duck even if the aliens had been a week's travel time distant. Looking at the huge warships that made up the center of the alien armada, superbattleships massing three times as large as the biggest human battleships, Geary had no intention of coming any closer to that armada than he had to. "Exactly what choices do I have, then?"

"Blow up *Invincible* or leave her for the, uh, whatever it is that lives here." Smythe looked and sounded unhappy at having to lay out those options.

Geary knew that his frustration was showing, but he tried to keep it out of his voice. No one liked delivering bad news, but he had learned long ago how easily a commander could discourage anyone from passing on important information by reacting harshly to the bearers of unpleasant truths. "We can't leave her. Not when the occupants of this star system have demonstrated such reflexive aggression toward us. I'll order *Invincible*'s surviving crew members evacuated immediately. Have your engineers prepare her for scuttling, and make sure it's complete. I don't want anything left intact."

Smythe nodded. "*Invincible*'s power core is still online. We can goose the output when we overload it to ensure nothing much is left but dust. However, I would very much appreciate the opportunity to take everything that I can off *Invincible* before then. She has a lot of equipment we can use instead of manufacturing new components for ships that need them."

It should have been an easy decision. To an engineer like Smythe, it simply made sense to recover equipment from *Invincible* to use as spare parts for other ships. But…"Tanya?"

"Sir?"

"How would you feel about having parts from *Invincible* used for repair or replacement on *Dauntless*?"

She shook her head. "We don't need that kind of bad-luck burden, Admiral."

He had expected that answer. Sailors hadn't changed for thousands of years. Why would they have changed in the hundred years that Geary had been locked in survival sleep? But he still tried to argue the point. "During the war with the Syndics, it must have been common to use salvaged parts."

"*Cannibalized* parts," Desjani corrected. "No. There wasn't much opportunity, and just as well. When I was aboard *Tulwar*, we had some components off of the wreck of *Buckler* installed over our objections during an emergency refit between engagements. The stuff *all* failed as soon as we went into action."

"Hasty work during an emergency refit—"

"It tested fine, but it was from a dead ship. We lost *Tulwar* when that gear went bad on us. No one in this fleet will want any pieces of *Invincible* aboard. *Especially* nothing from an *Invincible*."

He wanted to order the equipment salvaged anyway, but Geary knew that Tanya's attitude would be reflected on every ship in his fleet. Particularly given that the ship involved was the latest *Invincible*. Disbelieving popular superstition that ships named *Invincible* tended to be destroyed in action faster than other ships, Geary had looked up the statistics. And found in those statistics some grounds for supporting the superstition. Warships had come to have expected life spans measured in a couple of years at the most because of the bloody stalemate the war with the Syndicate Worlds had devolved into before Geary assumed command, but any warship named *Invincible* tended to have a significantly shorter existence than average. Maybe the living stars did find the name *Invincible* on a human warship to be too proud and provoking.

Turning back to Smythe, Geary shook his head. "No. Empty the spare-parts lockers on *Invincible*, but don't tear out any installed equipment. I can't afford the impact on morale of using anything that had been part of *Invincible*."

Smythe assumed the expression of an engineer having to deal with lesser and irrational mortals. "It's just equipment, Admiral. It's not alive. It's not haunted."

"Captain Smythe, it's not worth the headaches it would cause me." Morale in the fleet balanced on a knife-edge as it was. They should have all been at their homes, enjoying the fruits of victory over the Syndicate Worlds after a war that had lasted a century. But Geary had been ordered to take these ships far from human-explored and -controlled territory to learn more about the threats posed by a nonhuman intelligent species known as the enigmas. He had followed orders, the ships under his command had followed orders, but their officers and crews were war-weary and unhappy. Even a small thing could drop morale to disastrous levels, and to the sailors of this fleet, the use of parts from dead ships was far from a small thing.

"*Tsunami* is already coming alongside *Invincible* to take off her wounded," Geary told Smythe. "I'm going to tell *Tsunami* to evacuate the rest of the crew, but she may not have room. Since *Tanuki* is also close to *Invincible*, I want her to handle the overflow until we can redistribute the sailors through the fleet."

"Aye aye, sir." Smythe paused, then shook his head. "Those sailors are also coming off of *Invincible*," he pointed out. "You're going to reuse *them*."

"Thank you, Captain Smythe."

"Do you want me to leave Captain Vente aboard as a special case? I assume you are less than eager to reuse him, and Captain Badaya on *Illustrious* doesn't seem to want him."

"Don't tempt me." Even before his latest failure, Vente's arrogance and can't-do attitude had managed to get him on the wrong side of nearly every other officer in the fleet. Vente had also made a habit of balking at orders from Badaya, who was in charge of the Sixth Battle Cruiser Division, to which *Invincible* belonged. "Is that all, Captain Smythe?"

"Not quite." Smythe smiled. "We can rig *Invincible* so she doesn't blow until the aliens here try to board her."

That was even more tempting. Geary's eyes went to the casualty list from the recent engagement. These aliens had attacked without even trying to determine the intent of the human fleet and had thus far refused to communicate or respond to messages from the humans...

But a desire for vengeance was a lousy basis for making a decision of so much importance. "No, Captain Smythe. We don't know if it will be possible to eventually work with whatever these beings are. A booby trap like that might permanently poison any chance of relations, though I admit the odds of ever developing peaceful ones look pretty slim at the moment."

"A powerful lesson of what we can do to those who want to fight us might help convince them not to underestimate us, Admiral," Smythe suggested.

That was a good point. Geary pondered it for a moment.

Desjani spoke up while he was still thinking. "We don't know what these creatures can do. We don't know what tech they have. Maybe they could override whatever trigger we use on the booby trap. If that happened, they'd have *Invincible* and all of her human tech almost intact."

Smythe frowned, then nodded. "That is a very good point."

"Then rig *Invincible* to scuttle once our own ships are clear," Geary ordered.

"Very well, Admiral. We're on it. Oh, *Kupua* just reported to me that she has completed an evaluation of that main propulsion unit on *Orion* and estimates she will have the unit going again in ten hours. Until then, *Orion* can keep up as long as you don't do anything wild with the fleet." Just before breaking the connection, Smythe sighed theatrically. "All that equipment on *Invincible*..."

Geary looked over at Desjani. "I thought you would have supported the idea of turning *Invincible* into a trap."

She flipped a brief smile his way. "I have to keep you guessing. Besides, I was just being pragmatic."

On the heels of her words, another message arrived—the senior fleet medical officer beaming at Geary. "Admiral, uncrewed probes examining what's left of some of the alien attackers have found partial remains. Not a lot, and most of them are just small fragments, but we should be able to piece something together."

That sounded ugly. "Can you tell if they were human or enigmas?"

The doctor appeared startled at the question. "No. Definitely not. We're still trying to determine what they are, but I can tell you what they aren't."

So this was a second intelligent alien race, and it, too, was an alien race whose response to encountering humans was to attack. "Those ships that went after us had crews? All of them? They weren't automated?"

"Crews? Yes. The craft we could examine, that is. There isn't much left of many of the ships. We could have used more intact specimens, Admiral," the doctor added in an almost scolding tone of voice.

"I'll keep that in mind the next time we face an immediate

close-in fight with large numbers of attack craft belonging to an unknown alien species."

"Thank you," the doctor replied, oblivious to the sarcasm. "I do understand that things were a bit difficult, and, therefore, circumstances were not ideal for ensuring the best conditions for specimens. These craft were suicide attackers?"

"That's right." The tactics were disquietingly like those employed by the enigmas. Would every alien species they encountered turn out to be careless of not only human lives but also their own? "How long until we can get a picture of them?"

The doctor made a baffled gesture. "We're putting together a puzzle without knowing what the picture looks like, Admiral. There's no telling how long it might take."

"Thank you. Let me know the moment you have something recognizable." He might regret that order, since doctors could dispassionately examine things that churned the stomachs of average people. As a junior officer, he had learned the hard way that you should never sit down for a meal at a table occupied by doctors engaged in shop talk.

But that conversation brought up another matter. He was in danger of missing important things because so much was happening so quickly. Geary tapped his own communications controls. "Captain Tulev."

Tulev, aboard his own battle cruiser *Leviathan*, gazed back at Geary, Tulev's broad face betraying no excitement, just calm competence. "Yes, Admiral?"

"We can't leave anything behind here. I want you to use your battle cruisers, and any other cruisers or destroyers you deem necessary, to collect all possible debris from damaged or destroyed Alliance warships. Stay at the task until you're satisfied it is complete even as the rest of the fleet moves off." The battle cruisers, cruisers, and destroyers could much more easily catch up to the rest of the fleet than any battleships or auxiliaries. "In particular, ensure that no bodies are left floating out there."

"Yes, Admiral. I will ensure that no one will be left behind. All human remains will be recovered."

Geary leaned back, grateful that he could trust Tulev to coolly focus on picking up any human vestiges, whether bodies or equipment. But that brought thoughts of the aliens back to the forefront. He pivoted in his seat to look at the back of the bridge. Both emissaries of the Alliance government were still there. Retired General Charban was looking steadily forward with a bleak expression. Former Senator Rione stood beside him, her own face revealing little as usual. "Any responses yet to our attempts at communication?" Geary asked them.

"No," Rione answered. "These beings may be allies of the enigmas, Admiral. That could be why they attacked us as soon as they saw us. The enigmas could have used their faster-than-light communications ability to warn them that we were coming."

Charban frowned. "That is possible. But…" He looked forward again as if somehow seeing through *Dauntless*'s hull. "Those forts at all of the jump points, and in particular the fort at the jump point we arrived at. None of that was built overnight. The fortifications argue that if these creatures are allies of the enigmas, they are distrustful allies."

"Wouldn't you be distrustful of the enigmas?" Desjani demanded.

"To be sure, Captain, I would," Charban said.

Rione slowly nodded in agreement. "They could have gotten here by now. The enigmas who were pursuing us. But they have not arrived to join in the attack on us. My suggestion was wrong."

"Do you have any other suggestions?" Geary asked, wondering if Rione would finally break out of the odd passivity she had shown since the start of the mission.

"Yes. Leave this star system as soon as you can arrange it."

"I've already been advised to do that," Geary assured her. "And I have every intention of doing so. You emissaries keep trying to talk to whatever we're dealing with here. Tell them that all we want to do is leave, though we would be happy to establish peaceful relations with them. We'll leave quietly if we can, but if they insist on opposing us, we'll take whatever actions are necessary."

On Geary's display, the confused welter of human warships was slowly forming back into a recognizable formation, except where Captain Smythe's *Tanuki* and the attack transport *Tsunami* hung near the broken shape of *Invincible*, and where Captain Tulev was directing a scratch force in the task of collecting debris and bodies.

That left one more urgent task. Geary tapped his internal comm controls this time. "Intelligence. Is Lieutenant Iger down there?"

"Here, Admiral." Iger had a harried look but composed himself as he faced Geary. "We're analyzing everything we can, sir."

"Can you tell me anything about the creatures in this star system?"

"Not yet, Admiral," Iger confessed. "There's a lot of video being transmitted, but it's in some very strange format that we haven't been able to break so far. Not coded like the enigma stuff, just very different from how we do things. We'll get it. All I can say with confidence is that, whatever they are, there are a lot of them in this star system."

To one side of the intelligence officer's image, another picture appeared, that of the primary inhabited world orbiting this star. The image zoomed in at Iger's command, resolving into a curiously rectangular landscape. "Those are buildings, sir. All of it. They've got soil and plants on the roofs, but as far as we can tell, almost all of the land surface area on that planet is covered with buildings or roads. From a few construction or repair locations we can see, it appears that all of the buildings extend at least several stories underground and several stories above ground as well."

Geary tried to grasp that level of population density and failed. "Where do they get food?"

"The buildings, Admiral. Some of them, or some of the floors in them, are vertical farms. You can see the crops on almost all of the roofs."

"How many of these creatures are there?"

Iger almost shrugged, then caught himself. Junior officers did not shrug at admirals. "The planet is a little smaller than Earth-standard, sir, and has less land area. But it depends a great deal upon how large they are. As individuals, I mean. If they are roughly comparable to humans…" Iger looked to one side of the screen as he ran some numbers. "Something on the order of twenty billion."

"Twenty billion? On one planet of that size?"

"If they're roughly the same size as we are," Lieutenant Iger said.

"Let me know when you learn more," Geary ordered, then sat back again, rubbing his forehead. "What am I forgetting?" he asked Desjani.

"The fortresses," she answered.

"I haven't forgotten the damned fortresses. They're impressive as hell, but they're still targets in fixed orbits. We'll throw enough rocks at them to—" Geary stopped as Desjani shook her head. "What?"

"You're right," she said. "They are targets. So why were they built? Why are they still here? Why hasn't someone else blown them away already? I loathe the enigmas, but I know they're smart enough to throw rocks at minor planet-sized targets. Yet whatever lives here has gone to tremendous effort to build those fortresses. Have you noticed how few asteroids are in this star system? They must have used most of their asteroids to build those things, and, unless they're simply crazy, they shouldn't have done that if the fortresses were just targets."

Geary stared at the star system display. "They've got a defense against rocks?"

"We would be wise to assume so, Admiral."

"Let's find out. What's the biggest rock aboard *Dauntless*?"

Desjani grinned. "We've got a five-hundred-kilo kinetic round."

"Can we launch it toward that closest fortress without endangering any of our other ships?"

She ran the trajectory, then nodded. "Permission to fire?"

"Launch it," Geary ordered.

The kinetic round was simply a large slug of solid metal, heavy enough that even *Dauntless* jerked slightly when the object was launched at tremendous velocity on a trajectory aimed at the nearest alien fortress, the same fortress that had sent the attack force against Geary's fleet. "Sixty-five minutes to impact," Desjani reported, still smiling.

At least now she was in a good mood.

If he could have looked out a window in the side of *Dauntless*, if such a window had existed instead of sensors feeding into virtual windows and displays through the ship, and if *Dauntless*'s bridge had been near the outside of the hull instead of buried within it, the stars outside wouldn't have shown any sign of moving. If Geary called up an image of *Dauntless* seen from one of the other ships of the fleet, the large human ship would have seemed very tiny as it hung apparently motionless in space. There would have been no indications that the battle cruiser was moving at a velocity of point zero five light speed, or about fifteen thousand kilometers per second. Unthinkably fast on the surface of a planet, that speed felt slow among the vast distances between planets. If humans had been forced to use such velocities to travel between stars, the voyages would have required years and decades.

And he wouldn't have found himself stuck out here, much farther than any humans had ever gone before, dealing with another alien species that didn't seem to be thrilled at the opportunity to meet humanity face-to-face.

At least the Alliance government couldn't claim that he hadn't followed orders. He had definitely found the limit of space in this direction controlled by the enigma race.

Geary sat watching the fleet re-form around *Dauntless*, the other ships using the flagship as their point of reference. He took comfort in the familiarity and the expertise the ship movements demonstrated.

"Excuse me, Admiral," Desjani said.

He tried not to flinch, jarred out of a momentary sense of respite and wondering what he might have forgotten. "What?"

"There's something about those superbattleships these aliens have. Have you noticed their propulsion isn't proportionate to their mass?"

Geary glanced at her. "Less than in one of our battleships?"

"Yes." Desjani pointed at her own display. "Our systems estimate they maneuver compared to our battleships the way our battleships maneuver compared to our battle cruisers. That is, they need a while to get speed up, and they turn like pigs after a big meal."

He looked at where the massive alien warships, light-hours distant, were still orbiting, oblivious to the Alliance fleet, but which would surely turn to accelerate on intercepts with the Alliance ships as soon as the light from the arrival of the human fleet reached them. Then Geary looked at each of the jump points that offered escape from this star system, where the massive fortresses the size of minor planets orbited like deadly prison guards. "We can outrun them, but there's no place to run."

"Yes, but..." Desjani made an uncharacteristically indecisive gesture. "Those warships are designed that way for a reason. Some way they're employed. How would you use something like that?"

Geary shook his head, imagining an encounter with one of those superbattleships. "It would go through the fleet like a knife through butter. We couldn't stop it. Is that what they're designed to do? Charge into and through anything?" Another comm alert chimed. "Excuse me, Captain Desjani." The image of the fleet's senior doctor reappeared before Geary.

Dr. Nasr beamed with satisfaction. "We have a partial reconstruction of these creatures, Admiral, with a high degree of confidence as to accuracy."

"How do you stick the pieces back together?" Geary asked, hoping that the answer wouldn't upset his stomach too badly.

"There are various—Oh, you mean this time? We haven't had time to get the real remains and manipulate them. Those are still in quarantine. But we had virtual copies made and were able to play with those until we fit them together." The doctor made fitting together small pieces of once-living creatures sound like a fascinating pastime.

Next to the surgeon, a large image appeared.

Geary stared, speechless for a moment. Finally recovering, he tapped a control to forward the image. "Tanya, this is what they look like."

She gave him a curious glance, then sat looking for a while at the image Geary had sent before she could say anything. "You're kidding."

"No."

"Teddy bears." Desjani pointed at the chubby, furry image. "We were attacked by teddy bears?"

The creature, at least in this virtual reconstruction, was about a meter tall and covered with short, curly fur. The virtual image didn't display any blood or exposed internal body parts, just blurred filler in sometimes large sections where needed. The creature, with gleaming eyes set amid chubby cheeks, a shovel snout that seemed more cow-like than bearlike, and rounded ears above the skull, appeared to be... cute. "They're carnivores?" Geary asked the doctor.

"No. Herbivores."

"Herbivores?"

"Cows," Desjani said in a hollow voice. "Cute little cows.

Homicidal, cute little teddy bear-cows who build giant war machines."

Geary took another look at the image, his imagination supplying a malicious glint to the adorable eyes set in the chubby face of the teddy bear-cow. "Forward this to our experts on intelligent alien species," he told the doctor. The experts hadn't actually known anything about any real intelligent alien species until this fleet had penetrated enigma space recently, but they were still the best thing he had available. "And to Lieutenant Iger in Intelligence, please."

By the time he could watch the large kinetic projectile that *Dauntless* had launched reach the nearest alien fortress, the fleet had moved another three light-minutes farther away. Thus he watched the events unfold almost ten minutes after they actually took place.

The five-hundred-kilogram chunk of metal, shaped like an ancient image of a rocket in case it needed that streamlined shape to be dropped through atmosphere onto a planetary target, arced down toward the alien fortress. Traveling at thousands of kilometers per second, it held tremendous kinetic energy, which would be released on impact with its target.

But thousands of kilometers short of that target, the path of the projectile began bending quickly, so that it eventually raced harmlessly past the fortress, a clean miss.

"How did they do that?" Geary asked.

"Good question," Desjani replied. "Let's hope the sensors picked up enough to figure out the answer."

"Yeah."

"And we have to discuss whatever the sensors did or didn't see with different people for different insights," she added.

"I'm going to have to hold a meeting, aren't I?"

"I'm afraid so."

The main alien armada would be seeing the light of the human fleet's arrival in about another two hours, doubtless at the same time as they received messages from the orbiting alien fortress alerting them to the presence of intruders in this star system. Closer alien warships would already have seen the human fleet, but the light showing their reactions wouldn't reach Geary's ships for hours yet.

He had little doubt what those reactions would be. However, at the moment, the danger of further combat with these aliens was as distant as it would be for the remainder of their time in this system. There wouldn't be a better time for sharing his plans and receiving any inputs from the fleet's ship captains. Geary sent out the announcement, half-wishing he could just fight the aliens again instead, and half-fearing that all of his options from here on would be bad ones.

2

The conference room could really hold only a dozen people or so, but the meeting software allowed it to "expand" to fit the number of individuals attending meetings virtually. Geary looked down the long length of the table, which had apparently expanded in size to match the numbers of officers present. The commanding officers of every ship in the fleet looked back at him, along with other individuals such as Lieutenant Iger, the fleet's chief medical officer Captain Nasr, both General Charban and Emissary Rione, and some of the civilian experts on intelligent aliens.

A few others were hidden from sight and hearing by the rest of the participants except for Geary and Desjani. Those few, picked representatives from the former prisoners of war now berthed on *Mistral* and *Typhoon*, were being allowed to watch and listen to the proceedings. If their many high-ranking and self-important peers on those same assault transports knew, they would all clamor for seats (and voices) in the meeting as well, and that simply wasn't going to happen.

Far too many of the meetings held in here since Geary had assumed command of the fleet had involved far too much drama for Geary's taste. During the century he had been in survival sleep, fleet conferences had degenerated into political free-for-alls in which fleet commanders vied for support from their subordinates. When he was found and awakened, it was to discover that he, Captain Geary, was by far the most senior captain in the Alliance fleet, with a date of rank nearly a century before. That hadn't mattered to him, but it had meant that when Admiral Bloch died, Geary had been the next in line to command the fleet by seniority, by Bloch's own last command, and by the requirements of what Geary saw as his duty. Enough of the then-commanders of the fleet's ships had been swayed by one or more of those factors to agree to Geary's assuming command. The entire process, of not just soliciting advice from subordinates but of cultivating their support for his own position in command, had struck Geary as outrageously wrong. Back then, he had only dimly grasped how badly a century of bloody war had battered the structure of the fleet and the nature of its officers.

He was fixing that. Slowly and all-too-often painfully, but meetings now tended to be much more professional. "My first order of business," Geary said, "is to express my appreciation for the skill with which the fleet fought our last engagement. Well done."

He would have had a great deal of trouble saying that if Captain Vente of what had been the latest *Invincible* (but was now a rapidly expanding ball of dust following the controlled detonation of its power core) had been present. However, as Vente was no longer a ship's commanding officer, he had no right to attend this meeting.

Right now Vente was sitting in a spare stateroom on *Tanuki* oblivious to this conference. "We took some losses, too," Geary continued. "May the ancestors of the dead welcome them with the honor they deserve."

Captain Badaya scowled, his eyes on the table's surface. "We'll avenge *Invincible*. Perhaps the Alliance will finally stop giving that ill-omened name to new battle cruisers."

"It shouldn't happen again," Captain Vitali of *Daring* pointed out. "They've stopped building new ships since the war ended. There are no new battle cruisers under construction to give that name."

Geary's eyes went to meet the gaze of Captain Smythe, who made no gesture or expression but nonetheless conveyed his understanding of the same thing that Geary was thinking. There were new warships being constructed by the Alliance government if what Smythe and his staff had uncovered was true, but that fact was being kept secret from Geary and everyone else in this fleet. Why that was so was just one of the questions Geary had to resolve.

For now, it was best to get the conversation onto other tracks. "I want to make special note of the performance of *Orion* in the recent engagement."

Commander Shen nodded gruffly in acknowledgment of Geary's words as the other officers offered approving words and gestures. Most of the other officers, anyway. A few, perhaps out of lingering loyalty to the disgraced Captain Numos, kept their expressions neutral. And Captain Jane Geary seemed to be trying to suppress unhappiness at seeing Shen singled out.

"My crew deserves the credit," Shen said, his habitually dissatisfied expression in full force. Shen was no diplomat and seemed oblivious to the idea of currying favor with his superiors, but *Orion* had fought well in the recent engagement, fought well for the first time in Geary's experience with this fleet. Perhaps Desjani was right and, despite his rough edges, Shen would be the commander to finally turn *Orion* around.

"The second item," Geary continued, "is what we know about how the aliens diverted that rock we fired at their orbital fortress. The answer at this point is nothing. You've all been given full access to the sensor readings. I'd like to hear your thoughts."

Commander Neeson of *Implacable* spoke up first. "I thought initially that it might be magnetics. That is, a very powerful, highly focused magnetic field projected to divert anything fired at that fortress as long as it was the right kind of metal. But our sensors should have spotted a magnetic field that strong."

Captain Hiyen of *Reprisal* nodded judiciously. "Yet the activity matched what we would have seen if that were the case. Which means it was something that acted like such a magnetic field. Perhaps it would be equally effective against nonmagnetic substances."

"And this something would be...?" Captain Duellos of *Inspire* asked.

"I have no idea," Hiyen replied. "All I can say with confidence is that whatever it is must require an immense amount of power to generate."

"I agree. More power than any ship could produce," Neeson said.

Captain Tulev nodded, his voice somber. "So now we know why that fortress is so large. It must be to carry the power generators necessary to produce its defensive mechanism."

Since the death of Captain Cresida, Neeson and Hiyen were two of the best surviving scientific theorists among the fleet's officers. Having heard from the theorists, Geary looked to Captain Smythe. "What do the engineers think?"

Smythe spread his hands in a gesture of ignorance. "The consensus among my engineers is that the aliens can't do that without, as the commander remarked, projecting very strong and localized magnetic fields. Which they did not. Therefore, in a practical sense, we have no idea how they did it."

General Carabali, commander of the Marines embarked with the fleet, suddenly hit the table with her fist. "However they do it, their primary planet must have the same defense."

Everyone looked at her, then Desjani nodded back. "It must. Good thing we didn't waste any kinetic projectiles on a retaliatory bombardment."

General Charban was still staring at Carabali. "That kind of defensive system would be invaluable to us. To render our planets invulnerable to bombardment from space..."

He didn't have to finish the thought. During the century-long war with the Syndicate Worlds, uncounted numbers of human beings had died in such bombardments, and entire worlds had been devastated.

"How do we get it?" Rione asked, her voice harsh in the silence that had followed Charban's statement. "I agree. It would be of incalculable value to us. But how do we get it? They won't even talk to us. There's been no response to any of our messages."

"A raid?" Captain Badaya asked, but then answered his own question. "Even if we didn't have to worry about them launching another several hundred of those suicide craft against us when we approached that fortress, how do we knock down the surface defenses when our bombardment can be deflected? How do we land shuttles when they might also be tossed around by that defense system?"

Carabali shook her head. "Any group of shuttles trying to reach the surface of one of those fortresses would be annihilated by the weapons we can spot on the surface. If the fleet can't reduce those defenses, there's no way to get any Marines into those things. Not alive, anyway."

"What about full stealth gear?" Badaya pressed.

"I don't have enough of that to get a decent force in place. Even if they all made it down in one piece, it would be like throwing a thimble of sand at a mountain." Carabali paused, frowning. "We also don't know whether or not our stealth capabilities will work against the sensors these aliens use. Maybe they would. Maybe they wouldn't."

Badaya grimaced. "The only way to find out would be to try."

General Carabali's frown darkened into a thundercloud, but before she could erupt, Geary broke in. "I'm sure that Captain Badaya isn't suggesting that we try. He's just noting that we have no other means of being certain what the aliens can do. An actual assault in the face of those uncertainties would be a measure of last resort, and we're a long ways from such a point."

Carabali relaxed a bit, while Badaya seemed briefly startled at the reaction to his statement. "Yes. Of course that's what I meant."

"We do know one thing," Tulev pointed out. "The enigmas have been neighbors to these other aliens for unknown years. But they do not have this device. Our bombardments of enigma targets went home without hindrance. The enigmas, with all of their tricks and deceptions, with all of their worms and Trojan horses, with all of their combat capabilities, have not been able to acquire this thing."

"Maybe if we tell them that we're enemies of the enigmas—" Badaya began.

"We've tried," Rione broke in. "No response."

Badaya looked annoyed at the interruption by Rione, then focused back on Geary. "Admiral, what do we know about the species here?"

"We know they're bloodthirsty bastards," Captain Vitali replied. "Just like the enigmas."

Geary tapped a control, and the image of the reconstructed alien appeared over the table, the image seeming to be directly in front of every individual in the meeting.

There was a pause. Someone laughed. Someone else cursed. "Teddy bears?" Commander Neeson finally demanded.

"Teddy bear-cows," Desjani corrected.

Dr. Nasr frowned. "That's not medically accurate. Their DNA is unrelated to bears or cows. However, from the pieces we found and the use of them to reconstruct one of the creatures, we are certain that they are herbivores, they are intelligent, and their hands are suited to fine motor manipulation."

"Wait," Badaya said. "Herbivores? We were attacked by…" He looked at Desjani. "Cows?"

"Maybe they're slaves of some kind of predator that sent them on that suicide attack," a cruiser commander suggested.

Lieutenant Iger shook his head. "We've finally cracked the video system they use. So far we've seen a lot of images of these creatures but nothing that even hints at anything that dominates them or is an equal. Our observation of the primary inhabited planet also shows nothing consistent with the existence of a ruling predator class. Everything is uniform. Every building. Every square meter of land. There's no real variation in anything. A predator ruling class would have open areas around special structures."

Duellos frowned at Iger. "No variation? A monolithic culture?"

"That's what it looks like, sir."

"What's your estimate of the planetary population given what we've learned about these creatures?" Geary asked.

"At least thirty billion, Admiral. That's the lowest possible estimate." Iger heard the gasps of astonishment and looked around defiantly. "They're packed in. Shoulder to shoulder. Everywhere."

"Herd animals." This time everyone looked at Professor Shwartz, one of the civilian experts. "Herd animals," she repeated. "Herbivores. In the videos Lieutenant Iger has been able to access, we always see them in crowds, even when there is extra space in a room. They cluster together by choice. They are comfortable being in a tight group and uncomfortable being separate."

Badaya shook his head. "That may be, but cows? Attacking us?"

"You think herbivores pose no threat?" Shwartz asked. "They can be very dangerous. One of the deadliest animals on Old Earth was the hippopotamus. Others were... elephants. And... rhinoceros... es. Rhinoceri? The point is, all herbivores. But if they thought they or their herds were threatened, they attacked. Fast, determined, and deadly. Weaponry with sufficient hitting power could stop them. Nothing else could."

"That does sound like the engagement we just fought," Duellos admitted.

"And it fits the lack of communication," Shwartz added. "They aren't interested in talking. They don't negotiate because to them, any foe wants to kill them. Predators. You don't negotiate with predators! You either kill them, or they kill you."

"But they would negotiate among themselves," Neeson suggested.

"Or would they? Herd animals. They just do what the leader says, don't they?"

"At least thirty billion," Charban murmured, his voice getting picked up by the software and broadcast clearly. "What happens when the herd animals kill off all of the predators? The herds just get bigger and bigger."

"Why didn't they starve?" Badaya demanded.

"Why didn't humans starve when their population on Old Earth went from thousands to millions to billions? We were intelligent. We learned how to produce more food. A lot more food. And these are intelligent herbivores."

"We're a threat," Professor Shwartz said. "We've shown them images of ourselves when we tried to communicate. They can tell from what they could see of our teeth that we are at best omnivores, possibly just carnivores. They didn't become masters of their world by being meek or passive. They must have the ability to be aggressive when they feel threatened. That means they will keep trying to destroy us, before we kill and eat them."

"And they won't listen when we tell them that we don't want to eat them?" Duellos asked.

"No. Of course not. If you were a sheep, would you trust the reassurances of a wolf?"

"I don't think I would get the opportunity to do so more than once," Duellos replied.

"They're like the enigmas," Badaya said with obvious distaste. "They want to kill us, and they don't care about the lives of their own... people. They're willing to launch suicide attacks without hesitating."

The moment of quiet agreement that followed was broken by General Charban. "Captain, if you were a member of an intelligent alien species, and you had observed the behavior of humanity for the past hundred years as we fought the Syndicate Worlds, would you conclude that humans cared much for the life of other humans? Or would you decide that we were willing to spend countless human lives without visible signs of hesitation or remorse?"

Badaya reddened, searching for a reply.

"It's not the same thing," Captain Vitali objected sharply.

Tulev spoke, his words coming out slowly. "We know this, or we think we know this, but some of the actions of humans do not do us credit. We know this ourselves as well. To an outside observer, those actions might seem even worse."

The quiet lasted for several seconds this time. Everyone knew that Tulev's home world had been destroyed by the Syndics. The planet was still there, but the only humans left in that star system were a pitifully few die-hard survivors who had been occupying defenses in case the Syndics ever came back. Nothing else remained but craters and wreckage on a world that no longer held other life.

"I won't argue that," Badaya finally said, his voice stiff. "But the fact remains that *we* didn't immediately attack them when we arrived in this star system. *We* haven't refused to communicate. We have to treat these creatures as enemies because they give us no choice."

"If these are herd animals," Captain Jane Geary of *Dreadnaught* remarked, "and we're predators, then let's act our role and make them respect us."

"Absolutely!" Badaya agreed.

Wonderful. Now his grandniece was goading Badaya, who never needed a push to start being a loose cannon. Before Geary could reply, Desjani did, her tone dryly ironic. "These cows have guns. Big guns."

"I never liked cows," General Carabali added. "I like heavily armed cows even less. And I like at least thirty billion heavily armed cows least of all."

Duellos nodded. "It would take a long time to kill thirty billion of them. They have no lack of cannon fodder, and they're plainly willing to sacrifice members of the herd to protect the herd as a whole."

"All right," Geary said. "We're still mostly speculating as to the nature of these creatures. What we do know is that they possess a defense we don't against kinetic weapons, and they have a lot of very large warships as well as a lot of smaller attack craft. Since there are a tremendous number of them, we have to assume they have a lot of resources to throw at us. Right now we're cutting across the outer edge of the star system toward one of the other jump points in this star system. At our current velocity, which we have to maintain in any event while repairing battle damage, it will be forty-one hours before we reach that jump point. We'll remain on our current vector while I consider options and how to get us through that or another jump point without losing half of the fleet by going head-to-head with these bear-cows."

"What is our goal?" Jane Geary asked.

"Our goal is to exit this star system and proceed toward another star heading back toward Alliance space."

"That's a final goal, Admiral. As an interim goal, we need to eliminate the threat to us."

"Our mission is to explore and evaluate," Geary replied in what he hoped was a level voice. "These creatures don't seem to get on well with the enigmas, either, so I see no benefit for us in weakening them. The threat they posed may have kept the enigmas from turning all of their force and attention on humanity. Nor do I know how we can defeat them without taking serious losses. If necessary, we'll fight our way out of here and destroy anything that tries to stop us. But I would prefer not to lose any more ships or personnel."

Captain Bradamont of *Dragon* tapped a control before her, and a representation of one of the alien superbattleships appeared floating in front of her, clearly visible to everyone. Bradamont said nothing, letting the image of the alien behemoth speak for itself.

Badaya stared at the image, then nodded with visible reluctance. "Those superbattleships of theirs are very impressive."

"They *look* impressive," Jane Geary countered.

"Looks are all we have to go on. We know too little about what these creatures can do." Badaya turned a twisted smile on General Carabali. "The Marines have no enthusiasm for learning about an enemy's unknown combat capabilities the hard way, and I feel the same way about going up against one of those alien ships. Perhaps we can learn more, learn about vulnerabilities, but until we find those, Admiral Geary is right in choosing not to charge blindly into battle with them."

Desjani covered up a startled sound by coughing, then gave Geary a wondering look that he understood. *Badaya is saying we should avoid a blind charge into battle? Maybe he's becoming a bit less of a loose cannon.*

Captain Jane Geary, seeing that Badaya wasn't backing her, subsided, but only for a moment. "What about the enigmas, Admiral? Are we still worrying about them?"

"I'm still worried about them," Geary said, though in truth he hadn't spent much effort on that recently, with so many more immediate issues to deal with. "General Charban has suggested that the presence of defenses facing the enigmas indicates this species does not have good relations with the enigmas." He turned to where the virtual presences of two of the civilian "experts" sat. "What do you think?" he asked.

Professor Shwartz and Dr. Setin exchanged glances, then Setin spoke carefully. "The enigmas pursued us through space controlled by them, but this is not their space. Maintaining their privacy seems to have been a powerful motivation for them, but of course if they are not here, there is no danger of us violating their privacy in this star system."

"The species here was certainly ready for immediate action against anyone coming through that jump point," Professor Shwartz added. "As far as we know, only enigmas would be expected to be using that jump point, so as the general said, the defenses there must be against the enigmas."

"Which means we can focus for now on dealing with this species and the threat they pose," Geary concluded. "Anything else?"

Commander Neeson spoke up again. "A suggestion, Admiral. These aliens easily diverted the standard kinetic round we fired at their nearest fortress. Captain Smythe's engineers can fabricate some new kinetic rounds loaded with sensors. We can fire those at the nearest orbital fortress, too, one by one, and perhaps learn more about how that defensive system works by getting more readings about whatever field or force is generated by it."

"Good idea," Geary agreed. "Captain Smythe?"

Smythe glanced at the auxiliaries commanders. "I think we would enjoy the challenge, Admiral. We can also construct the new projectiles using a variety of casings. Different alloys, composites, and so on, to see how the defensive system handles them. I must add, however, that this will divert some of my resources from other assigned tasks."

"Understood." Other assigned tasks. Mainly the ongoing effort to replace equipment on every ship of the fleet that was reaching the end of its planned life span. It seemed that every time the fleet was catching up on that major problem, some other item demanded attention from the auxiliary force. "Get to it. Get my authorization before each launch, just in case we've seen some sort of advance in our attempts to communicate with the, uh…"

"Teddy bear-cows," Desjani said.

"Can we just call them bear-cows?" Captain Vitali asked. "I feel ridiculous talking about fighting teddy bear-cows."

"They are cute," Duellos said. "Not that it matters."

"It doesn't," Desjani agreed. "I can kill cute if it tries to kill me."

"We'll call them bear-cows," Geary said. He wished figuring out how to escape this star system intact was as easy as deciding what to call the species that was intent on wiping out his fleet.

"I have another question," Captain Hiyen said.

"Yes?" Geary prompted when Hiyen didn't continue.

"Why are we even here, Admiral? Why are we scores of light-years from Syndic space and much farther from our homes? Why are we facing this situation?"

A different level of tension came to life around the table. As Geary looked from face to face, the software automatically zooming in on anyone he looked at, he saw expressions range from unhappiness to stubbornness, with all too many clearly showing sympathy for the question.

He had dreaded that question's being asked openly because the answers were not simple ones. Not when a good portion of this fleet believed that Black Jack Geary was ruling the Alliance behind the scenes, and not when that belief was all that had prevented outright rebellion on the part of those military forces, which had suffered apparently endless casualties in an apparently endless war and blamed the civilian government for most of that. This fleet, for all its power and strength, had a hollow core born of war weariness, of too many demands for too long, of too many friends and family dead, of equipment being pushed past its designed limits, of an Alliance fraying at the seams from the strains of a century of all-out war only recently won, and of an officer corps that had been badly corrupted by internal politics while scorning the politics of the civilian government.

All Geary had to do was hold it all together despite everything that threatened to break it apart. And if he didn't hold this fleet together now, if portions like the warships from the Callas Republic, which included Captain Hiyen and the battleship *Reprisal*, broke away, then none of them might make it home.

Before Geary could answer Hiyen, Victoria Rione rose to her feet. "Captain Hiyen," she said, "if you wish to know why the ships of the Callas Republic are still with the Alliance fleet and still under the command of Admiral Geary, I am best suited to reply. I brought the orders from the Callas Republic, which set forth those commands."

"Why?" Hiyen demanded. "We have never been told why. And now we face death again, so far from the republic? Is it too much for those who have risked their lives and seen too many friends die to ask why we cannot return to our homes?"

Rione spread her hands in a helpless gesture, everything about her conveying an impression of sympathy. "I do not know, Captain Hiyen. You know that I was voted out of the government *before* those orders were issued, *before* those decisions were made. Because I was asked by the Alliance to serve in another role with this fleet, I was tasked to bring the orders from the Callas Republic with me. But I was not asked, and I was not consulted about the orders you were given. The new Callas government made the decision."

Captain Hiyen hesitated, then looked to Geary.

"The orders for your ships came as a surprise to me," Geary said. True enough. He had been planning on seeing those warships head for home along with those of the Rift Federation. "As I have told you before, I did not request them. I would be a liar if I said I wasn't happy to have your ships and your crews along with me when facing the challenges we have faced, but the Callas Republic, and the Rift Federation, are independent groupings of stars, which have only by choice aligned themselves with the Alliance. I can't tell them what to do. I don't want to tell them what to do. They and their people are free."

Badaya looked upward with a resigned expression. He had suggested using force to keep the republic and the federation with the Alliance, until Geary had pointed out how similar that would have been to the actions of the despised Syndics.

"Admiral." Commander Sinicrope of the light cruiser *Florentine* waved to indicate the officers near her. "This isn't merely a matter for the allied warships. All of us from the Alliance joined to fight the Syndics. We fought to beat them. And we did. I understand the need to learn more about distant threats before they become near threats, but this is far from the Alliance, Admiral, and we are facing foes who have nothing to do with the Syndicate Worlds."

Desjani was about to speak, but Duellos jumped in first. "Yes, we beat the Syndics. Under the command of Admiral Geary."

"No one disputes that, Captain Duellos. I would not have followed any other commander out here."

"And Admiral Geary had already announced that after this star, we would turn back for home."

"Yes," Commander Sinicrope agreed reluctantly.

Rione had remained standing and now spoke again, acting as if oblivious to the looks of barely veiled, or not-veiled-at-all, anger and contempt with which many of the officers regarded her. But her first words caused those expressions to shift to embarrassment. "I know I'm one of the enemy as far as you are concerned. Even though I have shared the dangers you have faced, even though I share them now, even though my own husband, a fleet officer, was thought dead and, though now alive and with us, has suffered greatly at the hands of the Syndics. Distrust me as you will. Think of me as you will. But think also of what we have seen in the space once controlled by the Syndicate Worlds. Think of the collapse of central authority, of spreading disorder, of worlds burdened by the human and material costs of the war and now facing the future without allies or friends.

"I want to go home, too," Rione said in saddened tones that echoed in the silence otherwise filling the room. Hearing how well she spoke, the emotion appealing to everyone here who shared those feelings, Geary finally realized how Rione had been able to reach the high political offices she had won.

"But I can't," Rione continued. "Because I need to continue working to ensure that the Alliance does not go the way of the Syndicate Worlds. This fleet is a mighty symbol of the Alliance. You represent the Alliance. You are in many ways the best of the Alliance. And if you go your own ways, if you declare that the time for sacrifice for others is done, what will become of the Alliance that has looked to you, that still looks to you, not just for protection but also for examples of the virtues our ancestors held dear? You will someday go home. All of you. Except Admiral Geary." She pointed to him so suddenly that he had no time to react and could only stand there as Rione went on. "His home is a century in the past, sacrificed in the first battle of the war, sacrificed for the Alliance. He saved this fleet, he saved the Alliance, and he will not betray you or the Alliance. I do not ask you to trust me. But trust him. Listen to him. Black Jack Geary will get you home, but if he asks you to leave that home, he has good reason. For the Alliance, and for our homes."

She sat down, apparently oblivious to the stares turned her way and to the openmouthed shock with which Desjani watched Rione until Desjani came to her senses and snapped her jaw shut. No one else but Geary, perhaps, could have spotted the way suspicion grew in Desjani's eyes as she banished her earlier surprise and hid her subsequent feelings about Rione's speech.

Captain Hiyen stood up, stiff at attention. "I withdraw my question, Admiral. Not because it should not have been asked but because it has been answered."

Feeling extremely embarrassed, Geary managed to find his voice again. "If that is all, thank you. I'll notify you all of our plans as they develop."

The images of the ship captains attending by virtual means vanished rapidly after Geary ended the meeting, the apparent size of the room and the table shrinking just as fast. Blinking to reorient himself to the actual size of the compartment, Geary turned to leave in Desjani's wake, only to find Rione standing waiting for him. "Thank you," he said.

She waved a dismissive hand. "I knew you were too humble and modest to say what needed to be said. Do you have a moment?"

"Is there something else?" He heard the accusatory edge in his voice, honed by Rione's enigmatic behavior for the last few months, and wondered how she would respond to that.

Desjani glanced back at Rione, her own face impassive, then, at Geary's gesture, stepped through the hatch and closed it, leaving Geary and Rione alone.

Rione nodded in reply to his question. "You know that the answer I gave in here is only a bandage on the wound. The problem still festers."

"Believe me, I'm fully aware of that."

"Once this fleet is on its way toward home again, it will help morale a great deal. You got them home once. They believe you will do it again." She paused to eye him speculatively. "You will do it again, won't you?"

This was the old Rione, taunting and sarcastic even as she offered assistance. "I hope so," Geary answered. "At the moment, I'm not sure how we're getting out of this star system, but I'm working on it."

"Not alone." She made the statement into something that sounded almost like an order.

"Tanya will help me, and I'll pull in whatever other help I need."

"Good. Working relationships sometimes suffer when they become personal." Rione looked to one side, her mouth twisting. "I'm ready to answer one question, Admiral."

He paused, eyeing her with renewed suspicion. "You've been acting like you've been carrying a lot of extra secrets ever since this mission began, Madam Emissary. Why are you willing to finally say something now?"

"Circumstances, Admiral. Assuming I did have orders unknown to you, the discovery of this new species of intelligent aliens might have triggered a different portion of them."

"I see. One question?" He got another nod. "Fine. What are your orders?"

She gave him one of her old looks, thinly veiled amusement with a hint of superiority. "I can't answer that one. Try another. I'd suggest asking what I will do, rather than what such orders might say." Geary sat down, gesturing her to one of the other seats. "Victoria, I'd be grateful to know what you'll do."

Sitting down, Rione met his eyes with her own. "I will do whatever I can to ensure that this fleet returns home."

"Is that a change?"

"In what I would do or in what my orders might have said?"

"Both."

"That's two questions," Rione said. "Or possibly three."

"Can you tell me where these orders came from?"

"No." She looked away then, her face suddenly bleak. "There's—I promise you, Admiral. I am on your side though my actions have been constrained up until now."

"Good." Could he believe her? At least she was talking. "Are you working with anyone? I assume you still have agents in my fleet."

"Perhaps."

"Do you know what happened with Captain Jane Geary? Why she started acting so aggressively?"

Rione raised an eyebrow at him. "I had nothing to do with that. I don't know of anyone's influencing her to act like Captain Falco's illegitimate offspring. That's not to say there is no one, but as far as I know, she's made that change on her own."

He didn't know why he believed Rione, but he did. Whatever had made Jane Geary change her behaviors couldn't be blamed on Rione's actions. "What do I need to know that I don't know?"

"That's another question." Rione wagged an admonishing finger at him. "You've become pretty aggressive yourself, Admiral."

He hunched forward, regarding her. "I've got a lot of lives riding on what I do, Madam Emissary."

"So you do." She paused, hidden thoughts passing behind her gaze, then focused on him again. "I honestly believe that you know everything that you need to know at the moment. You may know things that I don't."

"I wish I knew what was driving you these days."

Her expression went somber. "My priorities have never changed."

Which meant the Alliance, and one particular man. "How is Paol doing?" Her husband, captured during the war, presumed dead for years, and liberated not too long ago from a Syndic labor camp. Geary had received reports from medical on Paol Benan, so he knew Commander Benan's status, but he wanted to see what Rione said.

She didn't answer for a moment, then shook her head. "Medical is keeping an eye on him." It was a statement, not a question. "Watch him."

Geary felt unease at her tone. "Are you safe?"

"I don't know. I believe so. I suspect things were done to him by the Syndics, things he cannot recall, things invisible to those who examine him for harm. He is still a very angry man, Admiral." Rione looked directly at him again. "I have told him he must stay away from you, or I will leave him. That is why there have been no more confrontations. I am the last anchor to who he once was that he can grasp."

With the vast responsibilities weighing on him, with all the lives hanging on his decisions, Geary still felt a great guilt and sorrow over this relatively small human drama. "I'm sorry."

"Don't be sorry. I pursued you, and you cut it off before we knew Paol was still alive. Just get this fleet home." She was all business again. "You are properly focused on the current situation. I believe that General Charban was right that the enigmas will not pursue us here. But you cannot forget them."

Geary sighed, sitting back and rubbing his eyes. "There are a lot of immediate problems to address. What can the enigmas do now?"

"*I don't know.* Neither do you. *That* should concern you."

3

He glared at Rione, angered as much by his realization of the truth of her statement as by his own failure to spot that earlier. "I can only deal with so many issues at once." An excuse. Why was he offering an excuse instead of figuring out an answer?

Rione gave him an arch look. "A wise leader, which you usually are, doesn't try to do everything. I would suggest that you tell someone you trust to evaluate what the enigmas are likely to do."

"I can't spare Tanya for that."

"Is your captain the only person in your universe, Admiral? Is there no one else in this fleet who can think besides you and her?"

Geary smiled crookedly. "Maybe." He reached out to hit a command link but paused before completing the gesture. "Those prisoners of war we picked up at Dunai."

Rione nodded, her expression once again unrevealing. "The many generals, admirals, captains, and colonels who have made life difficult for you?"

"Yes. I want this question answered. Why did the government order me to pick them up on the way out here instead of letting me do it on the way home?"

"I'd just be speculating," Rione answered after a moment.

"Go ahead and speculate."

"There are undoubtedly some who would be happy if those senior officers never returned to trouble current high-ranking officers and officials."

Geary nodded, his expression hardening. "Then those same officers and officials would also be happy if this fleet didn't return?"

She stayed silent this time, as still and unrevealing as a statue.

"We are getting home," Geary finally said. "With all of those officers, assuming none of them do anything that requires me to order them to be shot." At the last moment he realized that statement applied very specifically as well to Rione's husband, Commander Benan, and couldn't avoid flinching.

Rione noticed. "You don't want to shoot anyone."

"I will order it done if it is necessary. You know that."

She sat back, looking thoughtful. "Do you know how many people there are who believe that gaining great power and responsibility means you get to do whatever you want to do, and you never have to do things you don't want to do?"

His laugh echoed harshly in the almost empty compartment. "Wouldn't that be nice?"

"Wouldn't it. Of course, some people who do attain such power believe the same thing. They get to do whatever they want." Rione eyed him steadily. "You know I feared Black Jack would be such a person. I was wrong. But now you want to know whether any of the

INVINCIBLE

former prisoners are cut from that cloth?"

"There have already been some attempts to interfere with the running of the fleet," Geary said. "I'm sure you're already aware of them."

"Unfortunately, I'm aware of nothing else. If their plots continue, they do not include me or anyone who reports to me in their confidence."

"Can you tell me anything about Admiral Lagemann? His record is spotless. Battlefield promotions got him to the rank of admiral, not politics."

Her gaze grew briefly puzzled. "Then why ask me about him? I know of nothing negative about the man. His name never appeared in any of the internal-security reports I've read in the past. Apparently he was too busy actually fighting the war to spend time politicking for advancement or maneuvering against the government."

"That was my assessment of him," Geary said. "But I've been wrong before, and if there was any dirty laundry in his past, I thought you would know of it."

"That hurts, Admiral." She almost sounded truly wounded by the suggestion.

"My apologies," he replied, letting the sarcasm come out clearly before finally activating his controls.

A few moments later, the figure of Admiral Lagemann appeared from *Mistral*. Lagemann, who had been among the few from *Mistral* allowed to view the recent fleet conference, cocked his head at Geary. "Something new already, Admiral Geary? We're already tossing around ideas for what to do to get through that jump point."

61

"Got any good ones?" Geary asked.

"Not a one."

"There's something else I need looked into besides the current situation here," Geary explained. "Something critically important. You and your fellow veterans gave me a very important heads-up about what tactics the enigmas might employ at Alihi. I would be very grateful if you could now assess what the enigmas will do knowing that we jumped to this star."

"You mean aside from celebrating that we jumped into this briar patch?" Lagemann asked.

"Exactly."

"That's a really interesting question." Lagemann stood silent for a moment, his eyes hooded with thought, then nodded. "We'll see what we can come up with. May I ask you something, Admiral?" Lagemann accompanied the question with a subtle glance toward Rione.

"Go ahead."

"Are we really heading back, or is that for public consumption to keep morale from heading for the nearest black hole?"

"We're really going back," Geary said. "And then all of you guys will be the government's problem."

"Not me. Get me home, and I'll retire and find a nice, quiet job on my home world." Lagemann paused again, thinking. "Something where I work inside at night. I've seen enough stars for one lifetime."

As Geary departed, leaving Rione alone in the room, Desjani stood away from the bulkhead where she had been waiting and walked at his elbow. "Did you have a nice chat, Admiral?"

"Yes, Tanya." They walked in silence for a while. "She says she's going to help get the fleet home."

"Oh, how wonderful," Desjani declared in perfectly flat tones. "That witch is still trying to use you for her own purposes. 'Don't do this because *I* want you to. Do it because the great hero Black Jack has sacrificed sooooo much for you.'"

"I don't think she wanted us to come out here, Tanya," Geary said. "I think she was forced as much as we were."

"You've said that before. You can go on believing what you want. I'll keep an eye and a weapon on *her*. Notice how I'm not even commenting on how quickly you decided to trust that woman again or how gullible you can be."

"Gullible?" Geary asked.

"Trusting. I said trusting, not gullible."

"You mean when you weren't commenting?"

Desjani turned a glare his way. "Someone has to watch your back, Admiral."

"And there's no one I trust more than you. But she wants the fleet to get home, too."

"When did that change of heart occur?" Still keeping step with him, Desjani gave him a sidelong glance. "Or is she just trying to distract you when you should be bore-sighted on resolving our current situation with the bear-cows?"

Geary waved one hand in frustration. "I'm going to refocus on that as soon as we're done talking. She said something about finding another alien species. Maybe whoever wanted to sabotage this mission put a higher priority on learning about another potential threat."

Desjani smiled. "Oh, darling, you admitted that someone is trying to sabotage this mission."

"I never denied the possibility." Had he? "And watch your language, Captain."

"Yes, Admiral."

"I think Rione is also worried about her husband."

"So am I. I still think he'll commit sabotage someday."

Geary barely managed not to glare at Desjani. He wasn't mad at her, he was angry with... fate, perhaps. Whatever had caused this to happen. "I've looked at Paol Benan's service record. He wasn't like this before he was captured. He had a good record. Now he's impulsive. Angry. Unpredictable."

"Well, duh," Desjani agreed. "The Syndics tortured him. There are ways to do that without leaving conscious memories or physical traces, you know."

He stopped and stared at her, finally grasping what Rione had only hinted at. "Lieutenant Iger told me we never sank to using torture though he also admitted that was partly out of pragmatism. Torture didn't produce worthwhile information. Surely the Syndics realized the same thing."

Desjani chewed her lip for a moment before replying. "What you and Lieutenant Iger, and the fleet doctors, are not taking into account is that for some people, torture isn't about getting reliable information. They do it because they like doing it, or because they think someone deserves it as punishment." She must have read his reaction on his face. "I do *not* believe that the Alliance ever permitted that. As far as I know, we always screened interrogation personnel very carefully to rule out those kind of tendencies. But do you honestly believe that the Syndics took such care?"

He had met some Syndics who didn't seem to be terrible human beings. Some had shown every sign of being decent and responsible. But he had met many others, usually senior leaders, who appeared to lack any sort of moral compass. "I'll tell the doctors to work on that assumption and see what they can do."

"It's a lot easier to break people than it is to put them back together," Desjani said, her voice low. "For the record, I wish it had not happened to him. Or anyone."

"I never doubted otherwise. I know Commander Benan is under medical surveillance. Do you have people watching him, too?"

"Twenty-four/seven." She paused. "They have orders to stop him if he starts to do anything wrong. I don't want grounds for court-martial; I want to avoid damage to my ship."

"Good." They reached the hatch to his stateroom. "I have a growing feeling that I need to talk to him again."

"That would be a very bad idea, Admiral."

"Just him and me," Geary added. "To see what he says when we're alone."

Her tone stayed remarkably even. "With all due respect, that would be a very bad and a very dumb idea, Admiral."

"I'll let you know before I try it, and it won't be until after we've figured out how to handle the bear-cows."

"That makes me feel so much better." Desjani shook her head. "The living stars must be guiding you. No human would consider a one-on-one with an unstable man *whose wife you slept with* a good idea."

She rarely talked about that directly, incidents which had occurred before he and Rione knew that her husband still lived and before he and Desjani had realized their own growing feelings for each other. Desjani's bringing it up now told him how upset she was. "I promise to discuss it with you again before I have a private conversation with Commander Benan. Now I'm going to forget that problem and work on ideas for getting out of this star system."

"Thank you." She smiled wryly at him. "One crisis at a time."

"Wouldn't that be nice?" The same phrase he had used with Rione now seemed apt as well, but it was just as well that Tanya didn't know he was repeating it.

He stood silently for a moment after the hatch closed behind him, alone in the stateroom that had once belonged to Admiral Bloch, before the Syndics killed him during "negotiations," and that had since been the only home Geary had in this time. What if Tanya had been captured by the Syndics while the war still raged? What if she were somehow captured now by the scattered and broken pieces that had replaced Syndicate Worlds' authority in much of what had once been Syndic space? What would be done to the person closest to the great Black Jack Geary in the name of gaining information or of pressuring him, or simply out of a desire for revenge?

He walled off the thought. Admitting such a possibility, considering such an outcome, would paralyze him.

As Geary watched the fleet brake at maximum capability past the looming bulk of the bear-cow fortress, the wave of hundreds of missile craft launched by the fortress caught the leading edge of the fleet. Massive explosions rippled down the length of the human formation as the suicide attackers drove their craft straight into scores of warships and auxiliaries.

He canceled the simulation with a grunt of disgust. *I've tried every possible angle of approach, every possible variation in velocity, but I can't get around the fact that the fortress is* there, *and I have to take the fleet* there *where the jump point is, and it can't be going faster than point one light speed when it gets there.*

There was something extremely aggravating about having literally the entire universe open before you and yet being unable to go where you needed to go.

Geary reached for the comm panel, then hesitated as he saw the time. It was well after normal working hours, the passageways of *Dauntless* darkened to simulate the day/night cycle that humans favored and almost empty of personnel, with only the night watch on duty. He wanted to talk this over with Desjani, but Admiral Timbale's warning that he and Tanya were being watched for any signs of unprofessional behavior couldn't be ignored. Tanya wouldn't do anything improper for a subordinate of his in the chain of command, but that didn't mean innocent activity couldn't be willfully misconstrued, especially if it involved her visiting his stateroom at such a time.

Hell. He had a job to do. Geary sent the request for a call, then waited until her window popped up nearby.

Tanya was in her own stateroom, which was good to see given the late hour. Sometimes he thought she lived on the bridge on the *Dauntless*, which wasn't the best thing for her or for her own subordinates. "Good evening, Admiral. What's up?"

"Are you busy?"

She looked back at him. "I'm commanding officer of a battle cruiser. Of course I'm busy. Why?"

"I'm stuck." Geary waved toward the display over the table in his stateroom. "I can figure out how to avoid the bear-cow warships, but I can't figure out how to get past the fortresses at the jump exits. If I didn't have to worry about the warships, I might be able to come up with a means of knocking out a fortress, but I don't have that luxury."

"It's all one problem," Desjani agreed. "I personally tend to focus on the warships, but the biggest problems are those fortresses. Do we have to get within range of their weapons?"

"No," Geary said gloomily. "We can pass outside the likely threat radius of anything mounted on the fortresses. What we can't possibly avoid is the swarm of missile craft that the fortress will launch to intercept us, knowing exactly where we have to go to get to the jump exit. Any ideas?"

"I'd tell you if I'd come up with any. But I'm just a battle cruiser commander. You're Black Jack Geary."

"You know I don't like that nickname. Can you come down and go over this stuff with me?"

Desjani laughed. "Oh, that would look good. Me sneaking into your stateroom in the middle of the night. Should I put on something sexy, like my full-dress uniform?"

"You do look awfully good in that. Dammit, Tanya, we're married."

"Off my ship we're married, Admiral. On my ship, we're captain and admiral. You knew that would be the case."

"It's the sort of thing that's easier to live with in theory than in practice," Geary complained. "Besides, this is purely professional. Tanya, you've got a great tactical mind. I need some of that."

"You sure know how to sweet-talk a girl." Tanya shook her head. "I think you need sleep more than you need my, um, tactical expertise. We've all been trying to figure out how to get past the fortress at the jump point we want to use. None of us has figured out how to do it. We need to try something different."

"Such as?"

"What else is there? The home world of these bear-cows... no. We've already been thinking about what their warships are like."

"We don't know how they'll employ those warships, though," Geary said.

"No, but so far we've seen them all turn and head for us. And we've seen how those missile ships engaged us." She shrugged. "It's not a lot to go on, but we know a little about how they think. Maybe that's what we should focus on. Tomorrow. You can't think without sleep. Go to bed now, and we'll talk in the morning."

"Are you going to sleep?" Geary demanded.

"I'm a battle cruiser commander. Didn't we already go over that? Sleep is a luxury."

"I could order you to go to sleep."

"Yes, you could," Desjani agreed. "You'd regret it, but you could. If you insist on staying awake, think about how the bear-cows think so you can try to understand the enemy. That's what you ended up doing with the enigmas, and that's my best advice."

After the call ended, he sat in his darkened stateroom, thinking about her advice. Know the enemy. That was a very old piece of wisdom. And Tanya was right. He had been focusing solely on what his own forces could do and, physically, what the enemy forces should be able to do. Never mind what these aliens *could* do, what *would* the bear-cows do? Thinking that he had never expected to be asking himself that question, Geary started searching for answers. There were still precious few things known about the bear-cows, mainly some short assessments from Lieutenant Iger and the civilian experts, which were filled mostly with words like "unknown," "assume," "estimate," and "possibility," so he started looking up information on actual bears.

The original bear had been found on Old Earth, but humanity had brought some bears with them into space, planting the species on distant worlds, and encountered on some other worlds animals which had bearlike characteristics enough to be added to the general term. Of course, technically, in terms of DNA, evolution, and countless other factors, those were all very specifically distinct species. But to the average human, all of those creatures were "bears" even though that attitude drove zoologists crazy.

None of what he found on bears seemed to be useful. Bears were fairly solitary animals, especially compared to cows. One thing that seemed clear was that the bear-cows liked living close together. Bears were also omnivores, and continued analysis of the remains they had recovered had confirmed that the bear-cows were pure herbivores.

He looked up cows, and cattle, and bulls, and herds, and everything else that came to mind, reading descriptions, analyses, watching videos (some of which were tagged as coming from Old Earth itself) and letting his mind roam free as he did so.

Geary found himself thinking about those superbattleships.

They weren't inherently slower than the much smaller human battleships. Given time, the bear-cow superbattleships could reach the same velocities as the human warships. They were doing so now, accelerating steadily on an intercept with his fleet. But that acceleration would take more time, significantly more time, and attempting to alter their trajectories using thrusters would also take more time. It wasn't just the relatively weak propulsion, it was also the greater mass of the superbattleships. Getting that much mass to turn took a lot of power or a lot of time, and the superbattleships didn't have the power.

Like this video he was watching. A charging bull, thundering ahead, missing his target, slewing around to face a more nimble opponent in the form of a man wearing some sort of garish costume, but the man danced away from the bull, anticipating its moves...

Geary looked at the frozen images of his last simulation, still floating above the table. The massive fortress, the wave of missile craft, the bear-cow armada outmaneuvered and out of position well off to one side. That was how he had done every simulation, outmaneuvering the bear-cow armada so it was out of the way. But if you could maneuver the armada into going somewhere, then maybe...

"Tanya!"

He had used the command override without thinking, blasting his message through her comm without her having a chance to wake and accept it, and now Tanya's image blinked blearily at him. "This better really be about my tactical expertise, Admiral, since you seem to have ignored my advice while I took yours."

"I followed your other advice. Tanya, I think I know how to do it, but I'm not good enough at maneuvering to make it work. I need you to work up the maneuvers and see if it's plausible."

"Now?"

Geary hesitated, suddenly aware of the time. Hours had passed while he flipped through research files. Yet Tanya had asked the question in all seriousness. She would jump right on the problem if he asked her because she was a damned fine officer. "Uh... no. We're still a long ways from the jump point we need to use, and that bear-cow armada is a long ways from intercept. You can look at it in the morning. Go ahead and go back to sleep."

That earned him a flat look that promised retribution at some future time. "You wake me up," Desjani said, "tell me you have a possible solution, then tell me to get back to sleep. Thank you, *sir*. Send me your idea. I might as well look at it since the odds of my getting any more sleep before the ship's day begins seem to be very remote. Not that there's much time left before the ship's day begins, is there?"

Maybe she would forgive him if the idea proved to be workable.

The bear-cow armada continued to grow in size as individual ships joined up, the entire force continuing on a path to intercept the human fleet. The human fleet hadn't altered its own vector, still curving through the outer edges of the star system toward the next jump point. If no one altered speeds or trajectories, in thirty-two hours, the fleet would come within estimated range of the missile ships based on the alien fortress, and in thirty-five hours, the alien armada would intercept whatever was left of the human fleet after that.

Geary sat looking at the display, wondering what Desjani would think of his idea. At least she hadn't already dismissed it as unworkable. Since no one had provided him with any alternative ideas as of yet, he had to keep hoping it could work.

Worn-out, but too keyed up to sleep, he left his stateroom to walk the passageways of *Dauntless* as the morning crew came on duty. They had to see him, had to see the admiral looking confident and calm. He didn't feel particularly confident or calm, but figuring out how to look that way regardless was an important part of being an officer. *Don't worry too much about the sailors seeing you get a little worried sometimes,* one of his chief petty officers had told Geary when he was a lieutenant. *That just tells them you're smart enough to know when to worry. Don't look too worried, or they'll think you don't know what to do. And, for the love of your ancestors, never look like you're never worried. That'll make the crew think you're either an idiot or a fool. They know officers are human, and no human with half a brain is never worried. But as long as you seem to know what you're doing, they'll follow you.*

The memory of a woman who had probably died eighty or more years ago in the first decades of the war with the Syndics, brought a smile to Geary's lips. The Master Chief Gioninni he had met a while back didn't have the same last name, but that didn't mean he couldn't have been a descendant of Senior Chief Voss. Certainly he seemed to have the same genes for conniving and chicanery that had made Voss extremely valuable to then-Lieutenant Geary, as well as a constant source of anxiety.

The crew members he passed saw Geary's smile, and their own worried expressions faded into confidence. The admiral obviously had the situation well in hand. *It's a good thing that Desjani is the only person on this ship who can read my mind,* he thought wryly.

His walk brought him past the worship spaces, where members of the crew could follow their own practices in privacy. Geary chose a small room and sat down alone, lighting the small candle that waited there. *Ancestors, help me make the right decisions.* What more could he ask? But he shouldn't just ask for things. *My thanks for helping to bring us this far.*

He was starting to stand when Geary remembered one other issue and sat back down. *Commander Michael Geary. We still don't know if you died when your ship* Repulse *was destroyed. Are you there with our ancestors?* He tried to sense a response and felt nothing. *Your sister, my grandniece, is acting odd. I don't know what's going on with her. It's more than just a much higher level of aggressiveness. That's just a symptom of something. But what? If you know, please help me understand.*

And if you're still alive, captive of the Syndics, I'll find you and liberate you someday. I won't stop trying. I promise.

Geary went back to his stateroom after that. He felt weary. Thinking about his grandniece and very-probably-dead grandnephew, the descendants of his own brother, who had aged and died long ago, had brought to the fore memories of that brother. The weight of the past had come down upon him again, and he could no longer smile, thinking of those who had died while he was in survival sleep for a century. Fortunately, there was always much to be done, and he could seek a small form of oblivion in the mass of work.

Once back in his stateroom, Geary paged through the multitude of messages in his queue. The fleet commander received hundreds a day, only a few dealing with major factors requiring decisions from him. But to make those big decisions he needed to know a lot of little things, so many other bits of information and reports were either forwarded to him or just passed on for background. Geary skimmed through message headers, sometimes pausing to also skim through the underlying material, only occasionally pausing to read through something of particular import.

The uncrewed probes sent to the wreckage of the alien ships to find traces of their former crews had also collected pieces of the wreckage. The report forwarded by Captain Smythe summarized what had been learned from those so far, which, unfortunately, wasn't much. *Unsurprising mix of alloys and composites... structural analysis of alloys reveals some intriguing signs of unusual casting techniques... composites tilted more heavily toward silicon than carbon, suggesting relative abundance of those elements on alien home world... no portions of equipment found large enough to provide critical information as to functions or design.*

Captain Tulev had reported on everything collected at the site of the battle. At least they didn't have to worry too much about the aliens analyzing any human wreckage or remains. Whatever the aliens might find after Tulev's cleanup effort would provide a lot fewer clues than the aliens' wreckage had provided to the humans.

Geary's eye caught on a disciplinary summary from *Dragon*. A petty officer caught selling drugs synthesized from stolen medical supplies. Six cases of insubordination, and three fights, one of them involving several sailors. Was Captain Bradamont having trouble controlling her crew?

He told the system to summarize all disciplinary reports and give averages for each ship type. *Dragon*, it turned out, was a bit better than average. Even *Dauntless* had seen a significant uptick in incidents.

Geary sat looking at the numbers, knowing what they meant. Fights. Insubordination. Failure to carry out duties. All signs of trouble, and they were getting worse. Sailors who were unhappy but had nothing specific to vent their unhappiness on, so they were turning on each other, letting minor events escalate to levels where official action had to be taken. All of it was still minor. Nothing was at a critical stage yet, but he had to try to keep things from getting that bad.

Which meant getting home.

He finally fell asleep in his chair for a couple of hours, waking with a jerk to see before him a message summarizing fleet junior officer qualification progress. Small wonder that had put him to sleep.

A quick shift to the star display revealed that nothing much had changed in the star system. The human fleet and the alien armada had moved a bit closer to each other, slowly converging, and this fleet had also gotten a bit closer to the orbital fortress guarding the next jump point; but that was all.

Shutting off the display, Geary checked his appearance, pondered appearing on the bridge looking like he had just come in from a wild night of liberty, thought about what Tanya would do if he did that, then took enough time to clean himself up and put on a fresh uniform.

Desjani was on the bridge, looking immaculate in her uniform even though her face displayed signs of fatigue. She yawned as she waved Geary to his command seat. "Did you get some rest, Admiral?"

"A little."

76

"Good. In exchange for your display of good judgment, I've got something to show you, Admiral."

He sat down, eyeing her. "A workable plan?"

"A workable plan? No, Admiral. I'm going to show you a great plan." She entered the commands, and Geary's display came to life.

He watched the maneuvers play out, running the simulation to its end, then let out a long breath. "It works."

"It *could* work," she corrected him. "If the bear-cows do what we think they will. If they don't, we can pull out of contact and try something else." Desjani frowned at her display. "We can probably do that."

"Probably?"

"I am fairly confident that we could, Admiral." Tanya yawned again. "Even against the Syndics, this probably wouldn't work, but I bounced some ideas off of Lieutenant Iger, and they match what his spooks have seen on the videos we've intercepted. But there's not a lot of room for error. It's a great plan, but it's a terrible plan."

Geary fought to keep from frowning. "A terrible plan?"

"Yes, sir. There's a lot of guesswork, and if the enemy behaves differently than we expect, it won't work. And if it doesn't work, we could be in serious trouble."

He was frowning now. Geary felt a mix of anger and unhappiness. He had hoped a solution had been found, and her first words had seemed to confirm those hopes. But if Tanya thought the plan was that bad… "So we need to try something else."

"No." Desjani shook her head, leaned back, and sighed with contentment. "First, because I already put a lot of work into this, and second, because even though it's a terrible plan, it's a lot better than any other idea that anybody else has come up with. You don't even want to look at what the combat systems developed using their little artificial minds."

"That bad?" Geary asked, his upset gone.

"Try projected fifty-percent losses." She shook her head once more, this time in disgust. "I can't believe people used to call that stuff artificial *intelligence*. It's still dumber than a deck plate."

"We couldn't aim our weapons without it," Geary pointed out. "Not with engagement envelopes measured in milliseconds. And I wouldn't want to try maneuvering at the velocities we move without automated assist systems."

"Yeah, but that's all physics! We can model that, after we figure it out. But actually thinking? Coming up with something new? Hah! Fast and stupid is still stupid. It just gets to stupid a lot quicker than humans could on their own. Which, I admit, is an accomplishment," she added, "because we're pretty damn good at stupid."

"That's something to take pride in," Geary agreed.

"I'll take whatever I can get." She waved one hand toward him. "Anyway, your plan isn't nearly as stupid as any other alternatives anyone has thought of. Congratulations."

He studied the display again, seeing every uncertainty, every assumption that Desjani had been forced to incorporate into the plan. If and if and if. It was up to him to decide whether to go with it despite all of those ifs. But they wouldn't learn all the answers even if they stayed here for months dodging the alien armada. His instincts told him that they needed to move fast, before fleet supplies diminished, before morale sank even lower, before the bear-cows could deploy even more forces, using their overwhelming numbers and resources. "We'll do it." Desjani nodded, her eyes closed for a moment. "Oh, by the way, you left out one step in the plan."

"What step was that?"

"The one where we pray this works, Admiral."

4

Geary sat in his fleet command seat on the bridge of *Dauntless*, watching the distance reading to the nearest alien fortress scrolling downward rapidly. From as far off as the fleet was, the fortress wasn't yet growing in size at any appreciable rate, but Geary still had the sensation that *Dauntless* and the entire fleet were diving down toward it. An odd sensation, born of human instincts that came from ancient ancestors walking the surface of a planet far distant.

Since the fleet was on an intercept course with the jump point guarded by the alien fortress, it was curving slightly around the edge of the star system. The fortress physically appeared to be just slightly to the right of Geary, or just off the starboard bows of the human ships. They were still forty light-minutes from that fortress. Since Geary had chosen to hold the speed of the human fleet to point one light speed, it would be nearly seven hours until they reached that fortress.

Much farther to the side, nearly amidships, hung the shapes of the alien armada pursuing the human fleet. To the human eye, those alien warships were still invisible, but the displays showed exactly where those other ships were, still about a light-hour distant. The relative bearing of the alien armada had not changed for hours, seemingly unmoving off to the side toward the alien star. But the distance to the alien ships steadily decreased as they held to a course that would bring them to intercept the human fleet in roughly eight hours.

Human fleet, alien fortress, and alien armada formed the points of a triangle with curving sides marking their trajectories through space to reach one another, the length of the sides constantly changing as the human and alien warships converged toward the fortress.

Geary shifted his gaze to the representation of the human fleet. Quite a few officers had been startled by the formation he had moved the fleet into. Unlike Geary's usual practice of breaking the fleet into multiple subformations that maneuvered independently, this time he had brought the entire fleet together into a single flattened box shape. The auxiliaries and the assault transports occupied the center of the box, while the battleships, battle cruisers, cruisers, and destroyers were arrayed along the sides and bottom.

"What exactly are we trying to do here?" Captain Duellos had asked.

"Give the enemy a clear, concentrated target," Geary had replied.

"You usually try to avoid doing that," Duellos pointed out.

True enough. But this time he wanted a target the bear-cows couldn't resist.

The biggest problem in the plan involved timing. He had to time everything the human fleet did in order to get reactions from the bear-cows when he wanted those reactions. Now Geary waited, trying to relax his mind, letting himself feel the right moment. "All units, turn starboard two zero degrees, up five degrees at time three zero." That should do it.

There wasn't any actual up or down in space, nor could ships, which could be pointed in any direction, agree on where their left and right were, so humans had imposed their own rules on trackless space. Upon arrival in a star system, the fleet's systems drew a plane along the orbits of the majority of the star's planets, designating one side "up" and the other "down," so every ship knew what those directions meant. Every ship also understood that starboard meant turning toward the star, while port meant turning away from it. Crude but simple, the arbitrary system imposed by humanity worked and so had remained unchanged for centuries.

Desjani sat in her own command seat near his side. "At least with the fleet this concentrated, everybody will get your messages quickly."

"That's one less thing to worry about," Geary agreed.

At thirty minutes past the hour, every ship in the human fleet turned simultaneously, the shape of the box not changing but its path through space altering to angle toward the alien armada. Geary watched the smoothly executed maneuver with a feeling of pride. "Damn, they move good."

"We always knew how to handle ships," Desjani reminded him. "You just retaught us the importance of moving in unison."

"Hell, Tanya, you can handle a ship better asleep than I ever could at full alert."

"You're only saying that because it's true." She tapped out some calculations. "All right, the bear-cow armada is fifty-nine light-minutes and a handful of light-seconds distant. They'll see that we turned toward them in about an hour. Since we're closing on them faster now, we should start seeing their reactions in another… fifty-six minutes after that."

"It shouldn't take them long to react. Lieutenant Iger and the civilian experts all think from the videos we've intercepted that the bear-cows are indeed herd organized. The herd leader is the leader, pure and simple. That leader won't consult with anyone before deciding what to do."

"And the big herd leader on the planet is five light-hours distant, so he or she can't, uh, horn in on what to do," Desjani added. "What are you going to do for the next two hours?"

"Wait," Geary said.

"I was going to suggest rest. Have you had anything to eat?" When he shook his head, she pulled out a ration bar in an unusually bright wrapper. "Try this."

He took it, frowning as he read the label. "This isn't a ration bar. It's a 'fusion cuisine hand-wrap.' VIP-issue only.'" Geary cocked a questioning look at her. "VIP-issue only? How many of these do we have?"

"Quite a few," Desjani said, chewing on her own hand-wrap appreciatively. "The crew is going to get a pleasant surprise in their battle rations."

"I know I shouldn't ask, but how did they get aboard *Dauntless*?" She shrugged. "I don't know."

"Meaning you didn't ask."

"Mama didn't raise a fool," Desjani said. "If you want to ask Master Chief Gioninni how he came across these, you're welcome, but he'll probably just tell you they were lying around about to be disposed of, and he rescued them from being wasted. Or something like that."

Geary took a bite. The hand-wraps were good. Much, much better than the ration bars the fleet was used to. "Oh, to be a VIP." He caught her amused look. "No, I'm not. So why did these wraps only show up now?"

"They've been available in the chiefs' mess since we left Varandal," Desjani said. "I—"

"Caught them?"

"I gained knowledge of the hand-wraps' availability," Desjani continued in a perfectly serious tone of voice, "and directed Master Chief Gioninni to immediately enter them into the ship's food inventory control system."

"I see." Geary took another bite. "Has the master chief reported anything regarding untoward activity among the auxiliaries?"

Desjani shook her head. "In his words, 'nothing to bother the admiral about.' Meaning the usual level of under-the-sensors, unofficial activity, I would guess, but nothing worse than that." She popped the last bit of her wrap into her mouth. "How about your green-haired lieutenant?"

"I haven't heard any reports from Lieutenant Shamrock since we got here," Geary said.

"Shamrock?"

"That's her nickname. I don't know why I keep remembering the nickname. Maybe it's that hair. Lieutenant... Jamenson."

Desjani grinned. "I'm glad my ancestors didn't think it would be a good idea to implant green hair in my genetic code."

"Me, too." Geary sobered, thinking again about the mysterious warship construction activity that Lieutenant Jamenson had discovered amid details and minor items hidden in hundreds of routine messages. "All of the engineers have been working around the clock getting damage repaired. I doubt there's been any free time to look into that more."

"Captain Smythe has probably run scams that Master Chief Gioninni has only dreamed about pulling off," Desjani warned.

"As long as he keeps my ships working, I can live with that." Geary took a final bite of his own wrap. "Right?"

"Well, yeah. Want another one?"

The crew wasn't happy, knowing that the fleet had turned toward a faster intercept with the bear-cow armada. Geary could feel on his back the worried looks of the watch-standers on the bridge. "Those bear-cows probably think we intend going head-to-head with them," he said to Desjani loudly enough for the watch-standers to hear.

"They're going to be disappointed," she replied at the same volume.

But then she lowered her voice. "If this works."

"Captain," Lieutenant Yuon reported, "we're receiving readings from the sensors on the latest kinetic projectile to be diverted by that alien defense system on their fortress."

"What's it telling us?" Desjani asked.

"Um, Captain, it…" Yuon shook his head helplessly. "It's telling us its course was diverted."

Desjani turned in her seat to look at Yuon. "That's all?"

"Yes, Captain. The sensors didn't detect anything except the

85

change in vector that caused the rock to miss the fort."

"Forward those readings throughout the fleet," Geary ordered. "I want to see if anyone can spot anything in them."

Yuon hesitated. "Sir, Lieutenant Iger said the readings are classified and need to be kept under single-user control."

Intelligence didn't want anyone seeing the new information? That made a strange kind of sense since the capabilities the bearcows had in certain areas would grant a huge advantage to any humans who could employ them against other humans.

But getting to that point meant getting this fleet past those bearcow capabilities, which meant he had to understand as much as he could as quickly as he could. "Inform Lieutenant Iger that I am overriding that order. In this case, the security of the fleet is best served by figuring out whatever we can about this alien technology."

Geary settled back again to wait. At the moment, there wasn't much else he could do.

"Here we go," Desjani said. "It took them less than a minute after they saw the vector we'd steadied on before they changed course to match."

Geary nodded, his eyes on the display where the warships of the alien armada had come to port to bring about an even faster meeting with the human fleet. "Hold on. How much are they reducing velocity?"

"Quite a bit." Desjani sounded thoughtful, one hand tracing out new data on her display. "Interesting. When we turned toward each other, it increased the combined speed we would meet at."

"That's right. To about point two five light speed if we both maintained our velocities. Too fast for our combat systems to compensate well for relativistic distortion." The faster a ship went in normal space, subject to the rules of the ancient relativity physics, the more that ship's image of the universe outside it was distorted. When it came to aiming weapons for millisecond-long engagement envelopes, even a tiny discrepancy between how the ship saw the universe and how that universe actually was would mean a clean miss. Human systems could compensate for that distortion fairly well up to point two light speed, but as velocities increased beyond that the systems increasingly developed too many errors to be accurate. "I expected them to slow at some point. But they've come down in speed immediately."

"Still braking," Desjani said. "Those superbattleships take a while to shed velocity. Lieutenant Castries."

"Yes, Captain."

"Keep an eye on the alien armada's maneuvering and let me know when their velocity steadies out." Desjani sat back, frowning now, her eyes intent as if aiming a weapon. "Earlier, they had stopped accelerating before I thought they would." She tapped controls. "Yeah. Our combined velocities when we came together would have been... point one seven light speed."

"Point one seven." Geary rubbed his chin. "I thought they were waiting to accelerate again when they were closer to us, but maybe they didn't want to encounter us going any faster than that."

"Want to bet they'll brake down enough to meet us at point one seven light?" Desjani asked.

"If they do..." Geary felt himself smiling. "Our combat aiming systems are better than theirs."

"Significantly better," Desjani said. "Why do you suppose they're changing velocity so early, though? Why not wait?"

"Good question." The answer might imperil his whole plan, based as it was on the enemy's charging his fleet. Geary passed the question on to the civilian experts, hoping they might come up with some insight.

It took nearly half an hour before Lieutenant Castries called out to Desjani. "They've steadied out, Captain."

"Thank you. What do the maneuvering systems say our combined velocities will be when we encounter the bear-cows?"

"If neither of us alters velocity or course again… point one seven light speed, Captain."

Desjani laughed softly. "Got 'em."

"Good call, Tanya." Geary was running some updates to his plan, taking into account the newly discovered fact that the bear-cow armada would limit its speed as it closed to contact. "That makes our next maneuver in one and a half hours."

"Admiral, someone on one of the assault transports wants to speak with you," the communications watch announced. "You've got your comms set to block him, though."

He didn't need distractions, but Geary checked to see who it was. Dr. Setin, one of the civilian experts. "Why is my software blocking Setin?" he grumbled.

Desjani heard, turning a glower toward the comm watch. "Have the systems people check the admiral's screening software and find out why it's blocking the wrong contacts."

Geary entered the override, seeing Dr. Setin's image pop up immediately, along with that of Dr. Shwartz. "Admiral," Setin said eagerly, "Dr. Shwartz has an interesting theory regarding the alien beings in this star system. It's based on a wide variety of observations and analysis—"

"Doctor," Geary interrupted, "I'm busy in the preliminary stages of an engagement with those aliens right now. Can you just summarize the theory?"

Dr. Shwartz spoke quickly. "As humans, we're used to dealing with creatures which, when threatened or pursuing something, start out with a quick burst of acceleration, trying to either get away or catch their prey by using maximum acceleration and speed for a short period. But an intelligent creature, and here I'm speaking of something as smart as the typical predator or prey, knows once it has escaped immediate danger or failed to catch its prey on the first lunge, that a prolonged chase might ensue. In that prolonged chase, both predator and prey adopt the pace best suited for them to maintain for long periods."

Geary thought about that, his eyes going back to his display. "That's what the bear-cows are doing? Instead of charging at maximum speed, they're adopting a pace sufficient to get to us using their best efficiency?"

"I think so, yes, Admiral."

"Dr. Shwartz, that doesn't make sense. They're not running after us. They're in ships. The propulsion systems won't wear out, the fuel won't exhaust unless their designs are ridiculously short-legged in terms of endurance. We'll be gone from this star system long before they could run out of means to continue chasing us."

"Admiral." Dr. Shwartz paused, then spoke quietly. "You are

assuming that these aliens only intend that pursuit to last as long as we are here."

He had to take that in, letting the idea settle, and not liking it at all. "You think they might follow us? Through that jump point?"

"Admiral, it's possible that they will follow us as long as they possibly can, trying to destroy us so that we cannot return and threaten the herd again. These herbivores gained control of their world. They built those fortresses. They must be persistent, able to focus for long periods on issues of security, and willing to devote whatever it takes to eliminating threats."

"Thank you. That's an... interesting interpretation, though I hope you're wrong." After the images of the doctors vanished, Geary turned to Desjani and passed on the theory.

"Oh, great." Desjani flexed her hands as if preparing for physical combat. "I wonder if they've got legs enough to follow us all the way back to Alliance space?"

"Without auxiliaries to transport and produce more fuel cells or whatever else they use?" Geary asked.

"Those superbattleships are big enough to have auxiliary capabilities," she pointed out. "Big storage capacity, manufacturing shops, that kind of thing. You know, they make more sense now that I thought of that. Maybe they even grow food on some of the decks. A self-contained warship that can make everything it needs, that has essentially unlimited endurance as long as it can pick up new raw materials occasionally as it passes through star systems."

He looked at the depictions of the bear-cow superbattleships with new eyes. "You're right. They may not be that big just for immediate combat capability. One more thing to worry about."

"We can take them as far as Syndic territory and lose them there so they can run amuck," Desjani suggested. "I'm joking, by the way."

"Thanks for clarifying that." He was only half-joking in his reply. When he had first encountered Tanya, she had carried many of the ugly legacies of a century of war within her. There were few things she would not have done to the hated Syndicate Worlds enemies, military or civilian. She still carried many scars of war inside her though she rarely let him see external signs of those. "But if they do follow us, we're going to have to take them out once we have them somewhere they don't have these fortresses and all of the other resources of this star system backing them up."

She nodded, smiling crookedly. "I notice you haven't been talking much about what might be at the star we'll be jumping to."

"Whatever is there is there. We'll deal with it."

"Admiral?" the comm watch-stander said. "Captain Smythe on *Tanuki* is trying to get through to you. He says he's getting a block notification."

"Captain Smythe?" Geary looked at Desjani. "I *know* my comm settings don't block him."

Her face grim, Desjani hit her internal comm controls. "Systems maintenance, this is the Captain. Something is wrong with the fleet commander's comm software. Find out what, find it now, and get it fixed five minutes ago. Understood?"

"Yes, Captain!" The systems maintenance personnel sounded worried, as well they should be when Desjani used that tone of voice.

"Forward Captain Smythe's call," Geary ordered the comm watch.

Smythe appeared, looking puzzled. "Comm problems, Admiral?

I'm guessing, but then I don't see how else I would have ended up unable to reach you directly."

"Apparently," Geary replied. "The systems people here on *Dauntless* are checking it."

"It's probably—Is it an isolated problem? Have you seen others?"

"At least one other recent problem with my comm settings," Geary said.

"Admiral, I don't wish to alarm you," Smythe said, though his expression betrayed a worrisome amount of unease despite his words. "This may not be a software problem. That is, the operating systems may be working fine. But if the comm system processors and memory tacks are developing physical flaws, it will cause erratic behavior in the software."

Everything else in the fleet was breaking as it reached the end of a short design life, but this particular problem hadn't occurred to Geary. If he started having comm problems now, as they were heading for an encounter with the alien armada... "Captain Desjani, Captain Smythe informs me that it would be a good idea for your systems people to check the hardware in the comm system. Processors and memory tacks."

As aware as he of the implications, Desjani stared at Geary for only an instant before reacting. "Systems! Check the hardware! Chief engineer! I want an immediate and full check of all comm and comm-associated processors and other gear."

Smythe, unaware of Desjani's words, was speaking to Geary again. "I was actually calling about *Orion*. *Kupua* completed her repairs on the damaged main propulsion unit and the fleet's readiness system will tell you that *Orion* is at one hundred percent again, but *Kupua*'s commanding officer, Commander Miskovic, told me that she is worried."

"Worried?" *She's worried? Try wondering whether or not your comms will work as you race to an encounter with an alien fleet.* "Worried about what?"

"The systems test fine," Smythe said, groping for words. "But… Miskovic told me they don't feel fine to her."

"What does that mean?" Geary demanded.

"It means there's nothing quantifiably wrong with *Orion*'s propulsion right now, Admiral, but a talented and experienced engineer has a bad feeling about it." Smythe gestured in frustration. "I don't have to remind you that *Orion* has taken a lot of damage in the last year and received a lot of repairs, sometimes very hasty ones. That sort of thing can add up in sometimes indefinable ways."

"I don't understand."

Smythe looked startled, then his expression cleared. "Of course. You didn't spend your career in combat, not until after the fight at Grendel. Your pardon, Admiral, but everyone today tends to assume that any officer they know has been in the fight all their lives. But that means you don't have extensive experience with combat-damaged systems that have undergone repeated repair. I'll be the first to admit that hasn't happened as much as it should have, because too many ships were lost completely or had to be scuttled. But it adds up, just like normal stresses add up over time."

Another headache was starting. Geary tried to relax himself. Letting stress impact *him* could lead to errors and misjudgments that he and this fleet could not afford. "What exactly does that mean in this case?"

"It means that while every test shows *Orion*'s propulsion systems working fine, the engineer who helped run those tests is of the opinion that *Orion* could suffer a significant propulsion problem at any time, with little or no warning. I thought you should know."

"Is there anything I can do about it?" Geary asked.

"Not apart from full rework, replacement, and rebuild of *Orion*'s systems," Smythe said. "Which is scheduled though that schedule keeps slipping."

Geary nodded, absorbing the information. "Thank you, Captain Smythe. At least if something does happen unexpectedly to *Orion*'s propulsion systems I'll be mentally prepared to deal with it." *Please, ancestors, ask the living stars to make sure that doesn't happen during a battle.* "Was Commander Shen informed of this?"

"Yes, Admiral. He didn't seem happy with the assessment, but then Commander Shen never looks happy."

Desjani leaned closer. "It was in the main comm coordination processors. Several of the memory tacks there aren't retaining updates."

Smythe heard this time and nodded in satisfaction. "That's it. They're losing memory-save capability. That's causing your comm system to keep falling back into default settings. Nothing anyone would notice at first, but the save problems will keep cascading through your systems."

"My system engineers are swapping out the tacks," Desjani said. "Should they be doing anything else?"

"Replacing the rest of the system," Smythe said with a sigh. "The tack failures are the canary in the coal mine for your comm system. Don't depend on normal physical equipment diagnostics and self-test schedules. Treat the system as sick until we can get everything replaced."

"Captain Smythe," Geary said with what he considered a great deal of restraint, "we're heading into battle. Are you telling me that I can't depend upon *Dauntless*'s comm system?"

He felt Desjani tense. She had always taken pride in *Dauntless*'s status as flagship, as well as her own reputation for keeping everything and everyone on *Dauntless* in top readiness. If he had to transfer his flag on the eve of a fight because he couldn't count on critical equipment on *Dauntless* working, Tanya and her crew would be humiliated.

Smythe simply viewed the question from an engineer's perspective, though. "I'd need to see a full inspection and test run before I could answer that question, Admiral. Obviously, there are already problems on *Dauntless*, though."

Desjani's face had darkened, and she appeared ready for a hot retort.

Should he let loyalty to Tanya, and his familiarity with and liking of *Dauntless* and her crew, override his responsibility to have a flagship with reliable communications? The consequences of letting sentiment decide the issue, rather than cold logic, could be extremely serious.

But there were other factors in war that had nothing to do with cold logic. Intangibles that could decide the outcomes of battles. What would be the impact in the fleet if everyone saw him making a last-minute shift of his flag to another warship when *Dauntless* was outwardly undamaged? How many reasons for such an action would fly around the fleet within moments, and how much damage could those rumors cause to the fighting spirit and discipline of this fleet?

Unaware of the emotional byplay, Smythe had continued speaking, his face intent and eyes focused elsewhere as he thought through the problem. "Obviously, too, *Dauntless* has already identified the problem and begun corrective work. Any other ship could develop the same issues at any time. But there's no telling how long or complex the repairs might be—"

"Thank you, Captain Smythe," Geary broke in, feeling the tension now not only in Desjani but within everyone on the bridge. For better or worse, he believed that this time the intangibles had to take priority. "*Dauntless* is working to correct the problem. I'll place my trust in the ability of her crew to get the job done. They've never let me down."

"All right, Admiral. It's your fleet. Oh, don't forget the bit about *Orion*."

"Trust me, Captain Smythe, I will remember that." He sat back, blowing out a breath he hadn't known was inside him. Glancing at Desjani, he saw her speaking on her internal comms, with brisk efficiency but no outward tension now. Around him, the rest of *Dauntless*'s bridge crew were at work with a sort of steady determination. "How's it look?" he asked Desjani.

She finished her conversation, turning toward him. "Another ten minutes, and the swap out of components and system checks will be done. A full inspection of the physical components will take a lot longer, but we're on it, Admiral."

"Thank you."

"No, sir. Thank you." She smiled. "You publicly expressed confidence in my ship and my crew."

He shrugged, uncomfortable with knowing his words meant so much to her and the rest of the crew. "I just told the truth. *Dauntless* has never let me down. If there is a ship in this fleet that is truly invincible, it's *Dauntless*."

Desjani's smile slipped. "And now you're trying to jinx my ship."

"I only meant—"

"Quit while you're ahead, Admiral. I'm sure you will apologize to the living stars later for the presumption, but for now let's pretend you didn't say that and just focus on the fact that Black Jack wouldn't have any other ship carry his flag."

He almost hesitated before sending the next maneuver orders, wondering if they would go out to the rest of the fleet as they should or if the comm system would suffer more problems. But Desjani's comm personnel had reported that the system was working properly for now at least. "All units, come port six five degrees down three degrees at time one five."

Every ship turned as ordered, the box formation once again pivoting its heading without changing its shape, the fleet curving around away from both the star here and the oncoming bear-cow armada, now only twenty light-minutes distant.

"The bear-cows are going to be unhappy," Desjani commented.

"As long as they do what we want," Geary replied.

"And what," Victoria Rione asked from the back of the bridge, "are we doing?"

He pivoted his seat to look back at her. "Trying to get them to do what we want them to do. I take it we still haven't heard from them?"

"No," Rione said. "Not even a bloodcurdling 'moo' of defiance. I believe your experts are right. These creatures do not speak with their enemies. They get rid of them."

General Charban came on the bridge as well as Rione finished. "And too bad for anyone or anything that wasn't actually an enemy, though I suspect their definition of enemy might be very broad. I just had a fascinating discussion with Dr. Shwartz."

"Any new insights?" Geary asked. It would be about forty minutes before they spotted the bear-cow reaction to their latest maneuver, so he might as well see if he could learn anything new during the wait.

"Nothing good," Charban said.

"Why is it that Dr. Shwartz's insights rarely bring comfort?"

Charban smiled. "That's a question I can't address. But I can tell you what our experts have concluded from more analysis of the surface of that inhabited planet here. You already know it is almost covered with buildings."

"Right. Buildings with crops on the roofs."

"The same crops, Admiral. There is very little if any variation in vegetation in all of the areas we have been able to view of that planet."

"Everywhere?"

Desjani got it, making a noise of disbelief. "They've wiped out everything else? That planet is covered with them and what they grow to eat?"

"Pretty much," Charban said. "They not only took out all of the predators, they've also apparently taken out everything else that might compete with them or be in the way. In the videos we've intercepted, we've seen birdlike creatures occasionally, and some small beasts that appear to be pets, but aside from that, it's just bear-cows. Oh, except for some shows that must be historical. The bear-cows in them wear primitive armor and engage in battles with other creatures, clearly digital special effects rather than real, probably the predators who are now extinct."

"Battles?" That might be another opportunity to confirm how the bear-cows fought. "Can you forward me one of those right now?"

"Certainly, Admiral." Charban tapped his comm unit, then nodded to Geary.

Desjani leaned in close to Geary to watch as well, pointedly ignoring the arch look that Rione sent their way at the physical proximity.

In the new virtual window that popped up before him, Geary saw serried ranks of bear-cows bearing shields and long spears, advancing steadily against foes that battered vainly against the shield wall. Occasionally, one of the maddened predators would leap high enough to clear the shields, only to be impaled on the bristling field of spears behind that.

"It's an impressive display of discipline," Charban commented. "The bear-cows all stay in position in the formation, all stay in step, all respond immediately to orders."

"I'm not seeing much drama," Desjani commented. "They're just using the weight of numbers to push back those predators, encircle them, and spear them."

"That's all that happens," Charban said. "All of these historical videos are the same. We haven't seen a single case where a lone bear-cow plays the hero. Apparently, the bear-cows get their pleasure from watching the mass movements of their own armies.

I checked, and there are rough analogues to that in human history. One ancient society on Old Earth, for example, who fought in similar tight formations with locked shields, and found heroism and drama in the simple question of whether or not each soldier could hold their place in formation as two forces clashed."

"They're not totally different from us," Rione said. "There are ways in which we could find common ground if they would talk to us. But our earlier estimate that these herbivores attacked us solely because we appeared to be predators was incomplete."

"There's another reason?" Geary asked.

She waved in the direction where the distant bear-cow planet lay. "We would be competition, Admiral. They don't allow competition of any kind. They've wiped out the competition on their home world, and if they had not been pinned here by the presence of the enigmas, they might have expanded to human-controlled space by now, plowing under every other life-form they encountered."

"What about in the other directions? Do we have to assume that the bear-cows are surrounded by enigma-controlled space?"

"We can hope," Rione said. "And, yes, I know none of us would have hoped for that before coming to this star, but now the enigmas do seem to be the lesser of two evils."

"Pandora," Desjani said.

"What?" Geary spoke for everyone else on the bridge.

"One of those old legends," Desjani explained. "The type that blamed everything that was wrong on women. Pandora opened some box and found all kinds of bad things in it. I think Pandora might be a good name for this particular star."

"Those old legends didn't blame all women for everything that

was wrong," Charban said. "They only blamed women who…
didn't do as they were told."

"A critical distinction," Rione said in dry tones. "It is, after all,
hard to overemphasize the importance of obedience in women."

Desjani grinned at Charban's discomfort, then suddenly realized
that she had allied with Rione in this matter and shifted her
attention back to Geary. "Five minutes until we see their reaction."

Not wanting to get involved in the discussion of historical views
on "appropriate" female behavior that Charban had unwittingly
opened, Geary simply nodded, focusing back on his display. The
bear-cows should react to his last maneuver by coming to port,
heading down very slightly, and accelerating again to set up another
intercept with the human fleet.

"There's always the chance," Desjani said, "that the armada will
peel off to let the fortress deal with us."

"I know. Our next maneuver will get us much closer to them,
though. If what we know and guess about the bear-cows is right,
they'll keep after us."

The bear-cow armada shifted vector exactly on schedule, making
the exact changes in course necessary to bring about another
intercept while the bear-cow warships began increasing their
velocity. Geary gave them time to steady out on their next course,
but ordered the next human maneuver while the bear-cows were
still accelerating. "All units come starboard one three four degrees
up five degrees at time two seven."

This time the human formation swung widely back toward the
bear-cow armada, every ship pivoting in place within the box.
"They're eighteen light-minutes distant," Desjani commented, "but

we're going to close that fast on this new course. Current closing speed is point two four light speed, and they'll keep accelerating until they see we've turned toward them."

Geary nodded, his attention back on the alien fortress. The human fleet had gradually closed the distance to that as well, so the fortress was now but twenty-two light-minutes away, its relative bearing on the port quarter of the Alliance warships as they steadied onto their new course. The bear-cow armada was off the starboard bows of the human ships, so that alien fortress, human fleet, and alien armada were now nearly in a line, with the humans between the two bear-cow forces. "We're going to be making quicker moves from here on, and a lot of it is going to be by instinct since we won't have time to see the bear-cow reactions before we make our next move. Let me know if anything feels wrong to you."

"You're better than me at fleet maneuvers," Desjani said. "A lot better."

"But you can judge whether or not *Dauntless* is moving the way we want. Just let me know how that feels. Every other ship in this fleet is keeping position on *Dauntless*, so if she's moving how we want, they'll be moving how we want."

"Yes, sir."

Seventy-five minutes left to contact, or more like seventy if the bear-cows kept accelerating.

He had briefed his ship captains on what was to happen. Over the next couple of hours, the human fleet made repeated turns, to port, to starboard, back around, forcing the oncoming alien warships to frequently change their own courses and speeds. If those creatures were human, they would be growing increasingly frustrated and angry as the human fleet kept alternately turning toward a faster meeting, then turning away to force a longer chase. There was also the risk that Geary's own captains would feel the same emotions. But each set of maneuvers left the bear-cow warships closer to the human fleet and brought both human and alien formations closer to the huge orbiting alien fortress. The twin threats of alien armada and fortress would hopefully help keep Geary's most aggressive ship captains in their places in the formation rather than charging the enemy.

As the fleet swung widely to port again, Geary thought about the virtues of the bear-cow way of fighting. Every combatant staying exactly where they should, doing exactly as their commander ordered. It would be comforting never to have to worry about someone doing the wrong thing or refusing to do what they had been told.

But then he would have a fleet of commanders who were even worse than Captain Vente, incapable of acting on their own when circumstances required, locked into waiting for exact instructions on what to do, blindly following orders even if those orders were clearly mistaken. Too much discipline and too little discipline were two sides of the same disastrous coin, which could only purchase defeat.

"The leader of that armada has got to be mad as hell," Desjani said. "You keep playing with them instead of charging in to fight."

"That's the idea." Soon now. The box formation of the human fleet had worked around so it was only a few light-minutes from the alien fortress, but on the nearly opposite side from the bear-cow armada, which was currently clawing around to starboard to come back at the humans, the massive bear-cow superbattleships requiring huge turning radii and the smaller ships around them keeping exact positions relative to the larger ships. Geary had dipped his fleet formation up and down slightly as he weaved back and forth, with the latest maneuver bringing the fleet aimed several degrees under the plane of the star system.

On Geary's display, he watched the elements of the so-far-bloodless battle all swinging toward the alignment he had been working for all that day. The heading of the human fleet sliding toward the alien fortress, and beyond that fortress, the jump point that he needed to reach now almost in line with the fortress, the current turn aiming to take the fleet short of the fortress. Off to the port side of the human fleet and the alien fortress, the curving path of the alien armada was gliding toward not only the human fleet, but also a close approach to the fortress. *That won't worry the bear-cow commander. He wants me. He wants this fleet, and he doesn't have to worry about being attacked by that fortress. And the fortress is watching me, too, waiting until this fleet gets into the right position so the fortress can launch hundreds of those suicide missile ships at us.*

They're not watching each other because they think they don't have to.

I hope.

Now.

"All units, come starboard three five degrees at time four nine. Accelerate to point one five light speed."

Thrusters fired at maximum power as the human fleet checked its turn to port and swung back to starboard in an enormous weaving maneuver. Main propulsion units flared, pushing the warships faster while they swung about. Geary kept his eyes on the ponderous auxiliaries in the center of the formation, knowing this maneuver would stress their capabilities to the maximum. If any of them failed to match the movement of the fleet, he would have to adjust courses on the fly to try to keep them safe.

But even though the largest auxiliaries screamed hull-stress warnings on the fleet alert net, they kept up with the turn. Geary took a deep breath, not even aware that he was crossing his fingers for luck. "All units. Immediate execute Modified Formation Hotel."

Off to port of the human fleet, the now all-too-close bear-cow armada would be seeing the latest human maneuver, turning away but not enough to avoid contact this time. They would also be seeing the human fleet finally altering velocity, speeding up to confuse targeting and make the intercept harder. And now they would be seeing the outer edges of the human formation dissolving as the human warships shifted positions at the same time as they kept turning and accelerating.

Hundreds of human warships dipped and climbed past each other, following individual paths that were coordinated and woven into a single fabric. The battleships not already at the top of the human formation climbed, joining the rest of the battleships in the top layer to form a wall of strength. The battle cruisers formed clusters at the front and back of the formation, ready to defend those areas or reinforce the battleships. Heavy cruisers swung downward to form a shell about the auxiliaries and assault transports, while light cruisers and destroyers scattered to mix with the battleships and battle cruisers.

But the mass of the human formation stayed relatively compact as it steadied out, heading straight at the alien fortress, but aimed to pass beneath it.

Dauntless's bridge was silent, everyone watching their displays, waiting to see how the alien armada would act, and when the fortress would launch its huge force of missile ships.

"Point of no return," Desjani murmured. They were too far committed to this course now, unable to turn away from the fortress and the alien armada quickly enough to avoid a clash.

"Here they come," Geary said.

The alien armada had come around and was braking velocity, its huge and cumbersome superbattleships straining to match the maneuver. The curve marking the armada's projected course drifted to the side, steadying directly under the alien fortress. But the massive bear-cow ships couldn't slow themselves fast enough. "Combined engagement velocity estimated at point one nine light speed," Desjani said, as unnaturally calm as usual in the face of battle.

"All units," Geary ordered, "engage any targets that enter your weapons envelopes."

It had been days, then hours, then minutes, and now only seconds remained as the three elements of the battle rushed together. Would the alien fortress launch its missile ships on time for a perfect intercept of the human fleet tearing past, or…?

"Here they come," Desjani said. "Get anything that comes close," she ordered her bridge crew.

The missile ships had begun launching, leaping upward from the surface of the fortress, but the launches faltered, staggering to a halt as the bear-cow armada in blind pursuit of the human fleet came blundering between the fleet and the fortress, fouling the path of the missile ships as the forces came together at a combined velocity of about fifty-seven thousand kilometers per second. Geary had planned it like an ancient bullfight, getting the bull enraged, getting it where and when he wanted it to be, until the final pass and away while the bull staggered past the place where it had thought to gore its opponent.

The actual shooting lasted for only milliseconds, too fast for human senses to register, automated combat systems selecting targets and firing at enemies who were there and gone in an instant. Particle beams seared deadly paths between ships, specter missiles launched to slam into targets too close to maneuver to avoid them, and sometimes even grapeshot was fired at targets close enough, the metal ball bearings striking with immense force against shields and armor. *Dauntless* rocked in the wake of explosions already far behind, Geary calling out new orders before he had time to assess damage to the fleet. "All units, brake at maximum to point one light speed."

The human warships slewed around in place, their main propulsion units struggling to get their velocity low enough to use the jump point looming just beyond.

"A lot of misses," Desjani commented, breathing slowly and deeply. "Looks like most of the bear-cow shots went wild."

Geary spared a quick glance at the fleet status readouts. The human warships had focused their fire on the missile ships that had managed to launch, annihilating the partial wave short of their targets though taking some damage from near misses. The bear-cows, hampered by fire control systems that couldn't match human capabilities at a combined engagement speed of point one nine light, hadn't scored many hits despite the tremendous amount of firepower hurled out by the superbattleships. He looked back at the maneuvering display, seeing velocities of his ships crawling downward, closer to point one light speed, the jump point approaching very, very quickly ahead.

"We'll make it," Desjani said.

"Not by much." But it would be enough. "All units, jump now."

5

"They're going to come after us," Desjani said. Outside of *Dauntless*, nothing was visible now except the dull gray emptiness of jump space. "Those civilian experts are right."

"Yeah." He had the same feeling. Geary watched one of the mysterious lights of jump space flare off to one side of the ship, then vanish. "The star we're heading for is a white dwarf. The odds of a habitable world are very small. Unless the bear-cows have heavily fortified a distant outpost, we'll be in a better position to take them out."

"We hit some of those superbattleships hard as we went past," Desjani pointed out. "But we didn't inflict much damage. They're going to be very hard to kill. And did you notice this?" She sent a record to Geary's display. "Watch the top layer of ships in our formation as they pass closest to the fortress."

He watched the replay, spotting what she had seen. During the moments when the human ships had been nearest to the fortress, passing beneath it though still thousands of kilometers distant, something had pushed them down and farther away from the fortress. "The bear-cow planetary defense. Whatever that is. At least those unexpected vector changes messed up some of the bear-cow fire aimed at those ships."

"And made some of the shots from those ships miss, too," Desjani said. "I think we've got a real good picture of the maximum range of that defense mechanism now."

"Good call." Tension was still draining from him. How long had he been up on the bridge, for how many hours had he been engaged in the bullfight with the alien armada? "We've got eight days in jump space. A really long leap."

"Are you finally going to get enough sleep?"

"That's my intent." He didn't have to tell Desjani to order maximum crew rest for the next couple of days. He knew that she would do that. Captains sometimes had to demand intense efforts from their crews for extended periods. All captains understood that. Good captains also knew the need to compensate for that extra effort when opportunity permitted, to let their crews know the additional exertion wasn't taken for granted. "First, I'm going to go down and give my thanks to my ancestors, though. We're going to need their help when we meet up with the bear-cows again."

It hadn't exactly been a victory, but it hadn't been a defeat. The fleet was clear of Pandora, and it was heading back toward home, even if that path back would be a somewhat crooked one of necessity as the fleet jumped from star to star. Once they reached Syndicate Worlds' space, they would be able to use the Syndic hypernet to get back to Alliance space quickly, but that option did not exist out here far beyond human-occupied space.

No one could claim that he personally and this fleet as an arm of the Alliance government had not followed their orders. Geary had done exactly what his orders called for, to learn more about the strength and numbers of the enigma race and to learn how far regions controlled by the enigmas extended beyond human-occupied space. Now it was time to take that information home.

The crew members whom Geary encountered in the passageways seemed cheerful enough in a "we survived that, and we're on the way home" sort of way.

He made his thanks to those powers who were hopefully watching out for him and the rest of the fleet, then made it to his stateroom, fell into his bunk, and finally let himself relax into blessed sleep.

"I'm going to have that talk with Commander Benan," Geary said. After three days in jump space, he had managed to catch up considerably on sleep and was not yet affected by the strange sensations of discomfort that grew in humans the longer they stayed in jump space.

Desjani raised beseeching eyes upward. It was odd, Geary thought, that humans still instinctively looked up toward the divinities they believed in. Even though humans had penetrated far into the heavens and among the stars, they still somehow thought of something greater being "up there."

"Admiral, I repeat that is a horrible idea."

"Understood. I think it's a horrible idea, too." He groped for the right words. "But I just have a gut feeling that I need to do this."

She eyed him. "A gut feeling?"

"Yes. Something keeps telling me that talking alone with Benan will accomplish something." Geary spread his hands as if trying to clutch at something insubstantial. "I owe that man. Personally, for what happened between me and his wife. And as a representative of the Alliance, for what happened to him in the line of duty. My brain tells me that there's nothing more I can accomplish, that I have done all that duty requires, but then something else says maybe honor requires a bit more. Requires me to try something that I have no right to expect will work. Because not trying something that *might* work would be safe but wrong."

Desjani sighed. "You're letting guilt drive you to this?"

"No. I don't think it's guilt. I did nothing against him on purpose, and I had nothing to do with what the Syndics did to Benan when he was a captive." Geary paused, thinking. "But he is one of my people, an officer under my command, who is suffering from some kind of injury. Nothing we have tried yet has helped much. One thing we have not tried is a private conversation with me. I need to do that."

She nodded, one corner of her mouth twisted in a rueful smile. "Duty is a hard horse to ride. All right. I might feel the same obligation. And if something keeps telling you that you need to try this… Our ancestors often speak to us in muted voices. Maybe one of yours is trying to tell you what to do. But"—the half smile disappeared—"you're not going to have that woman in there with you, are you?"

"No. Having Victoria Rione there would just emphasize one of the things between us."

"She could also serve to restrain him if he flies off the handle. Admiral, you know as well as I do that if Benan says something to you that is contrary to regulations, you are obligated to act on that even if no one else knows about it."

"I'm aware of that," Geary said.

Desjani shook her head. "Fine. Were you planning to have this little chat in your stateroom?"

"That is a private—"

"It's also where you and that woman spent a lot of time together. Remember?" Her voice roughened, but Desjani managed not to sound too angry at the thought. "Do you think Benan won't be aware of that?"

Geary grimaced. "We'll use a private conference room. Security-sealed."

"And I'll be outside the hatch. Along with that woman. If you hit the panic button in there, I'll have the hatch open and be throwing her between you two before you can count to three."

"All right, Captain."

Rione hadn't been any more enthusiastic about the idea than Desjani, but Geary had not relented. "Your instincts have been right often enough in battle," Rione finally said. "And mine have been just as often wrong. Perhaps you will be right in this as well."

Geary led Benan into the conference room, knowing that Desjani and Rione were just out of sight around a corner of the passageway and would come to stand by the hatch once it was closed.

Commander Benan stood rigidly by the table dominating the center of the room, his eyes wide like a trapped animal's. "Sit down," Geary said, realizing as he did so that the words had come out in the tones of an order.

Benan hesitated, his eyes fixed on the bulkhead before him, then sat rigidly in the nearest chair.

Geary sat down opposite Benan, keeping himself sitting erect, his hands resting on the table before him. There was nothing social about this meeting. It was purely professional. "Commander, you've been undergoing treatment since being liberated."

Benan nodded his head in a jerky motion but said nothing.

"Medical is very concerned at your lack of progress."

Another nod and continued silence.

"Is there anything I should know that is impacting your personal well-being, Commander? Anything that neither I nor medical staff is aware of?"

The commander's eyes went to Geary, meeting the admiral's gaze, something odd hidden inside those eyes. "There is nothing I can say." It came out haltingly.

"Nothing you can say?" Geary felt a flash of anger. *I'm trying to help. Why won't he let me?* "This isn't a personal issue, no matter what you may think. It is professional. You are an officer under my authority, and I am responsible for your health and well-being."

"There is nothing I can say," Benan repeated, his words sounding mechanical now.

"I am the commander of this fleet," Geary said, "and in that capacity and by that authority I hereby order you to tell me of anything that is complicating your medical treatment and recovery from prisoner-of-war conditions."

Benan seemed to stop breathing for a moment, then his mouth worked several times before words came. "The fleet commander. As the fleet commander, you order me to speak. Please repeat that."

"As the commander of this fleet I order you to speak," Geary said again, wondering what was happening.

Looking around, Benan paused to swallow. "We are alone. There are no recording devices active here."

"That is correct."

"Damn!" Benan swallowed again, this time convulsively, shooting to his feet. "I can talk. I can talk." He wavered where he stood.

"Sit down, Commander," Geary ordered.

Benan dropped into the chair again, his face working with emotions that changed too rapidly to read. "Yes, there is something inhibiting my treatment. I don't know how, but it must be responsible somehow. But I must explain. Do you know what I did, Admiral? Before the Syndics captured me?"

"You were a fleet officer," Geary answered. "Your record is a good one. Reliable, courageous, smart."

Benan gasped a short laugh. "That was who I used to be. Perhaps not the smart portion, though. No. A smart man wouldn't have gotten involved in it."

"Involved in what, Commander? The war?"

"We all had to get involved in the war." Benan stared at a corner of the stateroom. "Except Vic. She shouldn't have. It's changed her, too. Vic never would have—" His voice choked off, and Benan reddened, trembling, but didn't move otherwise, avoiding looking at Geary.

Since there was nothing useful that Geary could think of to say, he waited patiently. *I'm sorry I slept with your wife. We both thought you were dead. I'm sure that doesn't make you feel any better. But you already know it put your wife through hell when she found out you might still be alive.*

After a long pause, Benan spoke again. "I can tell you. Because if a fleet commander orders me to speak, I have to respond. If we are alone, with no witnesses."

"Are you saying that some order bound you from saying anything before this?"

"It wasn't an order, Admiral," Benan spat. "Have you been told about Brass Prince? Have they told Black Jack about Brass Prince?"

"Brass Prince?" Geary mentally ran through the many classified project and plan names that he had seen since awakening from survival sleep. "I can't recall hearing of that."

"You would remember if you had." Benan's voice had sunk to a whisper. "A very secret project undertaken by the Alliance government. Do you know what we were working on, Admiral? Biowarfare," Commander Benan said, his voice barely audible now. "Strategic biological warfare. You might have believed that's the one rule the Syndics and the Alliance didn't break during the war. But the Alliance conducted some research."

"Strategic biological warfare?" Geary repeated, not believing what he was hearing.

"Yes. Things able to wipe out the populations of entire planets. Things that could sit dormant inside human bodies long enough to be transported to other star systems before they became virulent, then wipe out populations so quickly that no countermeasures could be successful." Benan's hands shook. "Purely for defensive purposes, of course. That's what everyone said. If we had that capability, the Syndics wouldn't dare use a similar capability against us for fear of retaliation in kind. That's what we told ourselves. Maybe it was true."

Geary realized that he had stopped breathing and slowly inhaled before speaking. "Does the Europa Rule still exist?"

"Of course it does. But we were told that things had changed. That we needed to take into account new realities. The Syndics would do anything. Strategic biowarfare didn't seem beyond them."

"But… the Europa Rule," Geary said again, bewildered. "In my time, they showed vids of that in high school. To ensure everyone knew what happened. That colony moon in the Sol Star System wasn't rendered uninhabitable for humans for all time by an attack. The pathogen was accidentally released by a so-called defense research facility on Europa. If it hadn't been so virulent, caused death so quickly, it might have reached Earth itself before our ancestors realized what had happened."

"I know that! We all knew that!" Commander Benan glowered at the deck, then spoke in a more controlled fashion. "They still show the videos in school. Images, as clear as the day they were taken by surveillance cameras whose operators were already dead or by uncrewed probes sent down from space. The people on Europa lifeless, bodies strewn everywhere within the habitats. Some lying there peacefully, and others revealing final moments of panic and pain. If you've seen them, I'm sure you remember them as clearly as I do."

"I don't know how anyone could forget them. And the afterimages?" Geary asked.

"Yes. Centuries later, hallways and rooms still empty of life, filled only with the slowly crumbling remnants of those who had lived there." Benan shook his head. "We were told that we were working to prevent that by having the capability to do it. Is it odd, Admiral, what humans can convince themselves makes sense?"

"You were part of this?" Geary wondered if the revulsion he felt could be heard in his voice.

Benan bared his teeth in a grimace. "For a while. But one of my ancestors was aboard one of the warships enforcing the quarantine of Europa. His ship intercepted and destroyed a merchant ship packed with refugees."

"That's a hard memory to carry," Geary said.

"Harder than you think, Admiral. My ancestor knew that his sister's family was aboard that ship. They might have already been dead from the plague, but he never knew. And I... now I was working on the same sort of hell project." Benan slammed his fist down. "But I regained my sanity! I told them I would not work on it anymore. I told them it was criminal and insane, that it must be shut down."

"Did they?"

"I don't know. I was transferred out, given a fleet assignment." Benan bared his teeth in a grimace. "Doubtless in the hope that I would die valiantly in action and take my secrets with me. We were sworn to secrecy, but when I was transferred I was also mentally programmed for it. Not just an order. A block. Did they have blocks in your time?"

"Blocks?" What did personal configuration of communications have to do with—"What kind of blocks do you mean?"

"Mental blocks. Inhibitions implanted in the mind."

A memory finally flashed to the surface. "Mental blocks? But— Those are—They imposed a mental block on you?" Geary knew he sounded appalled again.

"Yes. I could *literally* say nothing about it. I knew what was working at me, eating at my head. *But I couldn't say anything!*" He yelled the last, then subsided again.

Geary rubbed his mouth with one hand, trying to find words. "But the block allowed you to talk if ordered to."

"Only if ordered by a fleet commander. Because regulations required that. And only if no one else was present. Small risk there. What were the odds that a fleet commander would talk to me personally, that the commander would order me to talk about something of which they had no knowledge, and no one else would be with us when that question was asked?" Benan stared at Geary. "Did you know?"

"No. I just had an instinct that I needed to talk to you alone. Something told me that was the right thing to do."

Benan nodded, much of the tension draining out of him, replaced by the slump of mental and emotional exhaustion. "Of course. Black Jack, sent by the living stars. As much as I hate you for what you did, they do seem to talk to you."

"I never claimed such a thing." Geary thought about what Desjani had said, that Benan must have been tortured by the Syndics. "When you were a prisoner, did the Syndics find out anything about this?"

"No." Benan laughed bitterly. "Blocked. I told you it was all blocked. I couldn't say anything. Not a thing. No matter what. No matter... what... they did." His voice fell to a whisper again. "I can't remember what they did."

Geary nodded to cover up his inability to find words again. "How can we help you now? What can we do?"

"I have no idea." Benan shrugged. "My fate isn't important. I had to stop caring about me. Victoria. She's all I care about." His gaze on Geary tightened with anger, and Benan looked away again. "Something is driving her. Something she does not want to control her. It's not you. I suspected that. It's not."

"She recently finally told me that someone she wouldn't or couldn't name gave her some kind of orders before she joined us for this mission."

"She's told me less than that," Benan grumbled, then laughed. "You'd think I wasn't judged stable enough to be trusted. What could anyone use to force Victoria Rione to do their bidding? She does not bend easily. What could buy her obedience and silence?"

Geary felt a sudden ugly certainty fill him. "She has told me, and I believe it, that you and the Alliance are everything to her. I've been trying to understand what kind of lever someone could use against her. Maybe this is that lever. Maybe someone with knowledge of your involvement in Brass Prince has threatened to make it public unless she does what they say."

"Yes! I am sure that has to be it! I would be demonized! They would blame me for Brass Prince, say that I had conceived it and pushed it along until they shut it down! She thought me dead, unable to defend myself!" Benan trembled again with barely suppressed rage, but Geary realized with surprise that this time the rage was directed at Benan himself. "Victoria compromised herself, was blackmailed to protect the memory of me, of who Commander Paol Benan once was. And look at me, Admiral! Look at what I have become! For this ruin of a man, the only woman who matters in all the universe has compromised herself!"

It all made sense, the pieces falling into place. He had no proof, only a growing certainty that this explained a number of previously inexplicable things. "You're her Achilles' heel, the one thing they could threaten to strike at that would force her do to what they wanted. But being who she is, she's followed their orders in ways that probably haven't furthered their aims. Do you think she knows who they are?"

Benan shook his head as he stared at the deck. "If she knew, I think she would have gone after them." He paused. "Or perhaps not. I am gradually learning that my wife can play the long game very well."

"When she first saw you, after we liberated you, I wondered if I had seen a flash of horror on her face," Geary said. "Now I know why. With you alive, if this information was leaked, your reputation would not only be destroyed, but you'd also be brought up on war crimes charges."

"Yes. Charges I couldn't deny or refute because I couldn't say one word about it." Benan stood up, his body rigid at attention. "There is a way out. You can free my wife, Admiral, and free me. You already have adequate grounds for sentencing me to die by firing squad. Do so. Once I am dead, declared a traitor, there is nothing else they can hold over Victoria."

Geary came to his feet as well, meeting Benan eye to eye. "I will not. You both deserve better."

"Have you understood nothing?"

"I understand that handing them this victory would accomplish nothing. Dead, your memory could still be smeared, and you'd be unable to testify in your own defense if we can get that block lifted."

"But—"

"Dammit, Commander! Think! You want me to execute you for treason? Or mutiny? A dead traitor? When your wife has already risked everything to protect your name and honor? That alone would destroy her. And if those charges are raised publicly, how many people would automatically believe a convicted traitor guilty as rumored? How many might accuse her of aiding and abetting in the crime?"

Benan sat down again like a balloon man who had been suddenly deflated. "There's no way out."

"There's always a way out. We just have to find it." He would do this. He owed it to this man.

Perhaps Benan understood, his eyes sharpening on Geary. "You think to balance the scales?"

"No. I can't do that. But even if I had never met Victoria Rione, I would not allow this kind of thing to be done to a good officer. And if this Brass Prince project is still running, I need to do what I can to get it shut down. I need you for that."

Benan shook his head. "You cannot depend upon me. I am not the man I was. I can see myself do things and not control them."

"Perhaps there is something that can be done now that we know the problem," Geary said. "I will pursue this. My orders to you, Commander, are to do everything in your power to remain stable. You can tell me what you need, and if that means telling me to lock you into solitary confinement in the brig, then tell me that."

"Admiral, I can't even talk about that aspect of it! I can't suggest things if those things are related to the block! Believe me, I have tried."

"*I* don't have a block." Geary stood up. "Since we are both convinced that your wife is aware of the blackmail charge that would be used against you, do you have any objection to my telling her the full truth?"

"She is not cleared for that information," Benan objected.

"She'll hear it from me."

Benan stood up, bracing himself on the table's surface with rigid arms. "I will always hate you, Admiral."

"I understand that."

"Why didn't you take her? You could have had anyone."

"She didn't love me. She never did. There's only one man Victoria Rione loves, one man she would sacrifice everything for, and that is you."

Commander Benan didn't answer, his head bowed, tears falling to splash onto the hard surface of the table.

Geary opened the hatch and stepped out, finding Rione and Desjani standing on opposite sides of the hatch. "I learned some answers." He leaned very close to Rione, his lips next to her ear, his words barely audible. "Emissary Rione, your husband has a mental block implanted by security." Her face went pale, then flushed with anger. "I think you know how that was justified, but if not, I will brief you privately."

He stepped back and looked toward Desjani, seeing her glaring at the hatch. "Is he safe now?" she asked.

"No. But we may have found the key to helping him."

Rione paused partway into the room, looking back at Geary. "Help may still be extraordinarily difficult. Thank you, Admiral."

She closed the hatch, leaving Desjani and Geary alone.

"Did he——" Desjani began in formal tones.

"No. He did not." Geary shook his head. "I need to talk with your ship's medical personnel, but I have a nasty suspicion that they won't know what to do. Once we get out of jump space, I can talk to the senior fleet doctor. If anyone should be aware of the proper treatment, or able to learn what that is, it should be that doctor. Meanwhile, keep watching him. By his own admission, Commander Benan is not mentally or emotionally reliable or stable."

"Those damned Syndics," Desjani muttered.

"The Syndics didn't do it to him, Tanya. The Alliance did."

She didn't answer for a long moment. "Because it was necessary?" Desjani finally asked.

"Yeah. One more thing that was 'necessary' to win but somehow didn't lead to victory."

A few days later, Geary sat once again in the fleet command seat on the bridge of *Dauntless*, waiting for the moment when the fleet would exit the jump point at the white dwarf star. If this was another bear-cow-occupied star, they would face a tough fight if more fortresses guarded the jump points. If it was an enigma-controlled star, they might face a fight with the enigma forces that had gathered to pursue the human fleet the length of enigma territory. And coming on behind them would very probably be that bear-cow armada they had outmaneuvered at Pandora. "Maybe there's no one there," he said out loud.

"That would be a nice option," Desjani agreed.

At the back of the bridge, both Rione and Charban waited.

Around the bridge, the different watch-standers stood ready. On Geary's display, which in jump space could only show the status of *Dauntless* herself, the battle cruiser glowed in combat-ready status, shields at maximum and all weapons ready.

"Ten seconds to exit," Lieutenant Castries announced. "Five... four... three... two... one."

The universe lurched, and Geary felt the disorientation that accompanied leaving jump. He struggled to recover, focusing on the display, where the gray nothingness of jump space had been replaced by the star-filled darkness of normal space.

Alerts were sounding from the combat systems as the ships of the fleet went into the automatic evasion maneuver that Geary had ordered programmed in before the fleet jumped for here. *Dauntless's* frame protested as the battle cruiser slewed down and to the starboard, evading any possible defenses at the jump point before the humans on the ships could clear their minds.

Desjani recovered before Geary, and he heard her words as his eyes finally focused on his display. "Ah, hell."

Geary blinked at the display, his mind realizing two things at almost the same moment.

The enigmas weren't waiting at the new star. Neither were the bear-cows.

Something else was.

"What are they?" Charban asked in a hushed voice.

"What they are," Desjani replied, "is far enough away that we don't have to worry about an immediate fight." She paused as the fleet's sensors provided more data from the analysis they had begun the moment the fleet entered this star system. "About one light-hour distant from us. They're not enigmas?"

"No, Captain," Lieutenant Yuon confirmed. "The combat systems are marking them as unknown. The characteristics don't match the enigma ships we saw. Nor are they like any human ships or anything we saw in the Pandora Star System."

"Another alien race," Geary said, past surprise by now.

"*Another* one?" Desjani echoed, then turned an accusing look on Geary.

He didn't answer, staring at the depiction of the force awaiting them here. About one light-hour from the jump exit, a grand array of ships hung in a complex formation that looked like multiple formations interwoven into a single grand scheme. It looked less like a formation than a work of art. "Damn," Lieutenant Castries blurted out admiringly.

"It is beautiful," Desjani agreed. "Now tell me what kind of ships make up that lovely little arrangement."

Geary waited as sensors studied the distant ships, combining readings taken from every ship in the fleet to produce composite images, which finally flashed before him on his display. "What?" If the presence of these aliens hadn't shocked him, the shapes of their ships did.

Desjani had a bewildered expression. "That's what I thought. What the hell?"

The ships varied in size from something half the mass of an Alliance destroyer to much larger ones about the dimensions of the late and unlamented scout battleships that the Alliance had tried as an unsuccessful experiment. But that was the only aspect of them that seemed familiar.

"Perfectly smooth ovoids," Lieutenant Yuon confirmed. "No protruding sensors, weapons hard points, launchers, shield generators, thrusters... nothing. Just smooth shells."

"What about propulsion?" Desjani demanded. "They've got to have visible propulsion systems."

"None we can spot from this angle, Captain. If those ships are all bow on toward this jump point, their main propulsion systems might all be facing away from us."

Desjani spread her hands in bafflement. "What's the point of having a ship that can't do anything?"

"They must have something we haven't spotted yet," Geary replied, grateful that these ships were a light-hour away. It would take an hour for that force to see the light from the arrival of the human fleet, and longer to react. That gave him a crucial margin of time in which to try to learn more about whatever crewed those ships. "What kind of creatures created such beautiful ships?"

Desjani shook her head. "They're not bear-cows, that's for sure. Admiral, would you please stop finding new, intelligent alien species?"

"I'm not trying to find new ones, Captain Desjani."

Her reply was interrupted by an incoming message. Captain Smythe had a look of bliss as his image appeared. "By my ancestors, Admiral, these creatures are engineers!"

"Why do you say that?"

"Look at what they did! Have you spotted the systems on the exteriors of the hulls yet?"

As Smythe spoke, the fleet combat systems began updating the images of the alien spacecraft, highlighting subtle features that were tentatively identified as the weaponry, sensors, shields, generators, and thrusters, which had been unseen earlier. "Look at them!" Smythe said. "They've faired everything into the hulls. It's all smooth, as unbroken as possible. The engineering required to do that and retain functionality for those features is… it's awesome, Admiral."

Geary tried to see it from Smythe's point of view. "You think the creatures here are excellent engineers?"

"Excellent and perhaps intuitive," Smythe agreed. "This work— the design, the construction—is simply elegant. There's no other word for it."

Geary turned to Desjani. "Captain Smythe thinks the creatures here are all born engineers."

"Oh, great," Desjani said. "Just what we need. Another species lacking in social skills."

"What do you think of their formation?"

She spread her hands. "It's gorgeous. The individual subformations and the interlinking patterns of those into the overall formation. But in terms of function? Assuming their weapons are roughly equivalent to our own, that formation will certainly work. Is it better than our cruder arrangements? I wouldn't say that. We achieve interlocking fire zones and concentration of fire without the same…"

"Elegance?" Geary asked.

"Yeah. That's a good word for it." Desjani pondered the images for a moment, then shook her head. "I'd be willing to bet that maintaining that beautiful arrangement would complicate maneuvering so much that it would create significant difficulty for them. We could do that. We could tell the maneuvering systems to generate formations based on fractals like a Mandelbrot set or by replicating Fourier series and stuff like that, but it would involve a lot of extra work when we maneuvered. I can't see any benefit from that to compensate for the complications."

"So they're doing it that way because they want to, not because it's superior in any absolute or physical way."

"That's my assessment," Desjani agreed.

"Captain Smythe, from an engineer's perspective, do you think the design of those ships produces better results?"

Smythe tilted his head slightly as he thought. "How do you define better results? In terms of pure functionality, they may perform less well. They probably perform less well. I mean, clearly, a hull as smooth as possible offers no angles or weak points where any force striking them can concentrate. Any force or object the ship encounters will more likely be deflected. But our own hulls are curved over the great majority of their surfaces to get the same results. Making everything else as flush with the hull as possible would create some major challenges in terms of effectiveness. I would think, and this is only from what I know as an engineer and not taking into account whatever the creatures who built those ships can do, I would say they've probably lost some functionality and added some complexity by fairing in everything so smoothly."

It added up to a consistent picture. Whatever these creatures were, engineering and perhaps mathematical aesthetics mattered a great deal to them. "They like beautiful things, the same sort of beauty we can appreciate."

"In terms of their ships, yes, Admiral."

"Thank you, Captain Smythe."

Geary looked over at Desjani. "Maybe that's a good sign, that they produce things we also find beautiful."

She raised one eyebrow at him. "May I remind the Admiral that we got chased to this star system by a horde of cute little teddy bear-cows who exterminate just about everything else they encounter?"

Geary pulled out the scale a little more on his display, studying the star system at which they had arrived. A white dwarf star, bright but unwelcoming to life. Only two planets, one a bare ball of rock orbiting rapidly less than two light-minutes from the star, the other a bloated gas giant, large enough to qualify as a brown dwarf. Based on the few minutes of tracking they had, the fleet sensors were estimating that the brown dwarf had a highly eccentric orbit. Right now it was ten light-minutes from the star, but according to system estimates, it would swing out perhaps as far as two light-hours before looping in again. "Unless they're a very exotic life-form, this isn't their home star system."

"They didn't evolve on that rock," Desjani agreed. "And that brown dwarf looks like a capture. If that orbit estimate is right, it got caught in the star's gravity field not too long ago. A couple of million years, maybe."

In terms of the life of stars, that was a very short time. Geary considered the implications. "They're out here, in a star system with no visible merits aside from providing jump points, facing a jump point that goes to the bear-cow star."

"The jump point might also be accessible from enigma space," Desjani pointed out. "I'm curious as to why they're positioned where they are inside this star system, though. Aha. So that's why."

The fleet's systems had finally identified the other jump points in this star system. There were three, one off to the left and ahead of the human fleet, a second to the right and above, and a third nearly on the opposite side of the star from the humans. Desjani ran some maneuvers, smiling with satisfaction. "Yes, indeed. See? From where they are, they can intercept anyone coming in here no matter which of those other three jump points they head for."

"And they'd have time to see what the other force was doing instead of having to react on the fly," Geary said. "All right. They're good at engineering, and they're smart tactically. Let's hope they're not hostile."

"We don't have a great track record in that respect," Desjani noted.

"Third time's the charm." Geary issued new orders to the fleet, bringing it around at a steady point one light speed to head for the jump point that should lead to another star on the way back to human space. As he did so, his eyes went from the human formation, a crude box disrupted by the final maneuvers and the fight at Pandora, to the gorgeous loops and spirals of the alien formation. "Let's try not to look too much like barbarians."

He searched among available formation choices in the maneuvering database before settling on one intended for a pass in review ceremony in which the individual divisions and squadrons formed into diamonds, those diamonds in turn congregating into larger diamonds to produce what he had once considered an impressive display. Against the alien formation here it would still look awkward, but at least it wouldn't be grossly primitive.

"All units, immediate execute, assume Formation Diamond Diamond Ceremonial."

Rione was standing beside his chair, her attitude tense. "Communicate with them, Admiral. Something short to assure them we come in peace."

"We come in peace," Desjani murmured sarcastically, "with a fleet of warships."

"Who are they guarding this star system against?" Rione demanded, ignoring Desjani. "They are facing this jump point, from which the bear-cows would come. Tell them we are not here to fight."

Maybe, for once, such a plea would have some success. As he thought about the bear-cows who would be arriving in this star system soon in pursuit of his fleet, Geary hoped that he had found allies, not more enemies. "Am I set up to send a broad-spectrum message?" he asked Desjani.

Desjani glanced at her comm watch, who nodded back immediately. "Whenever you want, Admiral."

Sitting straight and speaking slowly and calmly, Geary tried to convey strength and nonthreat at the same time. "Greetings to the people in the ships here. We are representatives of humanity on a peaceful mission of exploration." Hopefully, the weaponry and combat damage visible on the exteriors of many of the human ships wouldn't call that "peaceful mission" assertion into question. "We wish to establish friendly contact with you and pass through this star system on our way back to the regions of space controlled by our species. This is Admiral John Geary, to the honor of our ancestors, out."

He sat back as the transmission ended, unable to resist a laugh. "How could they possibly understand a word of that?"

"Hopefully, they will read attitudes," Rione said, but it didn't sound as if even she believed that.

Desjani had been running some data on her display, one hand moving rapidly to direct the calculations, and she now pointed to the representation of the new alien force. "We've got them in front, able to move to block us no matter which jump point we go for. According to our maneuvering system's best estimate, the bear-cow armada would have required anywhere from half an hour to an hour to get turned and come through the jump point at Pandora after us."

"Half an hour to an hour?" Geary checked the time. "We've been in this star system about twenty minutes now."

"Should we accelerate to get farther from that jump exit faster?" Desjani pressed.

"That would have us accelerating toward this other group of alien ships," Geary said. "That might look aggressive."

"If they want to fight us, they'll do it no matter what we do or don't do."

He shook his head firmly. "I won't push things toward the worst case because it might happen. The possibility of being caught between those things ahead of us and the bear-cows behind us is bad. Making sure we were caught between them would be worse."

She paused, decided that Geary wouldn't budge, and turned back to her display. "I'm going to stand down my crew then. We won't even see the reaction from those aliens ahead of us for close to another two hours, and if the bear-cows come out chasing us, they're going to have a long haul while we decide where to let them catch us."

He nodded this time, not wanting to face the necessity of a major fight with the bear-cows but knowing he would have to. He couldn't simply lead a force like that back toward human-controlled space, not knowing how long the bear-cows could continue in pursuit. If they were lucky, the bear-cows would have been content with chasing the humans out of the Pandora Star System.

Though he must have made the leader of that armada extremely angry with all of the maneuvers that had set up the human escape. Not to mention how angry that leader might be at the escape itself.

It took another twenty-five minutes, with the fleet about six light-minutes from the jump exit as it continued on at a steady point one light speed, before the answer to what the bear-cows would do became clear. Alerts sounded on the displays as the fleet's sensors spotted the bear-cow warships arriving at the jump exit six minutes ago, still in pursuit of the human fleet.

"I sure hope those guys ahead of us are friendly," Desjani said.

6

This was one of those times when the huge distances in space could only feed frustration. With one force of unknown aliens before them, and another force of too-well-known and hostile aliens behind them, Geary wanted to do something. Anything. But he could only wait, not knowing how the unknown aliens would react to the appearance of the human fleet and aware that anything he did might be misinterpreted by the unknown aliens. Meanwhile, the bear-cow armada had begun accelerating again, slowly overhauling the human fleet. At least there the distances involved were helping Geary. Even if the bear-cows took their velocity up past point two light speed, it would take them hours to catch the humans.

"Captain, we've got something coming in from ahead," the communications watch announced. "Broadcast signal repeating across a wide band of frequencies."

Rione laughed with sudden relief. "They want to talk to us."

"Maybe just to tell us they're going to kill us," Desjani muttered.

"Is it just audio or also video?" she asked her comm watch.

"Definitely video, Captain. It roughly resembles one of the old formats used by humans, so we can convert the signal into something we can view as soon as the system generates the right conversion protocol. The image might get jerky at times, but it should be clear, and audio should be fine."

"Give us a look as soon as you can," Desjani ordered.

"It should be less than a minute, Captain."

In fact, it only took a couple more seconds before virtual windows popped into existence beside Geary and others on the bridge, a sharp image visible in them. He gaped at what he saw, only gradually realizing that the entire bridge had gone silent.

"How big is that thing?" Desjani finally asked in a choked voice. "Lieutenant Yuon?"

"We... we can't tell, Captain," Yuon stuttered. "There's nothing to scale it against."

Geary forced himself to look closely at the image. If a very large spider had somehow mated with a wolf, the result might have been something like that. At least six appendages that might work equally well as arms or legs, a skin that appeared shiny and hard yet also sprouted patches of hair or fur, a head adorned with six eyes spread across the center, a flap above the eyes that might be for breathing, and beneath the eyes, a multijawed bear trap of a mouth. Two flaps on either side of the head made up of very thin skin rippled with veins might represent ears.

It was as if someone had searched for all of the most horrible-looking elements of living creatures and combined them into one.

"At least it doesn't have tentacles," Charban said.

Geary's gaze slid away from the hideous appearance to focus on the clothing the creature wore. Brilliantly colored bands of cloth that shone like silk were woven about the body in an intricate pattern, the colors never clashing as they wound about each other. Odd, yet beautiful in its own way.

The creature was speaking, a high-pitched, wavering sound, as it spread out four limbs to their full extent on either side of its body. Impressive claws tipping the ends of the limbs also spread out, the creature holding the pose as it kept talking, the sounds occasionally interspersed with clacking as jaws struck together.

"Ancestors preserve us," Desjani whispered, then swallowed and spoke in a nearly normal voice. "Is it threatening us?"

"I have no idea," Geary said.

"Something that looks like *that* made ships and formations that look like *that*."

"Yeah." He looked down, breathing deeply to regain his composure. "Forward this to the civilian experts and see what they think it is doing."

Rione finally spoke up, her voice the closest to normal of all those on the bridge. "It *is* talking to us. Whatever they are, they initiated contact. The enigmas have only spoken to us after a long period of hiding, and even then, very reluctantly. The bear-cows have never exchanged any communication with us."

"Maybe it's just asking us how we taste," Desjani muttered, then laughed. "I wonder how you say 'tastes like chicken' in their language?"

Geary found himself laughing, too, the dark humor a welcome release from the shock of seeing the creature.

"Captain?" The communications watch had managed to control his own half-hysterical laughter at Desjani's joke. "There's something attached to this communication. A program of some kind."

Desjani gave Geary a bitter glance. "A Trojan horse or a virus or what?" she asked the watch-stander.

"It doesn't seem to be any of those things, Captain. It's not concealed in any way. The attachment is very obvious. Either these, um... whatevers are incredibly unsophisticated about computer security issues, or they wanted to be sure we spotted that program."

"Run it by security," Desjani ordered. "I want our code people to analyze it and give me their assessment before we do anything with it. Wait a minute. That message could have been picked up by every ship in the fleet."

"Yes, Captain."

Without taking his eyes off the alien message, Geary hit his comm controls. "All units are to refrain from recording, running, or otherwise activating the software attached to the alien message. It will only be tested and activated under controlled conditions and as authorized by me."

In the comm window before Geary, the creature had ended its speech. Its four upper limbs folded back against its body, crossing over in front of it, then two rose again just enough to frame its head before the message ended.

"Now what?" Desjani asked.

"I don't know," Geary said. "Maybe it's easier to decide what to do when they *don't* talk to us."

"We've got the bear-cows on our tails. We can't just hang around waiting to figure out what these... spider-wolves want or need or whatever."

"You should send a reply," Rione said.

"A reply?" Geary questioned. "To what? I don't know what that thing just said." The idea of sending a message in the blind had made sense a couple of hours ago. But now, after viewing the spider-wolves' message, the gap between him and the creatures in those beautiful ships seemed vaster than the distances between stars. "They won't know what my gestures mean, they won't understand my words, and I may look as ugly to them as they do to me."

"Nonetheless, you should reply," Rione insisted. "Let them know we want to talk. Perhaps they know something about humans. They are neighbors of a sort to the enigmas."

Geary gave Rione a cross look. "I smiled at the bear-cows, and by showing my incisors seemed to them to be preparing to eat them."

"That is only a guess, Admiral," she reminded him. "A good guess, I admit. But I heard you earlier speaking of engineering issues, which apply also to living creatures. An attack posture is different from a defense posture, isn't it? Doesn't it have to be?"

Charban answered her. "It depends. There are a number of combat methods in which an individual balances, ready to attack or defend as necessary. However, those are fairly sophisticated as such things go." He paused, his expression thoughtful. "In human terms, we would indicate aggression by leaning forward, arms close to the body, ready to strike. Defense might look the same. But projecting peaceful intent is done by humans by standing erect, arms spread out, hands open. That posture does not suit either attack or defense."

"The way the, uh, spider-wolf stood," Geary agreed. "Arms out, claws open."

"Ready to grab us," Desjani said. "How do they do fine motor manipulation with claws, anyway?"

"Another good question." Geary scowled, knowing that Rione was right but wondering if he could talk openly and calmly when he now knew what his audience looked like. "Can we send a reply in the same format in which we received that one?"

"Of course *Dauntless* can do that," Desjani replied, looking off ended by the suggestion that her ship might not be able to do something.

"We can use the same conversion program, Admiral," the comm watch explained. "Only instead of converting their stuff to our format, we'll do it backwards and convert our format to theirs."

He nodded but sat silently, trying to get himself in the right state of mind to speak to those things without showing revulsion.

Charban spoke, his voice meditative. "You can partly judge someone by what they do, by what they create, and by what they surround themselves with. We did that with the bear-cows, looking at what they had done with their world and deciding from that they must be ruthless. Here we can't see the home world of these new creatures, but we can see what they created. We can see how they like to do things. That offers us some grounds for empathy."

"Empathy." Geary heard his skepticism clearly in this single word.

"Yes. Just as you could see aspects of humans in what we create and how we do things." Charban waved around. "We made this fleet. A mighty instrument of war. That tells you something about us, but it doesn't stop with the obvious. Not everything in this fleet reflects pure science or physics or engineering. Many things reflect how we want things to be done because that is how we like them. Not because they're most efficient but because we like doing things that way. It matters to us, though we might not be able to say why."

"The Golden Mean," Rione said. "It's a ratio between numbers. Humans use it in many things because we like seeing things with that proportion."

"A ratio?" Geary asked.

"It's an irrational mathematical constant," Lieutenant Castries reported, squinting at the results of the query she had run. "Derived from the ratio of a larger quantity to a smaller one. It's about one to one point six. Found in architecture, sculpture, the proportions of hard-copy books, paper, playing cards, music, and virtual windows among other things."

"Exactly." Rione gestured toward her display. "These displays probably default to such a ratio of sides because we like seeing things in those proportions. It is somehow part of us. Now look upon these creatures and what they have created. Somewhere within them is beauty."

"Somewhere very *deep* within them perhaps," Geary said.

"Look upon their works, think about those works, as you speak to them."

"Or maybe get drunk first," Desjani suggested. "That always makes ugly easier to accept."

"I won't ask how you know that," Geary replied. He sighed, then stood up, trying to maintain a nonaggressive stance. But then he stopped. "Images. We can try imagery. How do I get my display to show along with me?"

"We want to show them one of our displays?" Desjani questioned.

"Yes."

"Wait, Admiral," the comm watch said, his hands flying over controls. "All right. It's visible beside you if you transmit. Here's a secondary window that shows what you look like."

The secondary window popped up, so that Geary could see himself standing next to a display image. He considered how to do things, then tapped his comm controls. "Thank you for communicating with us. We want to pass through this star system peacefully." He pointed to the jump exit they had arrived at, then swung his finger to point to one of the jump points on the other side of this star system. "There are enemies who have pursued us." Now he held out an open palm in a shielding gesture against the representation of the bear-cow armada, his other hand poised to strike. "We will not fight you." Now he dropped both hands as he faced the representation of the spider-wolf alien force, his palms outward and empty. "To the honor of our ancestors, this is Admiral Geary, out."

"Captain?" Desjani looked over as the image of a lieutenant commander appeared before her. Geary recognized him as *Dauntless*'s systems security officer. "We isolated the attachment to that alien message and ran it on a physically quarantined system so there was no way it could infect anything. It took a fair amount of work, but we figured out how to run it since it contained its own operating system that seemed to adapt to our hardware."

"It adapted to our hardware?"

"Yes, Captain, but don't worry. It can't get to any other systems. There's no physical or electronic connection, and the unit is in an isolation box."

Desjani took a deep breath. "What is it?" she asked.

"I think..." The systems security officer scratched his head. "It's got pictures, and some kind of interactive routine. It kind of reminded me of a kid's book. You know, something for real young kids, to teach words and stuff."

"Words?" Charban cried. "A pictorial means of establishing communication!"

"Yes, sir," the systems security officer agreed. "That's what it feels like to me."

"Keep it quarantined for now," Desjani ordered, "and—"

"We need access to that," Charban insisted.

"This is my ship, and I decide what gets access to its systems."

"Captain Desjani," Geary said formally, "I agree it should be quarantined, kept isolated, but we need to get access to it as soon as possible for both General Charban and Emissary Rione as well as the civilian experts."

"We can put together a quarantined network," the systems security officer suggested. "It will take some work, and they'll have to access it in one compartment because we'll run short, physical connections between the workstations, but that way they can all play with it at the same time."

"Use one of the big conference rooms," Desjani ordered. "Assume a dozen users at one time. How long until it's up?"

"Half an hour, Captain."

"Do it, and make sure if you need more time to do it right you ask for it. I don't want that software having any access to the rest of the systems."

The lieutenant commander nodded. "Yes, Captain. I don't want something like that loose, either. If we can figure out how it adapted to our hardware, we'll get some really cool ideas from it, though."

Desjani twisted her mouth as she watched her security officer. "Their software does things our software can't?"

"Yes, Captain." The lieutenant commander grinned with almost childlike enthusiasm. "We don't know how yet, but it was amazing to watch. The software is really... cool."

"Thank you. Get on that network," Desjani said. After the image of the systems security officer vanished, she looked at Geary. "Some software that makes my code monkeys drool with delight, and those things just gave it to us."

"Maybe they don't think it's anything special," Geary suggested.

"Maybe not, but if that's so, I'd hate to see their special software." Desjani turned to Charban. "General, you'll have access to that program as soon as I get that isolated network safely set up."

Geary faced Charban and Rione. "They must intend for us to use that program to develop a means of communication. Here's what I most need to be able to communicate to them. I need them to know we don't want to fight them. Can we transit their territory in peace? I need to know their attitude toward the bear-cows. Are they enemies? Neutral? Or allies? Will they stand by if we engage the bear-cow armada, or will they take an active role?"

Charban nodded, his eyes intent. "Those will be our priorities. But aside from the time we must spend learning how to ask those things, there is the time involved in exchanging messages. We are still more than fifty light-minutes from the spider-wolf ships."

"I know we need time." Geary tapped another control. "All units, accelerate to point one five light speed at time five zero." That would buy some more hours before the bear-cows caught up, more hours to find out what the spider-wolves intended.

"How the hell are we going to take those things down?" Desjani wondered, looking at her display, where the bear-cow superbattleships were thundering in the wake of the human fleet.

"Has anyone here not seen the images sent to us by the beings in the ships ahead of us?" Geary asked, looking around the conference table.

Since the message had been broadcast to the fleet, he expected that everyone had seen them.

The expressions on his ship captains answered the question without words.

"We still don't know what the intent of the spider-wolves is," Geary said. "Our experts and our emissaries are working to establish meaningful communications, but, at best, such communications will be primitive and very limited for some time."

"Are they going to aid the Kicks?" Captain Badaya demanded. "That's what we need to know."

"The Kicks?" Geary looked around, seeing some of the officers nodding in recognition of the term and others looking as puzzled as he felt.

"It's a term the sailors came up with," Captain Duellos explained. "They started calling the bear-cows Killer Cows or Crazy Cows, which got condensed to KCs and CCs, which are both pronounced as Kicks."

"Works for me," Desjani muttered.

Geary couldn't really object to either name when it came to the bear-cows, and Kicks wasn't either obscene or a word that sounded like it might be obscene, so the term would work for him as well. But the byplay had distracted him. Geary took a second to recall Badaya's question, then activated a copy of the latest message received from the spider-wolves so that it played before everyone present, virtually or in person. The animation of spider-wolf ships attacking bear-cow ships could not be mistaken. "It looks like they are enemies. Watch the next scene."

Now the animation shifted, incorporating pasted-in images of human warships in this fleet. The animated human warships and the spider-wolf ships moved together, jointly firing on bear-cow combatants, which exploded in some nicely done computer graphics.

"They want to ally with us?" Captain Duellos said. "The ugliest creatures in the universe, and they want to be friends."

Captain Bradamont, who rarely spoke in these meetings, did so now. "As the admiral mentioned earlier, they're probably thinking the same thing about us."

Laughter erupted, born as much from release of tension as from the humor of the statement.

"If they think we're ugly," Captain Badaya added, "wait until they see some of the Marines!"

More laughter, accompanied by looks at General Carabali, who waved away the comment. "It's a well-known fact that when we hit planet-side, the Marines get all the available girls and boys while the fleet officers and sailors are left standing around alone."

"Taking the local populace prisoner is not a measure of social success by most definitions," Duellos observed.

Geary quieted the next burst of laughter. The relief that had given rise to the light mood could easily shift quickly to renewed realization that they faced a serious challenge here. "The important thing is, we have allies. Unfortunately, there's no way to coordinate our attacks. We'll have to operate independently, attacking the bear-cows while also avoiding interfering with the spider-wolves."

"And keeping an eye on the spider-wolves?" Tulev asked. "We have only their word that they are enemies of the bear-cows."

"We'll keep a close eye on our new allies and best friends forever," Desjani confirmed.

Geary hesitated as he saw how everyone accepted what Desjani said as a definitive answer, just as if he had given it. Were they accepting that she had already consulted with him on that subject, or did they assume that she could call the shots not only on the bridge of *Dauntless* but also in her professional relationship with him? "Yes," he finally said, hoping that didn't sound like a weak agreement. "We'll take nothing for granted."

He brought up the display showing this star system. Ahead loomed the spider-wolf formation, smoothly perfect ships in gorgeous intertwining loops, now only ten light-minutes away. "We're still in the middle, but not for long." Behind, the bear-cow armada had stabilized into an oblong that bore a disquieting resemblance to the head of a sledgehammer, especially since the face of the formation closest to the human fleet included the superbattleships. Since Geary had held the velocity of the human fleet to point one five light speed, the bear-cows had been steadily getting closer and now were less than two light-minutes behind the human fleet.

On the display, the human formation of interlinked triangles finally broke, individual ships streaming off on different vectors that gradually coalesced into three subformations of roughly equal size, each heading in a different direction. "We've been giving the bear-cows a single target to charge at. Now we're going to make them choose, and whichever one they choose, the other two subformations will be able to hit them while the targeted subformation evades."

"Or if those spider-wolves are indeed the enemies of the bear-cows," Duellos said, eyeing the display, "then when we pull away in different directions, the bear-cows may simply keep charging straight ahead at the spider-wolves. I'm not certain I would be pleased about that if I were the spider-wolves."

Geary paused again. He hadn't considered that, thinking that the bear-cows would continue their single-minded pursuit of the humans. But with the spider-wolves right in front of them, the bear-cows might shift targets.

He looked down and over at Desjani, who had helped develop the plan and was unsuccessfully trying to look like she was surprised by Duellos's suggestion. *Tanya, you obviously figured out that might happen and didn't tell me. We're going to have words about that.*

Badaya was frowning mightily as he thought. "If that happens, if the Kicks go straight for the spiders, it will be an excellent opportunity for us to observe whether or not these two sets of aliens are indeed enemies and how the spider creatures engage their foes in space combat. That's a clever approach, Admiral."

"Thank you," Geary said, not looking at Desjani. "We'll have to see what happens, but we'll be able to react appropriately no matter what the bear-cows do and remain clear of the spider-wolf formation just in case they're not as friendly as they say."

Commander Neeson hunched forward. "My systems security officer briefed me on the spider-wolf program we received. Our software specialists are geeking out over it."

"I understand it has capabilities beyond anything human software can do," Geary said.

"Is the rest of the spider-wolf technology superior to ours? My engineers are also enraptured by what they've seen of the spider-wolf ships."

Geary gave the only answer he could. "We'll find out. Right now, with the spider-wolf flotilla not changing its vector, we can't tell what their maneuvering capabilities are like. Their shield strength seems to match ours, but we don't know if they're at full strength or dialed back since their ships are not in action at this time."

Captain Smythe spoke up. "My specialists analyzed what could be seen of the spider-wolf equipment in the videos they have sent us. About the only conclusion they were willing to reach was that the bridge appears to be truly three-dimensional in its layout."

"Three-dimensional?" Tulev questioned.

"There doesn't seem to be a deck," Smythe explained, "a single surface that everything is arranged around. Instead, the arrangement of equipment seems to reflect no up-and-down bias. It's just wherever it best fits."

"They couldn't have evolved in zero g," someone protested.

"No, but however they evolved, they didn't think in terms of 'this has to be down and this has to be up.'"

"Have you passed that analysis on to the civilian experts?" Geary asked Smythe.

"Um…"

"Please do so as soon as this meeting is over." He took a moment to be certain he hadn't forgotten anything. "We know from our encounter at Pandora that the bear-cow superbattleships are extremely tough. Instead of focusing on them, our combat systems will be told to prioritize concentrating fire against the smaller warships accompanying the superbattleships. We'll peel away those escorts, destroy all of them if necessary, and once the superbattleships are stripped of support, we'll go after them one by one."

"What if they run?" Captain Jane Geary asked.

"Then we wave 'bye and watch them go back to the jump exit." He wasn't sure how that answer would be taken, not in this fleet, which had long ago fallen back on a single-minded emphasis on attack to replace the tactical expertise wiped out by bloody losses in decade after decade. "If they run, we've won. Pursuing a bigger victory would surely cost more lives in this fleet, and I believe that we've lost enough humans already at the hands of the bear-cows."

"We need to teach the Kicks a lesson," Jane Geary insisted. "Now is the perfect time and place to do that."

"We *need* to get home," Captain Hiyen grumbled in response. "The ships of the Callas Republic are part of this fleet for the purpose of defending our homes. Turning back the Kicks with a bloody nose so they can't follow us and have no idea where our homes are accomplishes that."

"The Alliance fleet," the commander of the heavy cruiser *Barding* began, "does not turn from battle and does not settle for less than complete victory."

"Speak for yourself," the captain of *Sapphire* replied. "That's

Black Jack, remember? If he says a victory satisfies honor, then I won't question him. How can any of us?"

"Even Black Jack was just a man," Jane Geary said, in the manner of someone who had made that kind of statement many times before. From what Geary had learned of her, his grandniece had spent her life resenting the Black Jack legend, which had constrained her and her brother Michael, forcing them into the fleet in the footsteps of their legendary great-uncle. "We do neither ourselves nor our fleet commander any credit by not raising appropriate questions—"

"This is not a debate." Geary didn't realize that he had said that, in tones that sliced across the conversation, until after every face turned toward him. "I am in command. This is the plan we will follow. Are there any other questions?"

There weren't. As the officers vanished around him, leaving only Tanya Desjani still with him, Geary struggled to get his temper under control.

"I tried talking to her earlier," Desjani said. "She was polite enough to me but no more than that. I made some joke about being part of the family now, and the temperature around her seemed to drop close to absolute zero."

"I don't get it," he said.

"I think I'm beginning to." Tanya stood up, her lips pressed tightly together. "She hated being a Geary, all her life she hated having to live in your shadow—"

"It was never *my* shadow!"

"All right. Black Jack's shadow. The point is, she might have hated it, but it was her. She was a Geary. Everyone looked at her as being part of that, even if she didn't like it. Now…" Tanya shrugged. "Now you're back. You're Black Jack himself, and don't bother interrupting again to deny it, and you suck all of the oxygen out of her world just by being here. She's just Jane now. And I'm your partner. Chosen to be with you. Where does that leave her?"

Geary stood silently for a while. "Trying to be something."

"Yeah. Because she thinks everything she was is gone. Something has to replace that. She changed after she went back to your home world, remember? What do you think people said there? In how many ways was she forced to measure herself against not a legend but against a real person? Now she's going to prove she's a Geary."

He stared toward the bulkhead before him, seeing not the surface there but images of other captains who had sought glory. Captain Midea charging *Paladin* to destruction at Lakota. Captain Falco, leading *Triumph, Polaris,* and *Vanguard* to their deaths at Vidha. Captain Kila, cold-bloodedly arranging the destruction of *Lorica* at Padronis, while also trying to cause the loss of *Dauntless* with all hands.

Those officers had thought themselves heroic, and ships and crews had paid the price.

There was a way to prevent that.

"I don't think that would be a good idea," Tanya said.

He focused on her. "What wouldn't be a good idea?"

"Relieving her of command."

"How did you—?"

She leaned in, one forefinger to his chest. "I know who you're thinking of. You think she's like Midea? I knew Midea a lot longer than you did. Jane Geary isn't close to that. She's been a bit reckless, she's pushed for more action, but she hasn't been stupid."

"What about Falco?"

"*Falco?* Falco was epically stupid, and he thought nothing of spending ships and the lives of crews in the pursuit of his victories." Her eyes narrowed at him. "You're thinking of someone else."

"You really are reading my mind, aren't you?" At the moment, it didn't seem a strange thing to believe at all.

"Don't be ridiculous. Who's the other one you're thinking of?"

"Kila."

Desjani glared at him silently for several seconds. "No one deserves to be compared to that murderous bitch, especially not your own grandniece. Keep this in mind, Admiral. I am death on incompetent officers. You know that. Jane Geary isn't incompetent. She's smart, but she needs a firm, guiding hand right now. You are her leader. *Lead* her."

"Yes, ma'am."

"That's not funny, Admiral. Now let's go teach some Kicks not to mess with the Alliance fleet."

"That reminds me." Desjani paused to look back at him as Geary frowned at her. "Why didn't you bring up to me the possibility that the bear-cows would aim at the spider-wolves when we split our fleet?"

"Because you already knew! I knew that you wouldn't want to admit knowing that could happen, but you know I know my job well enough to spot that, and I know you know enough about tactics to spot that as quickly as I did."

It took him a moment to work his way through her statement. "Tanya, I hadn't seen that before it was pointed out."

"Seriously?" She stared at him, then shrugged. "Sorry, Admiral.

You're good at tactics. You know that. I assume you know things that look obvious and, in this case, were just being diplomatic to avoid saying, 'Better those ugly suckers than us.'"

"You need to point out things like that to me rather than assume I already know them."

"So you can say, 'I know all that'?" Desjani demanded.

"I've said that *once*."

"I respectfully beg to differ, sir."

"I—Tanya, why the hell can you sometimes read my mind and other times not have a clue as to what I'm thinking?"

"I knew you were going to say that! No, I can't ever read your mind. Can we go fight the battle now?"

"Yes." Unlike this argument, at least he would have a chance of winning the battle.

He took his seat on the bridge of *Dauntless*, trying to put out of his mind everything except the coming battle. *We'll peel away those escorts, destroy all of them if necessary, and once the superbattleships are stripped of support, we'll go after them.* It sounded very easy. Actually doing it was going to be hard as hell.

But his attempt to concentrate was interrupted by a blip from his comm unit indicating that someone was trying to call. At least that was working right now.

No. It wasn't working right. The incoming call was from Captain Vente, who had apparently finally realized that he had been completely sidelined since the loss of *Invincible*. But a call from Vente should have been automatically blocked.

Should he tell Tanya? She didn't need distractions, either.

But if *Dauntless*'s comm system was acting up again, she needed to know, and he needed it fixed. "Captain Desjani, my comm settings aren't being honored by the system."

Her expression hardened. "Communications. The Admiral's comms are not working properly. You have fifteen minutes to get everything functional, or this ship will have a new comm officer."

"Yes, Captain."

Geary made another effort to get his mind into battle readiness, only to have an alert flash red on his display. Before he could acknowledge it, the image of *Spartan*'s commanding officer appeared before him. "Admiral, half of my ship just went dark. Preliminary estimate is several power junctions failing nearly instantaneously."

Damn. Damn. Damn. "Do you still have maneuvering and propulsion?"

"Yes, sir, we have propulsion. We're jury-rigging maneuvering circuits to get around the problem on the port side and should have adequate capability within five minutes."

It could be worse. It could be far worse. "How about replacing the power junctions?" Geary asked.

"We only have enough onboard spares to get five of the seven junctions that failed replaced." *Spartan*'s captain looked grim. "I am ensuring all records are sealed and damage sites maintained except for necessary repair work. If this was sabotage or negligence, we will identify how it was done."

"Thank you," Geary said. "Good thinking. There's a strong chance, unfortunately, that it was just equipment failure. Were you putting extra stress on your ship's power systems before the loss of power?"

"Extra? Just preparations for action, sir. Running shields up to full power for a readiness check and powering up hell-lance batteries."

Would he lose partial or full capability on other ships as they prepared for this engagement? "Let me know when you have full maneuvering capability again." As the image of *Spartan*'s captain vanished, Geary called the fleet. "All units, ensure when preparing for action that you power up systems sequentially rather than simultaneously so as to avoid putting extra strain on power junctions."

Captain Smythe was already calling in. "Admiral, preliminary analysis shows that the power junctions on *Spartan* failed one by one very rapidly. After the first went, the power distribution system automatically tried to route all power through the remaining ones. That overloaded another, there was another attempt to redistribute power, which sent even more power through the remaining junctions, one of those failed, and so on. One of the watch-standers in engineering on *Spartan* activated the manual override in time to keep the automated systems from blowing every junction on the ship."

Far from being able to relax himself, Geary now had an impressive headache developing. "I thought there were automated safeguards against that kind of thing."

"There are, but the power junctions aren't the only systems deteriorating, Admiral. In this case, the automated safeguards didn't kick in. It may take some time to figure out why, but I've already sent emergency engineering notices to all ships so they can be alert for that happening to them."

Another alert appeared. Smythe must have seen it on his display, too, as he looked to one side with a startled expression. "*Titan* just lost a main propulsion unit. Cause unknown."

Battle was looming, he hadn't even gone into action yet, and already his ships were taking damage. *Titan* was sluggish under the best of circumstances. Without one of her main propulsion units…

"Captain Smythe, I need that propulsion unit online and working again within the next twenty minutes."

"I don't even know what's wrong with it yet, Admiral! Let alone what repairs will be required!"

"Whatever it is and whatever it takes, you have twenty minutes."

"Very well, Admiral. But it has been months since I warned you of this problem developing. Be aware that as our ships boost power to systems and run tests in preparation for an engagement, we may see a sudden surge in similar failures popping up all over the place."

Smythe had barely signed off before his words proved prophetic. More alerts rippled across Geary's display. *Dependable*, ironically enough, reporting a sudden degradation of its combat systems during pre-engagement testing. *Dragon* and *Victorious* each reporting the loss of a hell-lance battery due to power-system failures. *Witch* losing partial shields capability. More hell-lance power failures on heavy cruisers *Parapet*, *Chanfron*, *Diamond*, and *Ravelin*, light cruisers *Assault*, *Forte*, and *Retiarii*, and destroyers *Herebra*, *Cutlass*, *Stave*, *Rifle*, and *Flail*. Another shield problem, this time on the light cruiser *Rocket*.

Geary sat back, his eyes on the bear-cow armada closing in and now barely one light-minute behind the Alliance fleet. A complicated battle had just become even more complicated.

7

"There's one good thing about this," Geary said as he waited through the last ten minutes before the first maneuver would take place.

"I'd love to know what that is," Desjani replied.

"The bear-cows can't tell how many of our ships are degraded and by how much. They have to treat every one of our ships as a full threat."

"Except," she pointed out, "the ships with degraded shields. The Kicks should be able to detect that."

"Except those," Geary conceded.

"What are you going to do if *Titan* can't keep up?"

"Improvise."

Desjani took a report, then nodded to Geary. "My comm officer swears on the honor of every ancestor he has that your comm system should be working perfectly, Admiral."

"Admiral!" Captain Smythe looked weary, as if the last half hour had been a long day of intense work. "We're helping to remotely direct repairs on the affected ships, but there are a lot of them."

"I'm very well aware of that, Captain," Geary replied. "How is *Titan*?"

"Commander Lommand has a fix in. He *thinks* it will work under stress."

"Commander Lommand has a good track record," Geary said. "I'm willing to trust his word on that. What about *Witch*? Can Captain Tyrosian get her shields fully up anytime soon?" The auxiliaries were as big a worry during a battle as they were a necessity between battles. As lightly protected as they were, any lowering of their defenses had to be a major concern.

"She's working on it," Smythe said.

That left nothing else to do but wait, watching as an occasional ship's status report upgraded as the sudden equipment failures were repaired. No, that wasn't the right thing to call them, Geary thought. "Sudden equipment failure" implied that there was something unexpected about them. But as he had learned not long ago, these ships had only been designed to function for a few years in the expectation that they would be destroyed in battle before that time was up. Geary, and the end of the war with the Syndicate Worlds, had thrown off that expectation by keeping these warships in the line of battle longer than they had been designed to operate. Now internal system components were wearing out. Smythe and his auxiliary force were working to get those components upgraded and replaced, but it would be a long and difficult process.

In the meantime, he had to go into battle with ships whose systems were increasingly prone to "sudden" failure after two, three, or even four years of combat life.

"All units, execute preplanned maneuver Alpha One at time three zero." He had trouble keeping his eyes off *Titan* as the remaining time elapsed. What would happen when *Titan* tried to use that balky propulsion unit? His first experience with *Titan* had involved propulsion problems, and now here he was again.

And that first time, his grandnephew, Michael Geary, had probably died aboard his ship *Repulse*, buying time for *Titan*.

Not again. Not this time.

"Here we go," Desjani announced, as *Dauntless*'s thrusters pushed her bow up and over, followed by the kick of main propulsion as the battle cruiser curved up and to port along with about a third of the other warships in the disintegrating fleet formation.

The bear-cows would see the maneuvers very quickly, within fifty seconds of when they took place, but it would take them a while to figure out what the human fleet was doing. Then the bear-cows would have to decide what to do.

Ships were forming up around *Dauntless*, which remained the guide ship for this portion of the fleet. Another third of the fleet had bent outward to starboard, forming around Captain Tulev's *Leviathan*, while the remainder of the human ships dove downward, using Captain Badaya's *Illustrious* as their guide.

Titan kept up with Captain Badaya's force, along with *Kupua*, *Alchemist*, and *Cyclops*. Accompanying the warships with Tulev's *Leviathan* were *Tanuki*, *Domovoi*, *Witch*, and *Jinn*. Accompanying *Dauntless* were the four assault transports, *Tsunami*, *Typhoon*, *Mistral*, and *Haboob*. "If the Kicks want to go after lightly armed support ships, they won't be able to focus on any one of the three formations," Desjani observed. "Nice."

The warships forming around *Dauntless* were taking up an oval-shaped formation, the assault transports on the side farthest from the bear-cows, as the path of the formation kept curving, turning back toward the Kick armada.

The humans were going at point one five light speed, while the bear-cows had pushed their own velocity up to point two three light speed. That had produced a closing rate for the Kicks of point zero eight light speed, but when the three new human formations turned toward the bear-cow force, the closing rate suddenly went up to nearly point four light speed. Geary saw the positions of the Kick warships on his display smear, going from pinpoints to blobs as the incredible closing velocity produced distortions in reality that the best human ingenuity could not compensate for. The human warships tore past the bear-cows before the enemy could even fully realize what had happened.

"They're staying straight on," Desjani said. "Heading for the spider-wolves."

"Then let's go help our new friends." Geary sent new orders. "Immediate execute. All units in Gamma One One, come starboard one nine zero degrees, down zero two degrees, all units in Gamma One Two, come starboard one eight five degrees, all units in Gamma One Three, come up one three degrees." He switched to personal comms. "Captain Tulev, Captain Badaya, once your formations come about, you are to operate independently. Concentrate on eliminating the escorts."

Desjani raised her eyebrows at him. "*You* won't be ordering maneuvers by Tulev's and Badaya's formations?"

"No. These Kicks, from what we've learned of them, believe in single-direction. If all of our ships are acting in accordance with my orders, we'll be meeting them on their ground, one mind versus one mind. But if all of our ships operated independently, hundreds of minds working on their own, we'd be at a disadvantage against their coordinated actions."

She nodded judiciously. "But three formations give us three heavy punches, while leaving the Kicks with three opponents who are working together but not in lockstep."

"Four opponents," Geary corrected. "If the spider-wolves don't just try to avoid action. I'm hoping the differences in temperament among the formation commanders will further confuse the bear-cows. Tulev is methodical and steady, while Badaya is quick and more daring."

"And you are unpredictable," Desjani said.

"Let's hope so."

Up ahead, the spider-wolf formation had begun breaking up, the intricate pattern shattering into shards that seemed to be re-forming into smaller whorls of ships. But then the smaller groupings also came apart, every spider-wolf ship racing off on a different vector. "Looks like they fight as individuals," Desjani remarked.

With the spider-wolf ships turning, accelerating, and maneuvering, the human sensors could finally get a look at their propulsion systems. "Hot stuff," Desjani said admiringly.

That sums it up pretty well, Geary thought. Baffles had spread outward, revealing impressive propulsion systems, and similar baffles at other points on the hulls had slid back to unmask powerful thrusters. The spider-wolf ships all seemed to have higher thrust-to-mass ratios than any human ships, giving them maneuverability close to that of the enigma ships. And they were all coming toward the bear-cow armada...

He clenched his jaw, thinking about how impossible it would be to avoid the spider-wolf ships swarming around the bear-cow formation. "They'd better stay clear of us because we can't stay clear of them and attack." That brought up something else, an omission that briefly appalled Geary as he thought of what might have happened. "All units, ensure your combat systems are set to not engage any spider-wolf ships unless specifically targeted in response to commands from me."

The bear-cows, without the spider-wolf formation to concentrate on, had finally chosen another objective. The Kick formation was braking as fast as the bulk of their superbattleships allowed, while coming around and down toward the subformation led by Badaya. Captain Badaya's ships in turn were rising to meet the bear-cows and pivoting so that a shield of warships remained between the bear-cow armada and the four auxiliaries with Badaya's force.

The Kick sledgehammer spread out as it turned, two super-battleships anchoring each side while the other six remained near the center. "They're not going to make this easy," Desjani said.

Geary adjusted the course of his formation, aiming it toward one of the superbattleships on the side nearest to his force. "Immediate execute, all units in Gamma One One, reduce velocity to point zero eight light speed." *Dauntless* and the ships with her pivoted, bringing their main propulsion units around to face in the direction the ships were going. Despite the inertial nullifiers, Geary felt pressure force him back into his seat as the propulsion units labored to brake the velocity of the warships.

The human subformations were all fairly close together despite the huge distances required for turns at the velocities they were traveling. With only about a light-minute separating the human forces, Geary could see what the others were doing almost as soon as it happened. Badaya had not yet changed course, still rising up straight toward an intercept with the bear-cows, while Tulev, like Geary, had steadied out, aiming for part of the enemy armada.

As his force rushed toward the bear-cow warships, Geary had a mental image of an enraged bull charging him, the horns and head made up of those colossal superbattleships. "Five minutes before we're in range," Desjani warned.

"Got it." He waited, wanting the Kicks to see his course change too late to do anything about it. At three minutes to contact, the time felt right at last. "All units in Gamma One One, immediate execute turn starboard four degrees, up one degree. Engage enemy escorts as you enter range."

The human formation turned slightly to the right and up, changing its vector from one aimed at the nearest superbattleship to a path that would clip the upper portion of the bear-cow formation about one-third of the way from the edge. The Kicks themselves had been braking as long as possible, trying to get down to engagement speed, but now were pivoting in the last moments before contact to place their heaviest armor and armament facing the human warships. The combined closing speed was down to point one eight light speed, well within human targeting parameters but just outside the bear-cow capabilities. "Too fast for them, but not by much," Desjani commented in the moment before contact.

Specter missiles were leaping out to home on bear-cow warships, then in an instant of sequential shooting, hell lances were firing, grapeshot was hurled at the closest enemies, and, in a few cases, the lethal clouds of null fields engulfed portions of their targets.

Dauntless shook with only one near miss, Geary's eyes on his display as it updated the status of the bear-cow fleet. Six of the lesser bear-cow ships—four about heavy cruiser–sized, one light cruiser–sized, and one equivalent to a human battleship—had been hit hard. Two of the cruisers were gone, blown to pieces, the crippled battleship spun off, and the other stricken warships wobbled to try to keep up with their formation, shields, armor, and weapons badly battered.

Desjani's shout and the blare of collision warning alarms sounded on top of one another. Startled, Geary saw twenty or thirty spider-wolf warships weave through his formation at tremendous velocity, some missing collisions with human ships by distances that would have scared the hell out of any human ship captain.

Once through the human ships, the spider-wolves pounced on the crippled bear-cow warships, making individual firing runs that rapidly reduced all of those damaged ships to wrecks.

"What. The. *Hell?*" Desjani glared at her display. "Those stupid spiders almost nailed us instead of the Kicks!"

"Captain?" Lieutenant Castries said in a voice that mingled awe and terror. "Our systems estimate the spider-wolf ships were on manual maneuvering controls. They weren't being guided by automated systems when they went through us."

"That's impossible. Nobody could—" Desjani shook her head. "Nobody human. Admiral, those things are absolutely insane."

"At least they're on our side," he said, trying to judge the right moment for his next maneuver. Tulev's force had just gone through a lower edge of the bear-cow force, leaving five mangled Kick escorts in his wake though taking more damage to his own ships than Geary's force had suffered because the closing velocity had fallen just within bear-cow targeting parameters. Geary saw another flock of spider-wolf ships weaving past any obstacles as they leaped to attack the victims of Tulev's strike.

Badaya had turned down again at the last moment, his ships raking the bottom of the bear-cow formation and knocking out four escorts while inflicting significant damage on several others. But *Illustrious* and *Incredible* had suffered some hard blows as well from two of the superbattleships.

"Immediate execute all units in Gamma One One come up one nine zero degrees," Geary ordered. "Increase velocity to point one light speed." He would bring his subformation up and over, back down in more than a half circle to close on the rear of the bear-cows, who had now slowed to point zero nine light speed.

An alert pulsed red. "*Titan* has lost that propulsion unit again," Geary said, adding some curses under his breath.

Badaya's formation had suddenly become limited in its ability to accelerate, slow, and turn. The bear-cows must have spotted the change in *Titan* because they began coming around to intercept Badaya's force. *Incredible* staggered into position near *Titan* as one of its own main propulsion units gave way after the damage it had suffered a short time earlier, and almost at the same moment *Illustrious* suffered shield failures along most of her hull.

Geary snapped out more orders, bringing his subformation in a tighter turn, the moan of the inertial nullifiers becoming audible along with the groaning of *Dauntless*'s hull under the strain. The other warships matched *Dauntless*, but the assault transports swung wider, unable to equal the maneuvers of the combatants.

If he kept this up, he would come into contact with the bear-cow warships with his formation disrupted and the assault transports dangerously exposed.

"Admiral?" Desjani asked.

"It can't be done," he muttered. "Not that way." But he had to do something to relieve the pressure on Badaya, who was unsuccessfully trying to hold his formation together as it turned to evade the head-on rush of the bear-cow armada. Tulev's subformation had been caught out of position when the Kicks turned toward Badaya, and now had to chase back into contact. Tulev couldn't make it in time to disrupt the attack on Badaya's subformation.

Geary had five battle cruisers in this subformation. *Dauntless*, *Daring*, *Victorious*, *Intemperate*, and *Adroit*. His hand hit the comm controls. "All units in Gamma One One, immediate execute come up two zero degrees. Shift formation guide to *Warspite*. *Daring*, *Victorious*, *Intemperate*, and *Adroit*, match your movements to *Dauntless*."

He turned to Desjani. "Captain, take *Dauntless* through the middle of the enemy formation at the best velocity you can manage."

She smiled in a baring of the teeth that would have surely unnerved any bear-cows who could have seen it. "Let's go!" she told her crew, then brought *Dauntless* screaming around, accelerating through a turn even tighter than that before, the other four battle cruisers following.

Geary watched red-line warnings pop up on his display as

Desjani pushed her ship into stress danger zones. Somehow, the other four battle cruisers stayed with her as the tiny formation dove straight for the bear-cow formation.

They went through at blinding speed, main propulsion units still at maximum. One of the superbattleships and a score of lighter yet still powerful Kick warships fired everything they had at the plummeting battle cruisers, but Desjani had gotten the relative velocity up close to point two light speed, throwing off the aim of the enemy. The human warships replied with lightning-fast barrages that pummeled two of the Kick battleships.

Then they were past, Geary reassuming control of *Dauntless* and bringing the battle cruisers back around to try to rejoin the rest of his formation.

A screen of spider-wolf ships had appeared between Badaya's force and the oncoming bear-cows, but they could only inflict minor damage before scattering in the face of the superbattleships.

Geary braced himself for serious losses, knowing that Badaya had been cursed with bad luck but had also fumbled this situation, reacting too slowly to the damage and not turning away far enough and fast enough. Nothing could stop the Kick armada now from inflicting major damage on Badaya's ships, not when those superbattleships were so hard to hurt or turn aside.

Without warning, battleships *Dreadnaught* and *Orion* broke away from Badaya's subformation, closely followed by *Dependable* and *Conqueror*. *Relentless*, *Reprisal*, *Superb*, and *Splendid* went after the other battleships in a rush, every battleship in Badaya's subformation now coming steadily and ponderously around on vectors aimed straight at the oncoming enemy.

The words of Captain Mosko came back to him. *It's what battleships do.*

"They'll get torn to pieces," Geary whispered. *My grandniece. Going to her death under my command just as her brother did. May our ancestors forgive me.*

Desjani wore a look of tragic pride. "Yes. But they might enable the rest of Badaya's force to get clear of that charge."

His eyes searched the display, looking for a miracle. Tulev's subformation still too far off, the spider-wolves only nibbling at the edges of the bear-cow force, his own battle cruisers climbing and turning back to join the rest of his subformation, which was still coming around to meet him and continue on toward the rear of the Kick armada.

No miracles. Just men and women doing all they could, knowing it wouldn't be enough.

"What are they—?" Desjani burst out.

Geary's gaze went back to the eight battleships making a suicide charge. It took him a moment to understand what he was seeing, hundreds of projectiles being launched from those battleships, curving on trajectories aimed at the oncoming bear-cow force less than a minute from contact. "Kinetic projectiles? In a ship-to-ship engagement? That's—" He got it then. "Brilliant."

Normally, ships could easily dodge dumb projectiles fired from a distance, but the battleships had pumped out every kinetic projectile they had, a field of death rushing toward the enemy armada. The battleships had even launched their big kinetic rounds, the ones called BFRs by the crews, which rarely got used because of the wide devastation they could cause when dropped on a planet, but they were now on trajectories going straight at the Kick superbattleships. Only a collection of that many human battleships could have pumped out a sufficient number of kinetic projectiles quickly enough to force evasive action by an armada the size of the bear-cow force.

If the Kicks didn't evade, if they held course to catch Badaya's formation, they would wade right through that barrage, and surely no one—

Geary watched with growing amazement as the final seconds to contact ticked down, the human battleships now also hurling out specter missiles as fast as they could launch them, the Kicks holding steady on their course and firing their own missiles. Just as in the bear-cow videos they had seen, no one would waver, no one would break the shield wall, no one would step away from their place in the line of battle.

As the two forces and the kinetic bombardment merged, space filled with chaos too intense for the fleet's sensors to pick out what was happening. Geary could only stare at his display, appalled by the amount of destruction.

One human battleship burst out of the bedlam, broadcasting extensive damage but still moving. *Dreadnaught*. On her heels came *Orion*, lurching with grim determination in *Dreadnaught*'s wake. *Dependable* and *Conqueror* followed, both amazingly lightly harmed. Then *Relentless*, *Reprisal*, *Superb*, and *Splendid* in a rush, armor pitted, shields in shreds, many weapons out of commission, but still going.

The bear-cow armada had kept on, but the energies erupting in its center had disrupted the other ships, breaking the charge. And Badaya had finally gotten the right maneuver in, twisting his formation up and climbing so that his ships were out of range of most of the surviving enemy warships as they blundered past.

Geary finally understood what had happened. Not a miracle, but something unexpected. "They blew a hole through the Kick formation. They made it through because everything in front of them got pulverized by that barrage instead of evading." Why hadn't they evaded? Just because bear-cow tactics didn't allow for individual action? Had the bear-cow commander been surprised by the new tactic? Had that commander tried to order evasive action but been unable to do so in time, while the individual Kick ships held to their places in the formation?

"Three of the superbattleships are gone, along with a lot of the ships that were near them." Desjani's pride was now mixed with glee. "May the living stars remember what happened here!"

"They're not beaten yet," Geary warned, watching the bear-cows re-forming. After every loss, they had simply tightened their formation, and now they did it again, ending up with a much smaller formation but still clearly ready to fight.

He could hear cheers echoing through *Dauntless* as word spread of what the battleships had done. There would be cheers on every ship in the fleet right now. For the moment, morale wasn't a problem.

"Why didn't they dodge?" Desjani demanded, and Geary realized that she was referring not to the human battleships but to the bear-cow warships. "The Kicks must have known what that many kinetic projectiles of that mass could do…" She turned a look of dawning understanding on him. "They don't. They don't have kinetic projectiles aboard their own ships, they don't use them because they have a defense against their being used against planets. Since ships can usually dodge rocks easily, there would have been no justification for their warships carrying rocks."

"The oldest trap in the book," Geary said. "Assuming that the enemy's capabilities, tactics, and intentions match your own. Thank the living stars that gives us an edge." They would need that edge, but he doubted that tactic would work a second time now that the bear-cows had seen it used.

The five battle cruisers merged with the rest of subformation Gamma One One again, *Dauntless* resuming her status as guide ship. The Kicks had swung wide to the left and up, trying to catch Badaya's force, but they were still hampered by the sluggishness of the surviving superbattleships. Badaya was accelerating straight up, unable to pull clear of contact with ships limited in their propulsion capability, but prolonging the time needed for the bear-cows to catch him. Tulev's force had come up slightly to aim for an intercept with the Kicks' new course, while the spider-wolf ships swarmed everywhere, zipping through human formations with crazy nonchalance and ripping apart any bear-cow ships that had been knocked out of the armada by damage.

The eight battleships from Badaya's formation were coming up and swinging back to try to catch up with their formation again, *Dependable* and *Conqueror* screening their more badly damaged sister ships, a welter of spider-wolf ships forming a weaving barrier between them and the bear-cow armada. *Who ordered that charge?* Geary wondered. *Did Badaya tell them to make that move, or did Jane Geary start it on her own initiative? Whoever did it, it was the right decision. And who came up with the idea of using their kinetic projectiles against this enemy?*

172

Putting aside questions he couldn't address now, Geary brought his formation nearly straight on, aiming to catch the bear-cow force as it steadied out on the new intercept with Badaya. He should get there minutes after Tulev hit them.

"How have the spider-wolves kept the Kicks at bay?" Desjani wondered. "From their firepower and their tactics, they could never have stopped the Kicks from parading through this star system and using one of those jump points."

"Good question. We'll have to ask them once this is all over." He could see the damage and casualty reports coming in from the eight battleships now, feeling a heaviness inside as the fleet systems automatically totaled up everything. The battleships had paid a heavy price for their success.

Here and there on his display, new damage warnings flickered to life as aging systems overstressed by the demands of combat failed on Alliance warships. But the burst of failures earlier had subsided. These failures weren't good, but at least his entire fleet wasn't falling apart as he watched.

Tulev's formation tore past one side of the enemy armada, hammering at the bear-cow warships there and knocking out two more. But the attack barely registered on the superbattleship there, and the armada continued its charge toward Badaya's force, closing at an increasing rate as the enemy continued to accelerate, and Badaya was held to about point zero six light speed by the propulsion casualties on *Titan* and *Incredible*.

Geary aimed his formation for the bottom side of the bear-cow force, *Dauntless* shuddering once again with hits and near misses as the Kicks threw out a heavy barrage. He half heard the damage reports streaming in to Desjani, telling of shields penetrated, hits on the battle cruiser's light armor, and a few penetrations but no systems losses. On his display, similar reports flowed in from the other ships in his formation. None had been hit hard, but many had taken damage.

One more bear-cow ship was limping, unable to stop a spiral out of its formation that left it prey to the spider-wolf swarm. Other enemy warships showed damage.

But it wasn't enough to turn aside the enemy.

Badaya had two battle cruisers left in good fighting shape, and now *Inspire* and *Formidable* swung away from the rest of his formation, twisting around to come at the Kick armada.

Geary weighed everything: Tulev coming around in a wide arc that took up large amounts of distance and time, his own subformation doing another swing up and over that would take too long, Badaya altering course to head directly away from the oncoming enemy and gain as much time as possible before being overtaken, and the eight battleships on the other side of the enemy from Tulev and Geary trying to claw their way back to Badaya, the entire battle heading upward from the plane of the star system. He ran some hasty maneuvers through the combat systems, coming up with an answer that was desperate but doable. "*Dependable, Conqueror*, this is Admiral Geary. Proceed at best speed on an intercept with the enemy."

Two light-minutes distant, the two battleships would turn and accelerate, leaving behind their much more heavily damaged comrades. That might distract the bear-cows, but Geary didn't think so. The important thing now was to hit that armada with everything. "Captain Tulev, I am assuming maneuvering control of your subformation."

No time to run this through the systems, no time to figure out the ever-shifting time delays and distances. He had to depend upon his own skills, his own experience, and the unmatched ability of the human brain to handle this kind of puzzle on the fly. "Captain Badaya, detach all of your escorts at time one seven, order them onto an intercept with the enemy formation at point one five light speed."

Desjani had noticed the moves, frowning at her display. "What are you doing?"

"Bringing a hammer down. If I don't, we lose all of the damaged ships and undamaged auxiliaries in Badaya's formation." Besides *Incredible*, *Titan*, and *Illustrious*, that included *Kupua*, *Alchemist*, *Cyclops*, two heavy cruisers, and several light cruisers and destroyers.

Inspire and *Formidable*, moving too fast for the bear-cows to target well, slashed at the enemy but didn't knock out any warships.

"Captain Duellos," Geary ordered, "coordinate the movements of *Inspire* and *Formidable* with *Dependable* and *Conqueror*. Make your next firing run in conjunction with them."

Desjani's eyes darted about her display. "You've got us all coming in together. We'll hit that armada almost simultaneously. Will that be enough?"

"It had better be." His gaze swept from place to place on his display. Badaya's core of damaged ships still going almost straight up, Badaya's cruisers and destroyers braking to fall behind their comrades and facing the oncoming enemy, the bear-cow armada curving in from the right and below to catch Badaya, Tulev swinging in a wide arc that ended where the Kicks would be, Geary's own subformation coming over the top of its own curve and steadying out to aim slightly upward at the Kicks, the small force under Duellos on the other side, also climbing but from the left of the enemy. "All units, we need to break their charge. Press your attacks and employ kinetic projectiles against the enemy formation as you close to contact."

"If anything will make them turn, that will," Desjani said.

"If they don't turn, and we hit them with that many rocks, they won't make it to Badaya." How badly did the enemy commander want the crippled human warships with Badaya? Did bear-cows suffer from the target fixation that could drive human combatants to fly right into obstacles ignored in their total focus on the objective?

"You know," Desjani remarked calmly as the several groups of ships rushed toward contact, "the Kicks haven't taken one important fact into account."

"What's that?" Geary asked, not taking his eyes from his display.

"They don't know how crazy humans can be. If we were sane, we'd be running. Badaya's formation would have scattered. They'd be able to chase us down and smash us. But we're crazy, so instead we're going to hold together and blow their butts off."

Geary smiled, watching Badaya's cruisers and destroyers volleying kinetic projectiles at the enemy.

The bear-cow ships shifted positions slightly, trying to dodge the rain of rocks. They probably would have succeeded, because no matter how many rocks there were, space was wide, but Tulev was coming in now as well, hurling rocks ahead of his ships, catching the bear-cows in a cross fire, and then Duellos's small formation was tossing out rocks as well.

"Here we go," Desjani said, as the combat systems in Geary's subformation also began launching kinetic projectiles, so that rocks came at the bear-cows from front, sides, and a bit to the rear.

The last seconds were gone as everything came together, the Kick armada trying to evade without breaking from its track on Badaya's crippled ships. The bear-cow commander had compromised, Geary realized in the instant before contact, trying to both continue pursuit and evade the human strike. It was the kind of compromise, the failure to choose one way or the other, that had doomed countless human commanders.

He saw one of the five surviving superbattleships lurch under several impacts, its powerful shields overwhelmed by the force of the kinetic projectiles before a single BFR tore into it and blew it apart. Then Geary's subformation was through the enemy armada again, tearing past with the other human warships in the immediate wake of the kinetic bombardment.

This time he felt few hits on *Dauntless*. Damage reports streamed in from Tulev's subformation, from Duellos's small task force, from the other ships in Geary's subformation, from Badaya's escorts. Geary took a sudden deep breath as he saw a dreaded symbol appear with names next to it. *No contact. Assessed destroyed. Brilliant.* A hard-luck ship since Captain Caligo had been arrested for conspiring with Captain Kila, but it was hard to believe that the battle cruiser was gone. Heavy cruisers *Emerald* and *Hoplon*. Light cruiser *Balestra*. Destroyers *Plumbatae*, *Bolo*, *Bangalore*, and *Morningstar*.

Not all of the destroyed human warships had been annihilated in the fractions of a second during exchanges of fire with the enemy, denying their crews any chance of escape. Some had survived, broken and helpless, long enough for their crews to take to the escape pods that now awaited rescue.

But the Kicks had paid for their stubborn stand. Even the superbattleships could only take so much, and the multiple firing passes coming close on each other right after the avalanche of kinetic projectiles had devastated the enemy armada. Two of the four surviving superbattleships were only drifting wrecks, a third crippled, with spider-wolf warships already swarming about it to administer the kill, and a fourth spinning away, trying to regain maneuvering control, its main propulsion units torn and mangled. The smaller bear-cow warships had been decimated, with maybe forty remaining, and those streaming frantically toward the jump point from which the enemy had come.

The shield wall had broken.

Geary slumped back, feeling no sense of triumph.

"We did it," Desjani said, but her voice was subdued, not jubilant.

"Yeah." He agreed with both her words and her tone of voice. "Isn't peace great?"

"Feels a lot like war to me," she said.

Geary roused himself. First priority, those escape pods that held survivors from his ships that had been destroyed in the battle. Many of those survivors would be injured and in need of medical care. "Second and Fifth Light Cruiser Squadrons, intercept and recover all escape pods. Notify me immediately if additional ships are required." That took care of the most immediate need. All that remained was to order the fleet to re-form, prioritize damage control, get help to the surviving ships that needed it most to deal with their dead and wounded and their battle damage—

"Admiral," Desjani said in a way that caught his attention.

The last surviving superbattleship had partially stabilized its motion, but now thrusters had ceased firing even though the huge warship was still rolling away uncontrollably.

"It's a sitting duck," Desjani said.

"Let the spider-wolves——" Geary began, then sat up straighter again. "It can't run."

"Will it self-destruct?" Desjani wondered.

"We haven't seen any of them self-destruct yet, have we? And there haven't been any——" He broke off speaking again, suddenly realizing something. "We haven't seen any bear-cow escape craft leaving any of their ships. None from any of the ships we crippled and destroyed."

"I guess they don't see those as cost-effective. When you've got that many billions of worker bear-cows, why worry about saving a few here and there? The herd is still strong." Desjani raised one finger to point. "But, Admiral, if they can't, or won't, destroy that superbattleship, it's ours for the taking."

A huge warship full of bear-cow technology, bear-cow survivors, bear-cow literature, bear-cow history, science, art...

"The taking won't be easy," Geary said.

But he knew they would have to try.

8

"Tell them to leave it alone!" Geary said.

The images of General Charban and Emissary Rione, locked all this time in attempts to communicate with the spider-wolves, exchanged looks. "We're not sure we have the means yet to tell them something like that," Charban said diplomatically.

"Try. You've got the civilian experts down there working with you, right? All of you get that message across. We do not want that bear-cow warship destroyed. It is *ours*."

Spider-wolf warships had clustered around the crippled super-battleship, but since the Kick vessel retained its shields, its armor, and its weapons, the spider-wolves were keeping at a safe distance, pinging shots futilely off the still-powerful defenses of the enemy.

Most of the spider-wolves, though, were harrying the surviving bear-cow warships still accelerating in a stampede for the jump point. It would be most of a day before the Kicks got there, even going hell-for-leather as they were, but the spider-wolves were making sure they kept going.

Ending his call to Charban and Rione, Geary sat back, rubbing his forehead. His eyes reluctantly went to his display to see the latest information. The human fleet was slowly drawing back together, licking its wounds, destroyers and light cruisers darting through the vast area of the recent battle to pick up escape pods carrying crew members from destroyed human warships. Geary hadn't spotted any spider-wolf ships destroyed during the battle, leading to a rising bitterness in him, but when he replayed the last charge against the bear-cows, he saw that the spider-wolves had joined in, diving into the heart of the Kick armada to help break the enemy and losing several ships in the process. Small lifeboats from those destroyed spider-wolf ships had been scooped up by other spider-wolf craft almost as soon as they ejected.

But his first impression had been right. There had been no lifeboats or escape pods from any bear-cow warship.

Escape pods. He checked the status of recovery efforts on his fleet's escape pods, seeing that the light cruisers ordered to carry out that task were well along at it. Except for—"Is there a spider-wolf ship picking up one of our escape pods?" He wasn't sure what to feel. Gratitude? Outrage? Fear?

"The pod was heavily damaged," Desjani said. "It's off *Balestra*. Maybe the spider-wolves are seeing if it needs assistance. *Quarte* is on its way to that pod but still half an hour from pickup."

"Get ahold of someone on that pod," Geary ordered. "Let me know as soon as you do."

Because of the distances involved, that meant nearly ten minutes of waiting before an image rendered jerky by damaged comm equipment on the pod finally appeared before Geary. He could see the interior of the pod, crowded with survivors from *Balestra*, both the survivors and the pod itself bearing wounds from the destruction of their light cruiser.

Some of the survivors drifted, too injured to act, while others flung themselves about the packed inside of the escape pod to patch up equipment and their fellows. Geary could see the emergency supply lockers open, their shelves already stripped of tools, medical supplies, and spare parts. The two rolls of duct tape that every escape pod carried as standard equipment were in use. A strip of duct tape already covered a patch on one wall, doubtless sealing a weak point or leak, and another band of tape was being used to help repair something inside an opened equipment panel. A corpsman, working frantically, was in the act of slapping duct tape over a chest wound on one sailor whose splinted arm was being bound up by another sailor.

At the air lock stood two shapes in space armor. Whereas the actual spider-wolves were incredibly repulsive to the human eye, their space armor resembled their ships in its smooth lines and beautiful engineering. The spider-wolves showed six limbs in the armor, but their appearance was otherwise concealed by the protective gear.

"This is Chief Petty Officer Madigan, combat systems, light cruiser *Balestra*," a sailor with a bruise covering one side of his face reported. "The... the... aliens have boarded us, but haven't done anything but watch. The situation in here is stabilized, but we need pickup soonest. Uh, senior officer aboard is Lieutenant Junior Grade Sidera, but she's unconscious."

Geary breathed a sigh of relief. "Chief Madigan, there's a

light cruiser on the way. Hang on. I think the spider-wolves came aboard to see if you needed assistance. I'll get a battle cruiser over your way." That was the fastest ship he could send with a large medical compartment and doctors aboard. It would take another several minutes for Chief Madigan to hear that reassurance, but he seemed to have the situation under control. "Good work. We'll get you picked up soon."

"*Dragon*," Desjani said. "She's the closest battle cruiser to them."

He ordered *Dragon* into motion, then clenched his eyes shut, trying to refocus on other issues.

"What's the name of the star?" Desjani asked. She looked tired, but relieved. *Dauntless* had taken damage, but aside from a few wounded had lost no crew members this time.

"I don't know," Geary said. "Why does it matter?"

"Ships died here, Admiral. Sailors died here. We should have a name for where they died."

He closed his eyes again, embarrassed not to have thought of that. Part of him wanted a dark name, but another part said that this star marked the graves of dead humans and should reflect their sacrifice and courage. Something that said humans had placed their mark here, far beyond their own borders, fighting to save their comrades. "Is there a star named Honor?"

"Honor?" Desjani questioned, then checked the database. "No. That's not a name… but you get to use any name you want, Admiral."

"It's for them," he said.

"I understand." She paused, then managed a smile. "It's a good name to remember them by. Permission to enter the name Honor for this star in the fleet database."

"Granted."

Jane Geary had survived the charge she had led though *Dreadnaught* had suffered extensive damage. Captain Badaya, looking unusually subdued, had volunteered that Jane Geary had made that move on her own initiative while he was still trying to figure out how to save his other warships. *Orion*, already beaten up from fighting at Pandora, had been hammered again, but Commander Shen had, with considerable annoyance at the question, declared his ship still fit for battle.

The amount of damage inflicted on *Dreadnaught, Orion, Relentless, Reprisal, Superb*, and *Splendid* proved the old maxim that while battleships might take a while to get where they needed to go, once there they were amazingly hard to kill. Still, had the bear-cow commander peeled off even one of the superbattleships with some escorts and sent it after those six beat-up battleships, they probably wouldn't have survived the fight.

Quarte reached the damaged escape pod from *Balestra*, the two spider-wolves on the pod withdrawing into their own ship as the light cruiser approached, the spider-wolf ship then soaring off in a grand leap back to its fellows. *Dragon* was still twenty minutes from reaching both *Quarte* and the damaged pod, but was coming on fast.

Geary thought about medical personnel all over the fleet, not just on *Dragon*, struggling with a tidal wave of injured personnel, sick bays and hospitals filled with those in desperate need of care for their wounds. Nowadays if someone made it to a hospital they were unlikely to die no matter how bad their injuries, but even then sometimes not enough could be done. "How do they do it?" he wondered aloud. Desjani turned a questioning glance his way, for once not reading his mind. "Doctors, nurses, corpsmen, medics, all of them," Geary explained. "Sometimes, no matter what they do, the people they're trying to help still die. How do they keep going?"

She pondered that. "How do you keep going? Knowing that no matter how well you do, people will still die?"

That stung, yet he saw her logic. "I guess I think about how much worse things would be if I didn't do everything I could."

"Yeah. Works for me, too. Usually."

Captain Smythe was once again proving his value, coordinating a huge amount of repair activity around the fleet, his engineers running on caffeine and chocolate to keep working ("The food of the gods," in Smythe's words. "When the old myths talked about nectar and ambrosia, they meant coffee and chocolate."), the eight auxiliaries each mated with or closing on one of the most badly hurt warships.

Commander Lommand of *Titan* had offered his resignation, which Geary had declined along with an order to Lommand to use his considerable talents to get ships fixed up, including his own.

The fleet administrative system popped up another alert, explaining in dispassionate terms that available storage for dead personnel had been exceeded and recommending burials be undertaken.

As he read that last, Geary knew that if he threw anything at the display or punched it the blows would just go through the virtual information, leaving it unmarred. He was nonetheless tempted. "General Charban, Emissary Rione, we also need to know as quickly as possible, *after* we get across to the spider-wolves to lay off the last superbattleship, whether we can safely bury our dead in this star system."

Rione looked away, but Charban nodded slowly. "I understand, Admiral."

He undoubtedly did understand, Geary reflected. The ground forces had also often taken hideous casualties in the war, waging battles across entire worlds and devastating wide portions of those worlds in the process. How many soldiers had Charban lost in battle? How many times had those soldiers spent their lives, only to have the ground they had died for be abandoned with the next shift in strategy, or when the Alliance fleet was driven away and ground forces had to leave before Syndic warships rained death from orbit upon them?

Geary had slept through a century of that, while such sacrifices formed the men and women around him. Desjani would occasionally remind him, sometimes angrily, that he could not understand them even if they needed his reminders of the things their ancestors had believed in before the war warped those caught in it.

And now more of them had died in as vicious a fight as any during the war. He had managed to help them survive that war. Could he manage to ensure that these men and women survived peace?

"Admiral," Rione called from the conference room aboard *Dauntless* where frantic attempts at communications with the spider-wolves continued, "we have gotten across to the people here that we will deal with the last superbattleship."

"The people here?" It took him a moment to understand that. "You mean the spider-wolves?"

"Yes, Admiral." Her voice took on a reproving cast. "We must think of them as people. Because they are people."

"Exceptionally ugly people," Desjani murmured.

He gave her a warning look before turning back to Rione's image. "Thank you. I'll do my best."

Rione's smile was pained. "I understand how hard that will be. Believe me."

"Make sure you and General Charban take some breaks. You've been at this continuously for hours now." Once Rione's image vanished, Geary bent to his display. He had to start moving ships toward the crippled superbattleship drifting through this star system, ensuring that the spider-wolves didn't question the human claim to it.

Some of the Alliance warships had only been moving toward an intercept with the superbattleship for half an hour when another alert pulsed. Geary, still anticipating a massive act of self-destruction by the bear-cows trapped on their ship, jerked as if he had been bitten.

But there was no marker showing a spreading cloud of debris where the superbattleship had been. Instead, that ship remained, but oddly changed. "Now what?"

A portion of the crippled superbattleship had been torn outward, making Geary think for a moment that an internal explosion had ripped the warship, too small to destroy it but enough to blow off a large piece. But within seconds it was clear that the detached piece was under power and shaped like a smaller version of one of the bear-cow ships. Where it had rested, cradled mostly inside the superbattleship, a matching depression now showed.

"Escape craft," Lieutenant Castries reported. "Accelerating for the jump point."

They had finally found an escape craft on a bear-cow ship. But only one? And configured for such speed and endurance? "Surely they don't have the whole crew on that," Geary said.

"No," Desjani replied. "That would be impossible."

The human ships were still too far from the superbattleship to intercept the escape ship, but spider-wolf warships were slewing about and leaping toward new prey.

"Do we want to warn them off that escape ship?" Desjani asked.

"I'm not sure we have time," Geary said. Just the amount of time needed for a message to reach those spider-wolf ships was longer than it would take the first of them to achieve an intercept.

Desjani nodded in tight-lipped agreement. "I guess they're going to blow the wreck now."

"Maybe." Geary frowned at his display. "That thing is big for an escape craft, but it's still less than half the size of a destroyer."

"About a third the mass and length," Desjani agreed. "Lieutenant Castries, get me an estimate of how many Kicks could be on that escape ship."

The reply took a moment. "Our systems estimate the escape craft was designed to carry a maximum of one hundred creatures the size of the Kicks," Castries reported. "That's if they were crammed in, and if their equipment took about the same amount of internal space as standard human layouts. At the lower end, it might service as few as twenty Kicks."

"One hundred at most." Desjani made a face. "That super-battleship could easily have a crew of thousands."

"Maybe a lot of automation," Geary speculated. "No. Some of the videos we've seen take place on ships, and those showed many bear-cows crowding them. But only a hundred at the very most had a means of escape." The answer came to him then. "The officers. The commanding officer, his or her staff, maybe family if they do that. The leaders of this part of the herd, leaving that herd behind while they head for safety."

"I prefer the term 'herd-leaders,'" Desjani said sharply. "Officers should never abandon their crews, and there are no signs that huge warship has any other escape craft."

"Some bear-cows are more equal than others," Geary said. "That shouldn't be a surprise. We knew they had leaders, and leaders can easily become an elite caste."

"Like the Syndics."

"Maybe. In some ways." Though even the Syndics had put escape pods on their warships. But then the Syndics didn't have at least thirty billion spare worker bear-cows packed cheek to jowl. "These herd-leaders may be running, but they won't get away."

Desjani smiled, letting out a small laugh. "Too many spiders blocking their way."

Indeed, right now the spider-wolf ships bearing down on the escape craft amid a welter of curving intercept vectors resembled a web rapidly ensnaring the fleeing bear-cow commander.

For its size, the escape craft had impressive shields. But it couldn't carry much armor, not and stay swift and agile, and it had few weapons, which fired desperately at the converging spider-wolf warships as they closed in for firing runs.

A score of spider-wolf ships slashed at the escape craft in attacks that collapsed its shields, penetrated its hull, then must have triggered a core overload. As the spider-wolf attackers curved away after their strikes, only a blossoming field of debris remained of the escape ship.

"I guess the spiders weren't interested in prisoners," Desjani remarked. "Why did the commander run? They'd have been safer staying on the superbattleship."

"That ship is doomed," Geary said. "Perhaps the commander panicked, perhaps we're going to see it self-destruct now, and the commander didn't want to go out that way."

"The commander went out that way anyway," Desjani said dryly, pointing toward the remnants of the escape ship. "Hmmm. They would have been well clear of that crippled ship by now. Even a worst-case estimate of the blast radius shows they would have been out of danger from that. Why hasn't it blown?"

"A booby trap? Like Captain Smythe suggested with *Invincible*? The bear-cows have rigged their superbattleship to blow up when we try to board?"

"Or something went wrong," Desjani suggested. "Or the Kicks left aboard aren't interested in being blown to pieces. Or they never intended doing an overload. I checked the records of the engagement. None of the crippled Kick ships self-destructed. The spider-wolves blew apart any that were crippled but still intact."

"When did you have a chance to go over the records of the engagement?" Geary wondered, thinking of everything that he had been doing since the battle ended.

"I used my copious free time. One second here, one second there... it adds up."

Geary clenched his fists. "There's still a chance we can capture that thing."

"Yes," Desjani agreed. "But whoever goes aboard will face the possibility of the superbattleship blowing up once they're inside, as well as fighting thousands of Kicks who will probably fight to the death to avoid getting eaten alive, which they would expect us awful predators to do. Have I ever told you why I didn't become a Marine?"

"I know you've led boarding parties," Geary said, recalling the Alliance Fleet Cross medal that Desjani never spoke about except in vague terms.

"When I was young and foolish." She shook her head. "Still no self-destruct. Hey, I thought of something. The spider-wolf tactics and weapons alone wouldn't have taken down that armada, even though the spider-wolves must have some way of stopping the Kicks."

"You already mentioned that."

"Did I? This part I just thought of. Maybe the Kicks haven't lost ships in hostile systems. Their battles have been at home or they've been able to get everyone who wasn't blown apart home. They wouldn't have procedures or plans for scuttling ships because it never happened. I mean, look at that thing." She waved toward the image of the superbattleship. "Would you expect to have that thing trapped and helpless?"

"It's not exactly helpless. Weapons and shields are still operational. And what about that escape ship?"

"Good point. The leaders aboard that thing must have had reasons to expect to need to be able to leave. Could that have been the armada flagship?"

"It could have been." A fleet commander would need some means of leaving a crippled ship during a fight so they could continue the battle from another flagship. "But even if you're right, that doesn't mean it would be impossible for the crew left on that battleship to rig up a means of self-destruct. We just don't know."

Desjani nodded toward her display. "The survivors of the armada are still running for the jump point. Forty-one ships. I'm glad the spider-wolves are chasing them because even I don't feel like that right now. But if the last Kick ship leaves this star system, and the superbattleship is still intact, we're going to have to decide whether to run the risks of trying to take it."

"I'm going to have to decide," Geary corrected.

The image of General Carabali gestured toward the display in Geary's stateroom. "This is about that ship?"

"Yes, General." Geary zoomed the display in on the crippled superbattleship. "Can your Marines take it?"

"Can we? Yes, Admiral, I am confident of that. What I can't be confident about is how much it might cost."

That was the big question. "I understand. In light of that, I need your best assessment on whether we *should* try to take it," Geary said.

Carabali paused, thinking. "There are a lot of unknowns. We have only a general idea of current Kick individual combat capability, based on some of the videos we intercepted. But you know how much movies can vary from reality, and we don't know if what we've seen are movies or documentaries. We also don't know how many Kicks are still aboard that ship. I wouldn't estimate less than a thousand, but it could be much more. A ship that size could hold ten thousand if they wanted to put that many aboard."

"Ten thousand?" Geary asked in amazement. "That's your estimate of the crew size?"

"No, sir. That's our top end. The most plausible estimate of crew size is five or six thousand. That's a lot of Kicks." Carabali paused as she found her train of thought again. "We know nothing about the layout of the ship. During a normal boarding operation, my Marines would head for certain critical areas, gaining control of the power core controls, the bridge, and other vital places. We don't know where those are in this ship or what form their controls take."

"We don't even know if they have compartments like that as we understand them," Geary agreed.

"The internal layout…" Carabali shrugged. "The Kicks are a lot smaller than us. The size of their passageways might be very tight for a Marine in combat armor. Even if we have a firepower advantage on a Marine-to-Kick basis, employing that firepower might be difficult. It all adds up to a very challenging operation, something more like an assault on a fort than a ship-boarding operation."

It wasn't a pretty picture, but the Marine general hadn't said it wasn't doable. Indeed, she had said it could be done. The question remained whether the gains from seizing that ship justified the risks of trying to capture it. Captain Smythe and the civilian experts had already weighed in, all of them enthralled by the prospect of being able to exploit such a capture for information about the bear-cows and their technology.

Conceivably, there might be the clues aboard the ship that could lead to human discovery of how to build that defense against orbital bombardment. The value of that one thing alone would justify almost any price. Almost any sacrifice. "But you can do it." Geary made that a statement, not a question this time.

"Yes, sir. Assuming the Kicks don't blow the ship to hell before we can stop them. Before the landing operation can commence we'll need to have the warship's external defenses reduced, and we'll need close support after that. That means significant fleet assets located near that huge ship, where they would also be endangered if it self-destructs."

"Understood." He would be committing a lot of his limited numbers of ships and Marines to this attack. If the bear-cows were just waiting to lure in humans, then they could destroy everything that Geary sent into or close to that superbattleship. There was a real chance that he could take hideous losses and gain nothing.

But if he didn't take any risks, he was guaranteed to gain nothing, guaranteed to pass up the sort of opportunity that might never come again.

"Begin your planning," Geary ordered. "Assume you have use of any available assets. I'll be planning to use every warship necessary to take down the alien defenses before the Marines go in. It's going to be a dirty job, but I know you can do it."

Carabali saluted, smiling sardonically. "That's why you have Marines along, to do the dirty jobs no one else wants or can do. When do you want my plan, Admiral?"

"As soon as possible, but take the time you need to get it right. We're not going anywhere until a lot more repairs have been done on our damaged ships."

"I understand, sir. Our planning in this case is going to be simplified by the lack of detailed knowledge. We're going to have to do a lot of this op on the fly once we get inside that thing. Fortunately, Marines are good at that."

Geary sat down after Carabali's image had vanished, lowering his face into both hands as he thought about how many men and women had already died in this star system and how many more might die as a result of this decision.

The superbattleship spun slowly through space, the depression where the escape craft had rested occasionally coming into sight as the warship rolled. It showed few signs of damage except at the stern, where the main propulsion units had been mangled by at least one powerful blow, which had apparently set off sympathetic explosions. "Their main engineering spaces may be destroyed," Captain Smythe had suggested. "If that's the case, they would have had to shut down the power core, or whatever they use."

"Why do they still have shields up and weapons working?" Geary asked.

"A secondary power source for those purposes. Both shields and weapons require less power than main propulsion at full drain. They could conceivably have several secondary power sources, each supplying different functions. Inefficient by our standards, but the backup that kind of redundancy provides would be a very nice thing to have."

The Alliance fleet hung stationary relative to the superbattleship, most of the ships thirty light-seconds distant in a cluster that minimized distances between units as shuttles flew between them bearing spare parts and repair teams. Much closer to the superbattleship, all of the human battleships along with half of the battle cruisers were arrayed around the enemy ship. Even though all of the ships were traveling through space, they appeared motionless to each other.

The fleet's combat systems and Captain Smythe's engineers had estimated what the worst-case damage radius might be if one or more power cores on the superbattleship overloaded. Geary had added half again that distance to the total and placed his battleships outside of that, the battle cruisers a little farther off still.

Much more distant, a good ten light-minutes away, the spider-wolf ships had re-formed into a beautifully patterned formation as the aliens watched the human action from a very safe distance. The spider-wolves were certainly respecting their previous agreement that the superbattleship was the property of the humans to dispose of. None of the humans who were "talking" to the spider-wolves had been able to tell what the aliens thought of the human decision to try to capture the bear-cow warship, but the fact that the spider-wolves were watching from so far off was a pretty clear sign that the aliens weren't interested in taking part or even getting caught in whatever mess the humans had decided to stir up.

"Maybe they are smarter than we are," Charban had commented.

Rione had been more direct, speaking privately to Geary. "I know you're aware of what can happen if you send thousands of Marines into that ship."

"I am painfully aware of the possibilities," he had answered. "What price would you pay for that planetary defense against space bombardment?"

She had read the anger behind his statement. "There's something else. What?"

Geary had fixed her eyes with his. "You pretty much confirmed for me that the governments of the Callas Republic and the Rift Federation didn't want their warships coming home."

"I never said such a thing."

"You didn't say I was wrong when I raised that possibility before this fleet left Varandal. A possibility I came up with because of hints you threw my way. Hints that those governments didn't trust what those warships might do, fearing they would launch their own coup attempts or act on behalf of a coup attempt by me. I suspect there are plenty of people in the Alliance government who fear this fleet for the same reason and sent it out here in the hopes that it wouldn't come home. And now I'm thinking about the ships and men and women who won't be going home, and I'm very, very unhappy that some people back home would be happy to know that."

It took a long time for her to answer. "I would expect nothing less from you. I *never* aided any goal of harming this fleet and its crews, regardless of what others may have demanded of me."

"Tell me who those others are."

"I can't because I don't know for certain! They are smart enough to use cutouts, agents who act for them but whom I can't tie to anyone. I am sorry, Admiral. I am sorry for those who have died because some of their own leaders don't trust them. But others do. Do not make the mistake of thinking the Alliance government is working against you. I have told you before that there are many minds trying to control that government. Some are your allies, and many of them want only what is best for the Alliance but differ on what they believe that is."

Now Geary sat on the bridge of *Dauntless*, wondering if he was doing the right thing but knowing he had to do it. "Send in the probes."

Automated probes launched from several of the human ships

around the bear-cow warship, approaching their target at a steady, unthreatening pace, each one broadcasting requests to surrender and promises of safety to the bear-cows still aboard their ship. The civilian experts with the help of some of the fleet techs had worked up an animated movie with the same messages, using images in the format used by the Kicks to convey the human offer, and those videos were being sent simultaneously.

The same messages, the same movies, had already been broadcast toward the superbattleship, with no response. Were the surviving members of the crew dead, or were they still refusing to communicate with humans?

Suddenly, particle beam and laser fire licked out from the super-battleship, and within seconds, probe after probe had been blown apart or rendered inactive, all systems dead. "We'll have to do this the hard way," Geary said.

"No surprise there," Desjani replied. She had been grumpy for some time, annoyed that the main effort of reducing the superbattleship's defenses had been assigned to the human battleships rather than the battle cruisers like *Dauntless*.

"Captain Armus," Geary said.

The image of Armus, commanding officer of *Colossus*, appeared before Geary. Armus was solid, unimaginative, and deliberate to a point just short of being too slow to act. Often that could be a problem. But in this kind of attack, those characteristics were a virtue, so Geary had placed Armus in charge of all of the battleships for the operation.

"My task force is ready," Armus said.

"Commence your bombardment."

Armus saluted in the slightly awkward manner of many of the senior officers who had spent most of their time in a fleet where saluting had once been a forgotten ritual, then his image vanished.

All around the helpless superbattleship, Alliance battleships turned bow on and began closing the distance, their shields at maximum and their weapons ready. *Dreadnaught, Orion, Superb,* and *Splendid,* all of them with weak shields and extensive damage, had been ordered to hold back until the majority of the bear-cow defenses had been knocked down; but they could still be called on earlier than that if necessary. Even not counting them, against the single superbattleship Geary could deploy nineteen human battleships. As mighty as the Kick warship might be, it was unable to maneuver and seriously outclassed by the firepower steadily drawing closer. He watched, feeling a surge of pride as the battleships headed toward the superbattleship by divisions.

He had led these ships in fights many times, but rarely with the opportunity to watch the slow majesty with which they went into action. *Gallant, Indomitable, Glorious,* and *Magnificent; Dreadnaught* bearing extensive recent scars from action, *Orion* as badly battered as her sister ship, *Dependable,* and *Conqueror; Warspite, Vengeance, Revenge,* and *Guardian; Fearless, Resolution,* and *Redoubtable; Colossus, Encroach, Amazon,* and *Spartan; Relentless, Reprisal, Superb,* and *Splendid,* the last four also scored by damage. Somehow, the wounds borne by the battleships made them seem even more imposing, more threatening, veterans marked by combat who would not let injuries turn them aside.

The superbattleship must have expended all of its missiles in the earlier battle and while fighting off harassing attacks by the spider-wolves. Now it opened fire again with particle beams and laser fire; but the human battleships didn't return shots yet, letting their bow shields absorb the shots while human sensors pinpointed the precise locations of the weapons on the bear-cow warship. "They're not concentrating their fire," Geary remarked. He had worried that shots would be focused on the already-most-hard-hit battleships, but with the Kicks lashing out at every battleship around them, no one human battleship was taking enough hits to cause serious worry.

"No leaders," Desjani replied. "Their leaders fled the ship, so there's no one to tell them what to attack. They're all just picking targets individually."

Having localized every alien weapon location, Armus gave the order to open fire, and twenty-three battleships opened fire at once with a tremendous barrage of grapeshot and some heavier kinetic projectiles as well since the superbattleship could not maneuver to avoid hits. The grapeshot struck all around the hull of the superbattleship, shields flaring in white-hot intensity as the energy from the solid ball bearings converted to force, battering at the enemy defenses. The alien shields flickered under the blows, weak spots appearing and growing.

The human battleships opened up with their hell lances in a staggered series of volleys that slashed through the remnants of the shields on the superbattleship, then into the armor and every place where weapons had been detected. The bear-cow shields collapsed completely, the superbattleship's hull itself now glowing with the heat of the hell-lance beams slamming into it.

Amazingly, the surviving Kicks kept firing, pumping out shots from every weapon still working in a frantic attempt to repel the human attack.

"Wow," Desjani breathed.

"It's an astounding amount of firepower aimed at one target," Geary agreed.

"I was thinking of the fact that the target is still there and still fighting in the face of that firepower," Desjani said. In her voice, there was grudging respect for the enemy standing firm against those odds.

The fire from the superbattleship fell off rapidly, becoming erratic, then finally ceasing as the human assault picked off every weapon almost as fast as it fired. The human barrage continued for another several seconds, then also halted except for a final vindictive volley from *Dreadnaught* as she, *Orion*, *Superb*, and *Splendid* closed in with the other human battleships.

Captain Armus appeared before Geary again, looking satisfied but not jubilant. Geary suspected that Armus had never worn a jubilant expression. "The external defenses of the alien warship have been reduced," he reported.

"Very well. Excellent job, Captain Armus. Keep your battleships in position, ready to engage any attempts to fire on the Marine landing force. Take out anything that fires as soon as it opens up."

Armus nodded in measured approval of his orders, saluted once more, then his image disappeared.

"General Carabali," Geary ordered, "you may begin your attack."

The four assault transports broke free from the mass of the fleet, *Tsunami* and *Typhoon* approaching one side of the still-slowly-revolving superbattleship and *Haboob* and *Mistral* coming in on the opposite side, the transports matching the rotation of the alien warship so that all five ships moved together like partners in a stately dance.

"Why is Carabali splitting her forces?" Desjani asked. "Isn't that a bad idea when we don't know much about what's inside that Kick can?"

"It's partly because we don't have deck plans," Geary explained. "Carabali didn't want to run into bottlenecks, places where she couldn't funnel too many Marines through too small an area. By coming in from opposite sides, she helps prevent that from happening."

General Charban had come onto the bridge unnoticed, taking a break from the ongoing efforts at communication with the spider-wolves. His eyes were shadowed with fatigue as well as emotion and memories as he watched the Marine assault begin. "Isn't she also complicating the enemy defense by hitting them in more than one place?" Charban asked.

"Yes. That was the other reason." Geary had wondered whether to let Charban, himself a retired ground-forces officer, look at Carabali's plan for any problem areas but had decided against that. It wasn't simply because he needed Charban to remain focused on the struggle to communicate. Marine operations had some significant differences from ground-forces assaults, and Charban wasn't with the fleet in a military capacity. No good could come of blurring lines of responsibility.

Though, Geary thought, no matter whom else he consulted, responsibility ultimately lay with him.

"You have three thousand Marines with this fleet?" Charban asked. "How many are being utilized in this operation?"

"The first waves will use two thousand," Geary replied. "A thousand on each side. General Carabali is holding five hundred in reserve, and we've got a final five hundred available on the major warships to reinforce the attack if that proves necessary."

"Two thousand," Charban repeated. "Against how many alien warriors? We will soon learn the answer to the age-old question of how many bear-cows a single Marine is equal to."

Geary fought down a laugh, recognizing a ground-forces soldier's crack at the legendary pride of Fleet Marines, who considered themselves the equal of any number of any other kind of combatant.

Desjani did laugh, turning to smile at Charban. She hadn't liked him, hadn't cared for his reluctance to use force when she thought it obviously necessary, but she did like people who could joke in the face of apprehension.

Flocks of landing shuttles burst from the assault transports, lining up and heading for the superbattleship like eagles swooping to a strike.

Here and there, shots from particle beams or lasers suddenly erupted from the battleship, weapons that had ceased fire before being destroyed or which had lain dormant until now, trying to tear up the oncoming ranks of shuttles.

A few shuttles staggered under blows, but the battleships had been watching, and now their own hell-lance batteries opened up again, silencing within seconds the defensive fire in an avalanche of counterfire.

Eight shuttles had taken hits, two seriously damaged, the ranks of shuttles wavering and disrupted by the defensive fire. Geary heard orders going out from the assault coordinators. "Shuttles 1210 and 4236, abort runs and return to base. All other shuttles continue approach."

Shuttle 1210 replied, her pilot sounding puzzled. "Say again. I didn't copy."

"Abort run. Return to base."

"Sorry. Can't copy," the shuttle pilot repeated. "Continuing run."

"This is 4236," another voice broke in. "I've still got control. Request permission to continue run. It's safer than trying to push back to base."

Everyone else had heard 1210 and 4236, and now the other shuttles steadied out, no one wishing to break formation while their more heavily damaged comrades hung on.

Even though the enemy fire had once again ceased, *Dreadnaught*'s main propulsion units lit off for a moment, pushing the battleship closer to the enemy superbattleship.

Geary activated a special circuit that allowed private communications with any ship's commanding officer. "Captain Jane Geary, this is Admiral Geary," he said. "There is nothing else you need to prove to anyone, not after your actions during the battle at this star. Pull back to your assigned position with your comrades."

He didn't wait for a reply, ending the message and sitting back.

Desjani made a sidelong glance in his direction. The special circuit had automatically activated a privacy field around Geary's seat, preventing anyone else from hearing what he had said, and she was surely curious as to what he had told Jane Geary.

Dreadnaught's bow thrusters fired, countering her forward motion and nudging the battleship back toward her assigned position.

"All right," Desjani said. "I'll give in. What did you tell her?"

"I told her that she didn't need to worry about proving to anyone anymore that she was a Geary."

"Let's hope she listens. Admiral, I can keep an eye on the external situation if you want to concentrate on following the Marine attack."

"I shouldn't—" As a rule, he shouldn't concentrate on one area, ignoring what was happening elsewhere. Especially he shouldn't get down in the weeds of a Marine operation, losing track of events in the space around his ships. But there was no battle under way elsewhere, no other hostile force in this star system. Anyone arriving via a jump point would be at least several light-hours away, and the spider-wolves were far enough off that even they couldn't stage a surprise attack if they suddenly and inexplicably became hostile.

"You need to learn more about how the Marines operate," Desjani pointed out. "You are an admiral now. And there's no better way to learn than by watching them."

"You're right," Geary conceded.

"I'm always right," she murmured in reply, then in a louder voice that others besides Geary could hear added, "I'll keep an eye on things while you overwatch the Marine action, Admiral."

No fleet officer would question that. As much as fleet officers respected the Marines, they also didn't entirely trust them around ships. The Marines were different, with different training and experience. They would sometimes push buttons they shouldn't, without knowing what those buttons would do. Everyone would be happy to know that the admiral was watching the Marines.

Of course, Marines felt the same way about sailors, and doubtless wished that General Carabali could supervise the actions of fleet officers.

Geary called up the windows that offered views from Marine combat armor and was surprised at first by the depth of the layers offered this time. But he had never overseen an operation this big, with this many Marines and this many squads, platoons, companies, and battalions to which they were assigned. He could touch a battalion commander's image and be offered access to the images of the company commanders below that, and below them the platoon commanders, then the squad commanders, and finally individual Marines. He could activate a huge window that contained thumbnails of the views from hundreds of Marines at once in a dizzying range of activity. And, of course, he could talk to General Carabali directly.

He didn't intend talking to her, distracting her when she needed to be commanding her troops. He didn't intend talking to any of the Marines and carefully moved his other hand away from the comm controls so he wouldn't accidentally do so. He needed to know what was happening. He needed to learn more about Marine operations. He didn't need to micromanage people who knew their jobs far better than he ever would.

A smaller window to one side briefly puzzled Geary, then he realized it offered views from the shuttles rapidly closing in on the hull of the superbattleship. He tapped one, getting a large view of the alien ship, its newly pitted armor looming on all sides as if the shuttle were flying toward a massive, slightly curving wall. Was that a large hatch sealed tight? It looked like a cargo hatch. Nearby was what seemed to be a personnel access, far smaller and not even as big as one intended for humans. Could a Marine in combat armor get through something that size?

The shuttle glided to a halt as its bow thrusters fired, hovering just short of the superbattleship. So close Geary could see the scars of impacts, could spot the place where what had probably been a shield generator had been before it had been blasted to ruin by fire from the battleships.

It all lay silent, as if the superbattleship were lifeless inside as well as out, a derelict crewed only by the dead.

That was possible. The defensive fire they had seen could have been the work of weapons set to fire automatically under control of computerized systems.

Geary didn't believe that, though. Neither, obviously, did the Marines.

He wondered how it would look, how it would feel, if the super-battleship self-destructed, while he was viewing it virtually from so close-up. The thought put a chill through him, and Geary looked for something to distract him from a possibility that he could do nothing about now.

Spotting thumbnails where activity seemed to be going on, he brought those to the fore, seeing views from the combat armor of Marines actually on the superbattleship's hull. The tags on the views identified them as combat engineers, and as Geary watched he saw them placing breaching charges to blow open one of the big hatches like the one he had seen earlier.

The view shifted rapidly as the Marines huddled by the hull, then shook as directional charges went off, blowing out portions of the hatch, the shock of the explosions transmitting through the hull to rattle the Marines clinging to it.

The view swayed again dizzily as the combat engineers swung back to the hatch, followed by curses over the comm circuits. "We didn't get through!" "How thick is this stuff?"

Then came orders from Carabali, sounding in every combat engineer's battle armor. "Double up the breaching charges."

The Marine engineers moved quickly, not really needing the "Move it!" encouragement from their squad leaders as they rigged breaching charges in tandem to get through the armor protecting the superbattleship. The delay had thrown off the shuttles, which were clustering near the superbattleship without anyplace to drop off their Marines. Views jumped again as the combat engineers put distance between themselves and the breaching charges. "Fire in the hole!"

How old was that warning, and what had it originally referred to? Geary wondered. Maybe it had once meant someone had physically lit a fuse with an open flame. Now it just warned of an explosion soon to come.

The view shook again, prolonged this time. Marines moved with cries of triumph to holes spearing through the armored hatch. "Five more! Here and here! That'll break this section free. Go!"

Geary scanned the other windows, seeing similar activity under way at every point where the Marines were trying to blast their way inside the superbattleship. One by one, the breaching teams were creating holes large enough for Marines to pull themselves inside.

He called up a different window, this one showing the view from a Marine who had made it inside a similar cargo-hatch area. There were no lights, just a dark void. "No gravity inside. It's broke, or they shut it off." Moving cautiously, the Marine moved to one side as more Marines entered, their infrared-beam lights providing ghostly images of a large compartment that bore some resemblance to that on a human ship. But then, why wouldn't it? The requirements for moving cargo were the same no matter what creature was doing the job.

"No internal gravity?" Geary heard General Charban comment behind him. "Marines train for that, don't they?"

"That's right," Desjani replied. "They prefer to fight with a gravity field, but they can handle zero g." She sounded proud of that, that the Marines could deal with something ground forces weren't trained to handle. Geary had heard her bemoan Marine behavior and mind-sets more than once among fleet officers, but when it came to outsiders like ground forces and aerospace defense, the fleet and the Marines suddenly became brothers and sisters in arms.

The Marines whom Geary had focused on were moving quickly but cautiously to check out the compartment, their heads-up displays highlighting anything that looked unusual or suspicious. In this case, surrounded on the bulkheads and overhead by alien devices of strange design even if they probably fulfilled familiar functions, the heads-ups were keying on almost everything that wasn't flat bulkhead. In some cases, even seemingly unadorned sections of the walls, overhead, and deck had something about them that made the sensors in the Marine combat armor unhappy.

"Pressure switches?" one of the Marines in the unit Geary was zoomed in on speculated.

"Maybe," his sergeant replied. "Maybe just cargo-tracking stuff. But maybe not. Keep off 'em."

"What the hell is this?"

"If you don't know, *don't touch it*! Stop playing tourists and find the air locks and their controls!"

Geary shifted from unit to unit, seeing pretty much the same thing everywhere. Units inside the compartments the combat engineers had breached, moving in zero g as they tried to find all of the hatches leading farther into the enemy ship. "Found one," a Marine cried. "Are these the controls? They're set real low, almost on the deck."

"Duh, brain-dead. These guys are short, remember?"

"Shut up," their corporal said. "Hey, Sarge, this looks like it. Some sort of knife switch instead of a button, though."

"Lieutenant?"

"Wait. Okay, Sergeant. The captain says open it up, but be ready for them to be on the other side. Weapons free."

"Got it. Cover the hatch, you slugs. Flip the switch, Kezar."

Geary waited, watching, as Corporal Kezar swung the knife switch upward.

And waited.

"Nothing's happening, Sarge."

"I can see that. Lieutenant?"

"None of the switches are opening hatches, Sergeant. Get your hacker to work."

"Cortez! Get that thing open."

Another Marine huddled by the switch, popping the cover with some difficulty and peering inside. Geary quickly changed views to see what Private Cortez saw, but he couldn't make out what he was seeing.

The lieutenant's voice came on again. "What's the word? Can you override the controls?"

"I can't even identify the controls!" Private Cortez protested. "This box looks like it oughta be them…"

"Then find the input, find some wires——"

"Lieutenant, there ain't no input that I can see except this swing switch, and there ain't no wires in this thing. There's just some kind of mesh in… what is that gunk? Gel or something."

"You can't—What's——" The lieutenant must also have been viewing what Cortez and Geary were both looking at. "How the hell does that stuff work?"

"I don't know, Lieutenant! All I do know is I can't hack something that doesn't work like anything we've got!"

Similar conversations were happening in Marine units at every penetration. "Captain, we're going to have to blow the air locks," the lieutenant reported after huddling with his sergeant.

"Are the outer hull penetrations blocked?"

"Sir, I don't know, but we can operate in vacuum fine——"

"Our orders are to take everything inside this ship as intact as possible, and there are a lot of things that don't handle vacuum as well as our combat armor," the captain said. "Hold on. Colonel, we need to know if the hull penetrations in this area have been sealed."

"Yuhas! We need a green light to blow the locks!"

Almost a minute passed as more and more Marines called up the chain of command for approval to blow open pathways into the ship.

"Colonel Yuhas reports his combat engineers say we're good to go," the relieved word finally came down the chain of command. "Blow the bulkheads, not the air locks. We don't know how they're sealed or locked. That's from brigade command. Everybody blow your way inside but avoid going straight through air locks. We're way behind on movement. Get inside that thing."

"What's going on?" Desjani asked.

"They're blowing internal bulkheads now to get inside," Geary told her.

"That's why I saw them plugging holes and rigging emergency air locks on the outside of the hull? Have they seen any Kicks yet?"

"No." He watched a hundred thumbnail views at once as Marines blasted their way through bulkheads and into passageways and other compartments. "Empty."

Everywhere the Marines were entering, the superbattleship seemed to be vacant of any crew. The Marines moved in rushes down passageways that weren't as wide or tall as those on human ships but were still large enough to manage a couple of Marines abreast. Smaller cross-corridors intersected the large passageways in what seemed to be a regular enough grid arrangement, similar to those used by humans. As in human ships, conduits holding wiring and ducts carrying air festooned the overhead, offering grips to the Marines as they pulled themselves along, swimming through zero g. As they advanced, the Marines spread out, penetrating deeper into the ship as well as to each side and up and down through the decks.

"Keep your eyes out for control compartments, power core compartments, a bridge, that sort of thing," a major reminded his unit. "It all looks the same," a frustrated captain replied. "There are markings all over the place, but they're nothing like the markings on our ships or the ones the Syndics use. They could mean anything."

"No ventilation," another one of the Marine officers reported. "The air seems okay. Breathable by humans, even though the pressure is lower than we're comfortable with. But they've shut down the ventilation systems."

"There are supposed to be thousands of 'em aboard this thing," another Marine muttered, her weapon seeking targets in another empty passageway. "Where the hell are they?"

On the thumbnails spread in front of Geary, bedlam suddenly erupted as Marines in scores of locations suddenly found the answer.

9

The Marines had penetrated about a third of the way into the super-battleship when the bear-cows suddenly appeared before them in dozens of locations at once. The once-eerily-deserted passageways filled with noise and the thunder of weapons as Marines traded shots with masses of Kicks filling the spaces from overhead to deck.

"They're in armor!"

"Look out! On the right!"

"Durien is down!"

"Keep shooting!"

"There are too damn many of them!"

"Accesses overhead! They're shooting down through them!"

"My grenade clip is empty!"

"Somebody pick up Sierra! She's still alive!"

"Eat this, you bastards!"

Gradually, the sergeants and corporals started to regain comm discipline, the initial ambushes settling into Marines holding their positions and pouring fire from every weapon they could bring to bear down the passageways where the bear-cows kept pressing forward behind weapons that combined assault rifles with rectangular shields.

"We're running low on energy and ammo."

"Fall back. Everyone fall back."

"The Kicks are using the bodies of their dead as shields!" a Marine yelled. "Pushing their dead ahead of them! Our shots can't get through to the live ones!"

"Fall back," the order came down again. "Don't do a staged withdrawal by fire teams. Get everyone back fast. We're feeding in the reserves and establishing defensive positions closer to the outer hull. Get back *now*."

Geary stared at the battle scenes, watching one where what seemed to be a solid plug of dead bear-cows whose armor had been ravaged by Marine fire was being pushed down a passageway. The muzzles of weapons stuck out from the bodies of the dead, carried by the living bear-cows behind, spraying fire at the Marines who were falling back toward the outer hull.

He pulled out of the close-up views, trying to grasp what General Carabali was doing. The image of the superbattleship on his display had gradually filled with more details as the Marines went into the ship, and now Geary could see the symbols marking Marine units heading back everywhere.

Why was Carabali ordering her units back so far, so fast? She was giving up precious gains, which might be very hard to retake if the bear-cows set up more defenses and ambushes.

Geary's hand hovered over his comm controls. *Has Carabali lost her nerve? I need to ask why she's reacting this way, why—*

His eye caught activity on a cluster of views in one area of the superbattleship. The Marines there had fallen back past a defensive barrier, which, after a furious burst of fire that tore apart the protective barrier of the dead and riddled the front ranks of the bear-cows, was itself falling back, toward where yet another defensive line was setting up heavy weapons. Similar activity was occurring all over the superbattleship, but Geary's attention focused on this spot as the retreating Marines were suddenly hit by Kicks who had infiltrated above, below, and to the sides of them, moving through the many side corridors and accesses too small for the Marines.

A minute later, and that platoon of Marines would have been cut off and swamped, but they were far enough back and close enough to the Marines behind them that a flurry of defensive fire and some vicious hand-to-hand fighting got the platoon through the danger.

Geary let his hand fall. *She knew. General Carabali realized what the bear-cows could do on their own ground with the superior numbers they have. Instead of standing firm while her strongpoints are surrounded, she's pulling them back faster than the Kicks can envelop them, taking a heavy toll of the attackers every step of the way.*

"Admiral? Are your comms working properly?" Desjani asked in a voice that promised serious repercussions for her comm officer.

"My comms are fine," Geary said. "The problem was with me. I almost forgot that General Carabali knows her job a lot better than I know her job."

As the Marines fell back toward the outer hull, the volume of space they had to defend grew larger as the diameter of the super-battleship's hull grew. But Carabali was feeding in reinforcements and pulling her forces together into hedgehogs at intersections of the largest passageways, able to fire to all sides with heavy weapons as the bear-cows kept pressing onward. Under the concentrated fire of those heavy weapons, augmented by the fire of the Marine hand and shoulder-fired weapons, the tight ranks of the Kicks dissolved as they tried to drive into contact with the human invaders.

"How many of them are there?" a Marine yelled.

Some of the bear-cows had pushed through to the compartments where the initial penetrations had occurred, rushing the combat engineers defending the bridgeheads there. The combat engineers lacked the heavy weapons of the line Marines, but they made up for that with demolitions and other tools of their trade. Geary winced as he watched the havoc wrought by the engineers as they wiped out the Kicks coming against them. Those portions of the enemy ship would yield little of use to those seeking to learn more about the bear-cows and their technology.

Geary, appalled by the carnage, couldn't take his eyes off the screens where the bear-cows pitted their numbers and their hand weapons against the concentrated firepower of the Marines. In some places, the Kicks actually managed to reach the hedgehogs, hurling themselves at the perimeters in solid ranks that threatened to submerge the Marines. Geary saw Marines being knocked down despite the superior strength of their combat armor, some of the Marine lines wavering as the hedgehogs were compressed on all sides. Packed in ever tighter inside their defensive perimeters, the Marines were unable to move, unable to do anything but keep firing with weapons glowing from waste heat.

Carabali had been watching, though. More Marine

reinforcements had been arriving, leaping from shuttles into the improvised air locks on the outer hull, being brought inside the hull as fast as possible. Those Marines were formed into shock teams, who now stormed into the passageways leading to the most heavily beleaguered hedgehogs, catching the attacking Kicks from behind.

One by one, the hedgehogs under the heaviest pressure were relieved, the Marines pushing out to form wider defensive positions and keep the bear-cows from being able to concentrate against isolated strongpoints.

The assaults against the Marine positions faltered here, then there, then at each point where the Kicks had surged ahead. The attacks paused, leaving a sense of a foe taking breaths and trying to regain enough strength to continue the fight. Before that pause could extend, Carabali issued new orders, and everywhere the Marines moved out of their hedgehogs and defensive lines, blowing holes through bulkheads to bypass passageways choked with dead bear-cows.

"Tough bastards," a Marine said as he skirted a solid wall of unmoving bear-cows, their armor torn, blobs of purplish blood filling the air in the absence of gravity.

"Good thing there weren't more of them," one of his companions agreed.

"There *are* more of them," their sergeant barked. "Keep your weapons ready, your mouths shut, and your eyes sharp."

As the Marines moved farther into the ship, they encountered scattered pockets of Kicks, who hurled themselves forward in hopeless, desperate attacks that ended only when the last of them was dead. Geary watched the symbols of the Marine units spread back through the superbattleship, then onward past the points where the crew had counterattacked.

"What the hell?" a lieutenant asked as her unit entered a very large area near the center of the ship, a vast compartment whose ceiling soared six meters high. But the deck of the compartment wasn't a deck, it was vegetation, row upon row of crops set into growing containers, the tops of multiple stems on each plant heavy with seeds or fruit or maybe something that was both seed and fruit.

"Food and oxygen resupply combined in one," a sergeant remarked, pulling himself down to examine a long line of growing containers. "My father worked on a farm like this in a sealed city before Huldera Star System was abandoned. And, unless I miss my guess, this is how those bear-cows recycled at least some of their waste products, as fertilizer. Good things these troughs are sealed so stuff couldn't float away when the gravity went off."

The sergeant's squad made noises of revulsion, suddenly taking great care where they put their hands and feet.

More units stumbled across similar compartments, then one platoon sounded an alert that drew Geary's attention. "Lieutenant, I think we found a control station. It doesn't look big enough for a full power core."

"How would you know, Winski?"

"I helped take a Syndic battleship at Welfrida, that's how. That was a lot smaller ship than this thing, and it had a bigger control station than this one."

"Tanya," Geary said, "take a look at this." He also forwarded the image to Captain Smythe. "What do you think?"

Desjani sounded doubtful. "A secondary control station, maybe.

That's not big enough even for the power core of a ship the size of *Dauntless*."

Smythe agreed but added something else. "It may be that what we find will all look like secondary control stations. I've been watching as the Marines fill in the deck plan on that superbattleship, and I am ever more convinced that the bear-cows avoided using one or two major power sources, instead choosing to use multiple lesser power sources. Maybe that was for backup. Redundancy. Or maybe in a ship of that size it made sense to distribute the power sources rather than run lines all over from one or two sources located in one area."

"Why didn't they blow it up?" Geary asked the question again.

"Maybe it didn't occur to them. Maybe they beat the predators on their world by refusing to give up, instead fighting to the last breath and the last Kick to kill their opponents." Smythe blinked, his expression twisting. "When you showed me the images of that control room, I saw some of the passageways on that ship. What they're like now, filled with so many dead. Why would they keep fighting? Why die in a hopeless struggle?"

"I guess they thought they'd die anyway and wanted to go down swinging." Geary had disliked the bear-cows. No, he had hated them for forcing the fights in the Pandora Star System and here, but he had to feel grudging respect for them as well, just as Desjani did. It was easy to see why they had overrun their world, wiping out all competition.

But that was just one more reason why they couldn't be allowed to follow this fleet back to human space.

The Marines spread through the superbattleship, breaking down into smaller and smaller forces, wiping out smaller and smaller gatherings of remaining Kicks, who still refused to surrender and attacked until they were killed. Occasionally, a tiny group of bear-cows stampeded away from the Marines, but the moment the aliens hit a dead end, they turned and charged their pursuers.

The human invaders found vast barracks, subdivided by airtight hatches but otherwise sprawling for long distances. Everywhere, there were compartments set up for eating, as if the bear-cows grazed nearly constantly. The Marines found what could only be hospitals, the operating equipment undersized so that the complexes seemed oddly and disturbingly like children's playrooms. Armories empty of weapons. More control rooms.

Finally, a squad came across the bridge of the superbattleship, a compartment where command seats were backed up by what seemed like stadium seating, as if dozens of spectators routinely watched events there.

"That is so weird," Desjani said. "What is that about?"

"Beats the hell out of me," Geary replied.

General Carabali called in, professionally deadpan as she made her report. "Organized resistance has ceased aboard the superbattleship, Admiral, but I can't say it's safe yet. Not until we've gone over it much more carefully. My Marines aboard that ship will remain in a combat footing, and any fleet personnel coming aboard will require Marine escorts."

"Thank you, General," Geary said. "Damned good job. My congratulations on your success and my condolences on your losses."

"Thank you, Admiral."

"Are there any bear-cows still alive?"

"The Kicks fought until they were killed, or if we started to physically overcome them they died. We don't know if there's a suicide device on them or in their armor, or if it's some mental thing. They also slaughtered their unconscious wounded if there seemed a chance of their being captured."

"Ancestors preserve us."

Carabali made a face. "If you think about it, Admiral, if you were a cow, and you knew the fate awaiting any of your fellow cows who were captured, then the Kick actions make sense. They were protecting their injured from a fate worse than death. My Marines are searching through the enemy dead for any Kicks who were injured so badly they were rendered unconscious but weren't subsequently killed by their own comrades to 'save' them from us."

Now Carabali hesitated. "Speaking of the enemy dead... Admiral, after any battle there is the matter of enemy remains to address. Our policy on that varied during the war, as you know, even though our opponents were fellow humans. But since you assumed command, we have dealt with remains with all due dignity and respect. But now... Admiral, there are so many dead crowding that ship. Long stretches of some passageways are impossible to get through, and there's a tremendous amount of blood floating around so we don't dare restart ventilation even if we knew the right controls. What should we do with them?"

How could they give decent burials to that many enemy dead, especially when many of the bodies weren't intact but blown into pieces?

But they had to get them out of the ship, or, within a few days, it would turn into an unlivable hell.

"General, we'll treat them as best we know how. Working parties will have to collect the enemy dead. Fleet medical will want to retain some specimens; but otherwise, they are to be gathered at one of the cargo docks. A service will be said each time the dock is full, then the bodies will be ejected en masse on a trajectory aimed at the star, and we'll start filling the dock again."

"Yes, sir. It would help if we could get sailors to assist in those working parties. It's not a pleasant job, and there's a lot to collect."

Geary shook his head, looking at the fleet status readouts. "General, every sailor I've got is working almost around the clock either repairing their own ship or on tiger teams assisting other ships. I have to give priority to getting my ships as combat-ready as possible as soon as possible." What other resources did he have? The senior officers rescued from the Syndic labor camp on Dunai. The Syndic citizens rescued from the enigma race. There weren't that many of either, but it was something. "I will ask for volunteers among our two groups of passengers to assist in the cleanup and will see if the auxiliaries have any equipment that can handle the task on its own."

Carabali let her disappointment show but nodded. "I do understand. No one is taking it easy right now. But even a few personnel besides Marines assisting in the task would be welcome."

"I'll have someone there, General."

It took nearly two days of careful exploring, using Marines assisted by small, robotic probes that could get into any area of the ship before it was declared officially taken by General Carabali.

Long before that, human engineers who were desperately needed to help conduct repairs on Geary's ships had been hauled off those jobs to try to figure out the controls on the superbattleship and render everything safe.

The engineers on the auxiliaries had offered up a half dozen decontamination units, mobile devices designed to enter ships and remove any sort of contagion or pollution. They vacuumed up blood from the air, scrubbed it from bulkheads, decks, and overheads, collected pieces of what the engineers called random biological remains, and scooped up relatively intact dead bear-cows in large numbers to deliver to the designated cargo dock, giving relief to tired and resentful Marines. Midgrade fleet and Marine officers rotated at the dock, each reciting the words of the standard burial service over each mass of dead Kicks before they were sent on their final journey to the star here.

The Marines had found amid the bear-cow dead six who were still alive but too badly injured to arouse to consciousness. The six were transferred to medical quarantine on *Mistral* while the fleet doctors tried to figure out how to keep them alive.

"What the hell are we going to do with that thing?" Desjani grumbled on the third day. She was exhausted, they were all exhausted. "We are taking it with us, right?"

"Yes. We have to." Geary knew that she knew the answer as well as he did.

"How?"

That question was a lot harder. "I'll ask Captain Smythe." Geary rubbed his eyes, realizing how woolly his mind was after so many days with too little sleep as he supervised so much repair work and everything else. "All units, this is Admiral Geary. Tomorrow is rope yarn. All hands are to relax, sleep, eat, and recharge. To the honor of our ancestors, Geary, out."

Desjani frowned at him in disbelief. "We can't afford a day off. And why do they call it rope yarn anyway?"

"I know we can't, and I don't know."

"What?"

"My point exactly," he said. "We're all running on empty, our minds fuzzy from fatigue. We need rest, we need a reset, so our efforts can be a lot more effective."

Captain Smythe protested as well. "My engineers don't need a rest, Admiral. It will blunt their momentum. They can easily go two or three more days without a break."

"Are you saying your engineers are fully effective and will remain so if they keep working without a break for two or three more days?" Geary asked.

"Absolutely. Of course, the frequency of hallucinations and erratic behaviors will go up a bit more on an accelerating curve—"

"Give them a rest, Captain Smythe. That's a firm order. I will be checking to see that the stand-down is enforced."

Of course, even though Geary made an effort to sleep in, he couldn't avoid all work that day.

"I request a personal conference," Captain Badaya said, his image standing in Geary's stateroom.

Badaya looked as subdued as Geary had ever seen him. "Granted. Sit down, Captain."

"Thank you, Admiral." Badaya took a seat in his own stateroom, leaning forward with his elbows resting on his knees. "You already have my formal report of the recent action."

"Yes. You didn't spare yourself."

"Nor should I have!" Badaya sat back. "I blew it. I could not have anticipated that *Titan* would lose some of her propulsion when she did, or that *Incredible* would take damage to one of her main propulsion units at the same time as the shields on *Illustrious* collapsed, but I should have reacted better and faster when that did happen. If not for Captain Geary, the majority of the ships under my direct control would probably have been destroyed and the rest severely damaged."

"That decision of Captain Jane Geary's should not have worked out as well as it did," Geary pointed out.

"It was still the right decision," Badaya insisted. "I was busy trying to figure out how to save my entire formation, which I couldn't do, but she recognized that some sacrifice would be necessary. Now, I realize you don't publicly humiliate officers, even those who deserve it, and you and I both know some of those I speak of in that regard. But I wanted to tell you that I will not contest any other officer being put in command of a subformation in which my battle cruiser is a part. I understand that everyone will see that as a demotion, but I understand that I failed in a higher command position. Perhaps with time, I'll figure out how to handle things better. If you feel it is appropriate, I will also not object to giving command of the Sixth Battle Cruiser Division to Captain Parr of the *Incredible*. He is not as experienced as I am, but he is a fine and skilled officer."

Geary watched Badaya for a few moments before answering. "It could have been done better. It could have been done a lot worse."

"Thank you, Admiral."

"I was remembering my first commanding officer on my first ship," Geary said. "I was still a new officer, only about a month after reporting aboard, when I made a big mistake. My department head almost took my skin off. The executive officer almost popped my eardrums. That took most of the morning. Then the captain called me in."

"That must have been one hell of a mistake," Badaya observed.

"Oh, yeah. Big enough that I won't say what it was. But my captain called me in, junior officer me all quivering after the dressing-downs I had already gotten, and he said to me in a calm voice, 'Mistakes are how we learn.' He let me stare at him in amazement for a long moment, then he added in a voice like frozen nitrogen, 'Don't ever make *that* mistake again.' Then he dismissed me."

Badaya laughed. "The hell you say."

"The point is, I learned more from those two sentences from him than I did from the screaming directed at great length at me by my department head and the executive officer. That captain managed to chew me out and convey continued confidence in me with those two sentences. After that, I never let him down. I wanted to be certain I never let him down." Geary leaned back, deliberately relaxing his posture. "Yes, you screwed up. You know you screwed up. I will make further decisions on subformation commanders taking that into account, and you know I have to, but I will also take into account what you did right and have done right. There will be no changes in command of the Sixth Battle Cruiser Division. I have no problems with Captain Parr, who as you say has proven himself a fine officer, but you still have my confidence as commander of that division."

It took perhaps half a minute for Badaya to answer, his voice rough with emotion. "You really are him, you know. I've heard people say no one could actually be Black Jack, but—"

"I've made my share of mistakes." Geary paused, realizing this was a moment he could use for other reasons. "Especially in areas I'm not trained in. Captain Badaya, the fact that many of the politicians running the Alliance aren't doing a very good job of it and haven't done a very good job of it doesn't mean you or I would do better than they have."

Badaya looked back at Geary steadily, thoughts moving behind his eyes. "That's a point," Badaya finally conceded. "Do you ever feel overwhelmed during a battle, Admiral? Like too much is happening, and you don't know what the right thing to do is?"

"Of course I do."

"As you were saying that last, about the politicians, I imagined myself making political decisions in a crisis. It was all too easy to imagine feeling overwhelmed." He paused. "That's why you're still letting them do most things, isn't it?"

"Yes." A partial lie, which made Geary cringe internally. Badaya thought Geary was actually directing the government now, behind the scenes. That had been necessary to avoid the chance of a coup in Geary's name though without his approval, but Geary had been wanting to work his way out of that perception ever since he had been forced to adopt it. "As bad as they may be at it, most of them anyway, they're still better at it than I am. There are some who are terrible by any standard, but there are also some who are good by any standard. And, most important, they derive their power from having been chosen by the people of the Alliance."

Badaya bent an arch look at Geary. "The people of the Alliance would choose you if you asked for that openly."

"I know." Give him the full truth now. "That scares the hell out of me."

"Understandably." Badaya stood up, saluting. "Thank you, sir."

His comm panel chimed the moment Badaya's image vanished. "What did he want?" Desjani asked.

"He apologized," Geary said.

"He apologized? Foot-in-mouth Badaya? Damn." Desjani had never taken well Badaya's often clumsy comments about her and Geary. "You are a miracle worker, aren't you?"

"Very funny. Are you resting?"

"Resting? Me? Oh, yes, sir. I'm resting so hard that I'm sleeping in my sleep."

"Tanya, set a good example for your crew."

She offered him a rigidly proper salute. "Yes, Admiral. I hear and obey."

With both Captain Badaya and Captain Desjani gone, Geary rubbed his eyes, thinking about trying to sleep...

Six bells chimed in spaced pairs across the ship's general announcing system, followed by a voice saying "Admiral, Alliance fleet, arriving."

An admiral. There were only two other sources of Alliance fleet admirals in this star system, among the liberated prisoners of war aboard *Mistral* and *Typhoon*. But none of them should be coming to *Dauntless*.

Geary was reaching toward his comm panel when it came to life, Desjani once again gazing out at him. "Admiral Lagemann has arrived on a shuttle and requests a meeting with you, Admiral."

"Admiral Lagemann?" His sudden tension just as quickly gave way to relief. A personal visit was unusual, but not that strange with so many shuttles winging between ships. "Certainly. Send him to my stateroom."

Admiral Lagemann took only five minutes to reach Geary's stateroom, nodding in greeting as he entered. Geary was actually meeting him in person for the first time. "There was a shuttle run between *Dauntless* and *Mistral*, so I thought I'd take advantage of that to see you. I owe you a report, Admiral Geary."

"About what?" he asked, unable to recall with his mind cluttered by everything he had to deal with in the aftermath of the battle and the capture of the bear-cow superbattleship. "It's nice to meet you at last. Have a seat."

"Thank you." Lagemann sat down, looking around Geary's stateroom with a small smile. "Nothing fancy, but it's home, eh?"

"That's a good way to describe it." He didn't have any other home. There was his home world, Glenlyon, where the cult of Black Jack had burned the brightest. The idea of going back there, to a world filled with familiar places but empty of all of the people he had once known who had died during the last century, to a world that would treat him as some superhuman hero, was more frightening than facing battle.

"It's not too different from my last flagship." A wry look crossed Admiral Lagemann's face. "Also a battle cruiser. *Invincible*."

"*Invincible*? I wonder how many *Invincible*s ago that was," Geary said.

"Probably a dozen. I was in Syndic hands long enough, and everyone knows how long *Invincible*s last. I don't know why I was foolish enough to put my flag on one of them. May I?" Lagemann reached for the display controls, bringing up the regions of space that the fleet had traversed. "You asked for an assessment of what we thought the enigmas might be up to."

And had then forgotten about it. Thank goodness he had remembered to delegate that task. "What did you conclude?"

"A stab in the back." Lagemann grinned lopsidedly. "Big surprise, huh?" He highlighted one star. "We jumped from here to the bear-cow star, Pandora. The enigmas were following us there with a fair-sized force, but they didn't chase us to Pandora, doubtless knowing exactly what awaited us there. Now, since they knew what defenses the bear-cows had, the enigmas would have been justified in concluding that our chances of getting out of Pandora in one piece were pretty damned small."

"It wasn't a situation I'd want to be caught in again," Geary agreed.

"So, if we fought our way back to this enigma star, going back the way we came, what remnants of our force reached them would be chewed up. A reasonable conclusion for the enigmas to make. They could leave a blocking force there to deal with whatever made it back to them. But that wouldn't prevent another human fleet from showing up and driving through their space in the future."

Lagemann shifted the star display back toward human space. "No. If they are going to ensure that no more humans come knocking, they need to lock the front door."

"Pele?" Geary asked. "There's nothing there."

"No. But for us to get to Pele we had to go through—"

"Midway." He stared at the star display, appalled. "The enigmas will try to eliminate our ability to use Midway as a stepping-stone into their territory."

"That's our assessment. At the least, they could move in and collapse the hypernet gate there the old-fashioned way, by shooting out all of the tethers. Are you sure the Syndics have systems on their gates that ensure a collapse doesn't devastate the whole star system?"

"I'm certain of it," Geary said. "We spotted the equipment on the hypernet gate at Midway when we came through there last."

Lagemann chewed his lip, looking morose now. "You could have knocked me over with a feather when I found out how much damage a collapsing hypernet gate could do. Nova-scale energy bursts. And we built those damned things in all of our most valuable star systems."

"That's what the enigmas wanted when they secretly leaked the technology to us," Geary said. "They wanted the Alliance and the Syndicate Worlds to build huge bombs in our own star systems. Either we and the Syndics would figure out they were weapons as well as transportation devices and use them to cripple or even exterminate humanity, or the enigmas would use them that way if we humans were too smart or moral to engage in self-genocide."

"I wouldn't have placed a lot of bets on us being too smart to do that," Lagemann said. "But that plan fell through. Now the enigmas have to stop us one star system at a time. And the way to stop us is to take out Midway as a place we can use to stage new incursions into enigma territory. They could well have started that retaliation force on its way almost as soon as we jumped for Pandora."

Midway couldn't repel a strong attack by the enigmas. The Syndics there, if the authorities at Midway still answered to the Syndicate Worlds' government, had only a small flotilla of cruisers and Hunter-Killers to protect the star system. Nor would reinforcements likely be coming, not with the Syndicate Worlds' mobile forces crushed by Geary during the last stages of the war and the remnants of its military overstretched as the Syndicate Worlds' government tried desperately to hold on to star systems breaking away from it everywhere.

The only other thing that Midway had to muster in its defense was a promise that he, Admiral Geary, had made to defend them against the enigmas.

But he was very far away from Midway now, with either spider-wolf or enigma territory blocking his way back.

10

Admiral Lagemann spread his hands in apology. "I know that's not a welcome assessment."

"It's an incredibly valuable assessment," Geary replied. "I don't know whether I can do what I need to do in time for it to make a difference, but at least I know I need to do it." He measured with his eyes the distance back to Midway, knowing it was much too far given how little time he might have. "It may be impossible. Especially with that superbattleship we have to haul along with us."

"We can't risk losing that," Lagemann agreed. "Have you been aboard it?"

"Only virtually. I've seen a few compartments, some passageways, and during the capture of the ship, of course."

"Hell of an operation," Lagemann said. "The colonels and generals with me on *Mistral* all agree that your General Carabali did a fine job. But, anyway, I've been on that ship in person. While the other members of my assessment group were finalizing their conclusions, I volunteered for some of the cleanup duty because I wanted a chance to see an alien ship. Besides, it never hurts for sailors and Marines to see an admiral doing real work, does it?" Lagemann paused in memory. "Being on that alien ship was like a dream. Literally like that. Familiar, and yet strange. I'd be walking down a passageway, everything feeling right about this ship I was in, normal, then I would encounter something utterly weird but which belonged in that place. You never really appreciate how many things we do in certain standard ways because everyone does them that way until you get around a totally alien creation built by someone who doesn't share any of our understandings of how things should be done."

Geary nodded. "It's got the engineers alternately thrilled at the new approaches and pulling their hair out at things they can't figure out."

"If we're taking it back, who's going to ride it, act as commanding officer?"

He hadn't even considered that yet.

"You'll need at least a captain," Lagemann suggested. "Maybe even an admiral if one volunteered."

"Where would I find an admiral dumb enough to volunteer for that?" Geary asked, smiling. "It's going to be hardship duty. The bear-cow life support is erratic after all the damage we inflicted taking that ship, the only food will be battle rations, and the furnishings are all sized wrong for us."

"Sounds like a little slice of heaven," Lagemann said.

"Can anyone on *Mistral* keep an eye on things if you're on the superbattleship?" Lagemann had been a reliable source of information and a steady presence among the former prisoners, some of whom had reacted very badly to discovering that they no longer had any role to play in the destiny of the fleet or the Alliance.

"Admiral Meloch. Angela has a steady hand and a steady head. Or General Ezeigwe. He's aerospace defense forces, but don't hold that against him."

"I won't." Geary thought only for a moment, feeling the prod of having to get moving on the assessment that Lagemann had brought. "All right. Consider yourself assigned to command of the prize crew on the superbattleship. Coordinate with the Marine on-scene commander and the officer in charge of the engineers aboard it. I'll notify General Carabali and Captain Smythe."

Lagemann stood up, smiling with enthusiasm. "It'll be nice to be really responsible for something again! Any idea when the next shuttle from here to the superbattleship will fly?"

"I'm sure we can arrange something fairly soon."

"Is there an official designation for the superbattleship yet? Some name a little less cumbersome than 'the Captured Kick Superbattleship'?"

"I hadn't thought about that, either. I'll get back to you."

"Great. With all due respect, Admiral, I've learned that one of the officers aboard *Dauntless* is the daughter of a man I served with. Before I take the shuttle back to the CKSB, I'd like to see her and let her know—" Lagemann's smile wavered, then vanished. "I'd like to let her know how her father died. It was something I wanted to do in person."

After Lagemann left, Geary sat, trying to think what he could do. One thing overrode everything else. He couldn't possibly get to Pele or Midway in time unless the spider-wolves agreed to let him pass through their territory, which hopefully extended a fair way back toward human space. Which meant he had to talk to those who had been trying to talk to the spider-wolves.

He called Rione, finding her in her cabin going over pictograms. "You're supposed to be resting, Madam Emissary."

"So are you. And since when did you expect me to follow your orders?" She still looked tired and obviously wasn't in the mood for banter.

"I know you've been talking to the spider-wolves about getting us clearance to head back toward human-controlled space through spider-wolf territory," Geary said without further preamble. "That has now become an urgent priority. We need to be able to get back to the vicinity of Pele or Midway as quickly as possible."

Rione eyed him, then nodded. "The enigmas?"

"Very likely, yes."

"I understand. I should have thought of that. General Charban and I will make that our highest priority now. Oh, you or someone else had asked how the spider-wolves manipulate small objects with those claws. It turns out they have small… wormlike tentacles inside each claw that they can extrude for fine-motor tasks."

"Small wormlike tentacles? Inside each claw?"

His reaction must have been showing because Rione smiled crookedly. "I know. Could they possibly be any more physically repulsive to us? That's something we have to overcome. Speaking of which, I recommend you call Dr. Setin and Dr. Shwartz. They have an intriguing theory about the spider-wolves that I think you want to hear."

"All right. Thanks." He punched in the call to *Mistral*, quickly getting a reply from a guilty-looking Dr. Setin.

"Admiral! Is there something?"

"Yes." Geary studied the expert on nonhuman intelligent aliens, trying to figure out why he had the appearance of an undergraduate caught cheating on an exam. Cheating... "Are you working, Doctor?"

"Yes, Admiral," Setin blurted out. "But it is so important, we didn't think we could afford to pause. I knew that you would understand."

Which is why you didn't tell me? "Emissary Rione said that you and Dr. Shwartz have a theory about the spider-wolves?"

"Oh, yes. It's not really at the stage where—"

Dr. Shwartz expanded the view of the comm screen on their end so that she was in it, too, looking haggard but gleeful. "I think we should tell the admiral. This is more of a gut instinct, a belief, than something scientifically provable at this point. We can puzzle over exact words and phrases the spider-wolves seem to be employing until new stars replace the old and not find any certainty. What I feel to be true of these beings, and Dr. Setin agrees this is a real possibility, is that they think in patterns."

"Patterns?"

"Yes. General Charban and Emissary Rione and all of the rest of us keep trying to talk in terms of specific things. It took me a while to understand that the aliens were always talking about *connections* between things. You and I are seeing a forest made up of individual trees. They are seeing the forest as the primary thing." She paused, grimacing unhappily. "Maybe that is not the right analogy because they use terms that seem to refer to balancing of forces. Like spiderwebs. That's what made me think of this. Our academic bias is to assume that something that looks like a spider can't actually be a spider. It needs to be deconstructed and broken down to learn what it really is. But what if the spider-wolves are indeed descended from the thing they resemble to us? Something spiderlike. Something that makes webs, in which everything is tied together, all the tensions and forces in equilibrium, a picture of beauty and stability. Imagine a race of beings that sees everything in those terms."

Geary frowned in thought, leaning back. "Like their ship formations. Not just functional, but also beautiful to our eyes. And if they come from something that could build webs like spiders, that would imply natural instincts for the sort of engineering that humans look at in awe."

"Yes! Something that thinks differently from us but in a way we can still touch, still grasp in our way."

"Humans can see patterns," Geary objected. "That's not alien to us."

"We can," Dr. Setin broke in, "but that's not our bias. This was what led me to consider Dr. Shwartz's ideas to be intriguing because humans don't instinctively think in terms of patterns. We think in terms of opposites. Black and white, good and bad, yin and yang, thesis and antithesis, yes and no, right and left, friend and enemy. What matters to us are opposites, and everything that isn't a clear opposite is evaluated on a scale of where it lies between opposites. Lukewarm. Maybe. Gray. When we stretch our minds, we can see patterns, but that's not our natural way of seeing things."

He had to think about that some more, the implications gradually growing apparent, while the doctors waited. "Then to these aliens, we're neither allies nor enemies. We're part of some pattern."

"We think so," Dr. Shwartz said. "There was one sentence they sent that I kept puzzling over. It seemed to say, 'The picture is changed but remains.' And then I thought, what if they mean not picture, but pattern? Our arrival changed the pattern, but the pattern isn't gone, it has just altered. And then the spider-wolves said, 'Together we hold the picture.' Well, if that really means 'together we hold the pattern,' then that explains what they expect from us. Our part in this pattern, I think we can speculate, is in their eyes to provide another anchor so that the pattern through which they view the universe can retain stability."

"You think these creatures see humanity as a force for stability?" Geary asked.

The two doctors both hesitated, then exchanged glances. "That does sound odd, doesn't it?" Dr. Shwartz said. "We don't see ourselves that way. But then how many outside observers have ever evaluated humanity? Perhaps, compared to the likes of the paranoid enigmas and the rapacious bear-cows, we look pretty good to the spider-wolves."

"There's a term, a pictogram," Dr. Setin added, "that they keep using. The software they gave us interprets it in various ways. Anchor or foundation or bond or keel or buttress. Those are all things that lend stability to something. It keeps coming up when they talk to us. This concept of having firm anchors appears to be critically important to them."

He understood then. "Because without anchors, any pattern is going to unravel, come apart."

"Exactly."

"I think," Dr. Shwartz continued in a cautious voice, "that their idea of an anchor may include intangibles as well as physical objects. Ideas. Theories. Philosophies. Mathematics. All of these things contribute to the pattern, all of these things help keep it in place."

If only they weren't so ugly... "It sounds like the spider-wolves and we can understand each other. Or at least understand enough to coexist in peace and maybe exchange ideas."

"I think so, Admiral, yes." She made an uncomfortable gesture. "Of course, this remains a theory. It's not always clear at all how they react to something we try to say. Reading emotion on them is... challenging."

"There are subtle color shifts," Dr. Setin explained. "We've spotted those on the spider-wolf people, changes in hue on the head and body, but we don't know which color means what. It is possible there are other cues to feelings, like scents or hormonal emissions, but since we're carrying on all of this by remote communications and are not physically in the same room with them, we can't know that."

"I... understand." What did the spider-wolves smell like? He wasn't sure he wanted to know. "Have they said anything about the ship we captured?"

"The ship?" Both doctors appeared uncomfortable now. "We haven't talked much about that..." Dr. Setin said.

"Why? Are the spider-wolves upset about that?"

"No. It's..." Setin looked downward. "The... attack. We've seen... the aftermath. So many... so very many..."

Geary got it then. "The bear-cows we had to kill. I know that's not easy to contemplate. It wasn't something we did by choice. They chased us here, they attacked us here, and they refused to surrender."

"But, to meet a new species, and then to... to..."

"Have you given the same amount of anguish to the men and women who died because the bear-cows wouldn't even talk to us?"

That had come out harshly, more angry than he had intended. "I'm sorry. But the ugly truth is that the bear-cows cared less for the lives of their fellow bear-cows than you and I did. That's a difference in the view of the universe between our species that left us no alternatives. If you think I am happy about that, you're mistaken."

"We know that, Admiral," Dr. Shwartz said. "We regret that it had to be so. It's not a criticism of your actions."

Dr. Setin didn't look as if he entirely agreed with that, but if so, he had the good sense to remain silent.

"What about the six living bear-cows, Admiral?" Dr. Shwartz asked. "We keep being told the matter is classified."

"They're recovering, as far as we can tell, but remain comatose," Geary said. "They're totally isolated from human contact to try to keep them from panicking if they wake up. That's all I know right now."

After that call ended, Geary sat staring at his star display, thinking that he should try to rest. Or maybe do something just for fun. Read a book—

His comm panel buzzed.

Dr. Nasr, the senior fleet medical officer, looked like he hadn't slept in days. He probably hadn't, despite Geary's orders that everyone stand down for a day. Doctors had always considered themselves above the military discipline that governed everyone else, making no secret that they thought their oaths as physicians held more important status than the rules binding other officers. "You left me a message, Admiral?"

He had? When? Prompted by the doctor's statement, Geary finally recalled. The message had been cached in the comm system on *Dauntless*, set to transmit when the fleet left jump days ago. Neither he nor the doctor had experienced the luxury of time for dealing with that message until now. "It's about one of the fleet's officers. Commander Benan."

"Benan?" Nasr's eyes went vague as he searched memory. "Injured during the battle?"

"No. This pertains to the reasons for his difficulties in adjusting to having been liberated from the Syndic labor camp at Dunai."

Nasr sighed. "Admiral, I fully appreciate your concern for all of your officers, but we're still heavily engaged in dealing with combat injuries right now."

"Doctor"—something in Geary's voice caused Nasr's gaze on him to sharpen—"what do you know about mental blocks?"

The doctor stared silently back at Geary for several seconds. "Not much."

"Do you know if the nature of blocks has changed in the last century?"

The doctor paused again for a long while before replying, his face increasingly grim, then finally shook his head. "In every way that matters, no."

"But they're being used now." Geary made it a statement.

"You know that, Admiral?"

"I know that. I didn't know it until very recently."

The doctor closed his eyes, then opened them again to focus on

Geary. "Officially, on an unclassified level, and even for most levels of classification, blocks are not used. I couldn't discuss this with anyone else but you, because you're the fleet commander. I'm not blocked, I would have left the service rather than agree to that, but I have taken an oath to follow security procedures."

"Commander Benan also could only discuss it with me because I was the fleet commander."

"Commander Benan? Why would a line officer—*he* has been blocked?"

"Yes." Geary wondered what else to say, what else he could say. "Purely by chance I satisfied the conditions under which he could tell me."

"He couldn't tell *me*." The doctor slammed his open palm onto the table before him, his face working with anger. "Damn! Do you know, Admiral, that by discussing a specific case of mental blocking with me, *you* are violating security regulations?"

"Are you telling me that security regulations don't allow you to know what's wrong with one of your patients, a patient who is a fleet officer?"

"I'm not even allowed to tell you *that*." Geary had grown used to this doctor's being professionally unflappable, but now Dr. Nasr was openly bitter. "There might be one or two other medical personnel in this fleet who know about the use of blocks, but even I don't know who they are."

"Ancestors preserve us," Geary said. "Does that at least mean the use of blocks is rare?"

"As far as I know." The doctor loaded that statement with irony as he tapped a query into his console. "It certainly explains the problems we're seeing in Commander Benan. Personality changes, problems with controlling anger and impulses, occasional confusion."

"He had a good record before he was captured by the Syndics," Geary pointed out.

"Did he?" The doctor pulled up some records, scanning them rapidly. "I see. Yes. He reported aboard his new ship, and three months later, he was captured. Two weeks' leave prior to reporting to that ship, and about three weeks in transit before he joined the ship. All told, a little more than four months." The doctor paused, his brow furrowing. "Yes. Six months. That's the usual time before symptoms of a block start manifesting clearly. Commander Benan got captured before they showed."

And if he hadn't been captured, his performance aboard his ship would have deteriorated, he would have committed offenses against discipline and good order, all for no known reason, and eventually he would have been expelled from the service. "I remember something about suicide," Geary said slowly. "When I went through commanding officer capture and interrogation survival school a century ago, they didn't tell us much about blocks, but there was something about suicide when they talked about why blocks weren't used."

"Yes." The doctor's mouth worked with distaste. "It's common in blocked individuals. They're suffering from the symptoms, they know what's wrong, but they literally can't tell anyone else, any attempts at treatment fail because the real underlying cause isn't known to those directing treatment, and..." He shook his head. "An impulsive decision, the only way out, the only way to find peace, and that's it. I'm about to make a statement that would get me in great trouble with security, Admiral."

"Feel free. I'll defend you."

"Thank you. It has occurred to me on those rare occasions when I thought about blocks that they are indeed aimed at keeping secrets by the oldest and surest means. They eventually drive those given blocks to suicide, and once those individuals are dead, the secrets they carried can never be divulged."

Dead men tell no tales. How old was that saying? Geary let out a slow breath, trying to calm himself. "Why not just kill them?"

"But we are civilized people, Admiral. We wouldn't kill someone out of hand." This time, the doctor's voice dripped with sarcasm.

"I see why they keep this so secret," Geary said. "If more than a very few people knew about Alliance use of mental blocks, then the facts would come out somehow, and the blowback would be ferocious. How often do the Syndics use mental blocks?"

Dr. Nasr shook his head. "They don't. I'm sure I would have been told if they did. Being less civilized than we are, the Syndics apparently simply shoot anyone who inconveniently knows the wrong things. It's a much more efficient way of eliminating the problem if you look at it in a sufficiently cold-blooded manner."

What could he say to that? "Thank you for your information, Doctor. With what you now know, can you provide any better treatment for Commander Benan?"

"There are some measures I can try, but I doubt they will help much. The block has to be lifted, Admiral. Then we can try to start undoing the damage."

"Can I order you to lift the block?"

"No, Admiral." The doctor spread his hands helplessly. "Even if you could, I don't know how to do it. I know, in a theoretical way, how blocks are impressed upon individual brains. I don't know how to do it in practice, though, and I wouldn't have accepted such training. That means I also have no idea how to lift a block."

"So Commander Benan has to wait for effective treatment until we get home."

"If he lasts that long, and if once we get there, you can get authorization to have the block lifted. The only ones who will know how to do it will also be people who will only do it if they receive proper orders through proper channels." Dr. Nasr shook his head. "I am sorry, Admiral."

"It is in no way your fault."

"If that is all, I'm needed in surgery in fifteen minutes."

"Are *you* getting enough sleep?"

Dr. Nasr paused. "My patients need me, Admiral. If you'll excuse me, I have to—" He stopped speaking, staring to one side as another message came in to him. "One of the bear-cows became fully conscious, Admiral. He is now dead."

"Dead." Geary felt a bitter taste in his mouth. "As soon as he realized he had been captured."

"Yes. He shut down his entire metabolism. I don't know how. But given the isolation in which we've kept them by the time we could react it was too late."

"I had hoped that one of them would take the time to realize that if we had patched them up, tried to make them well, it would indicate we didn't mean them harm."

The doctor hesitated again, then spoke heavily. "Admiral, the creatures here, the…"

"Spider-wolves."

"Yes. Have you considered the possibility that they eat like the spiders with which we are familiar?"

"To be perfectly frank, Doctor," Geary admitted, "I've tried not to think about what they eat and how they eat it."

"That's understandable." Dr. Nasr grimaced. "Some spiders don't kill their prey at once, you know. They paralyze it, perhaps, or just wrap it in webbing to immobilize it. Then they leave it, keeping it handy for when they want to eat. They don't want their prey injured. They want it alive and ready for consumption."

He didn't get it at first, then the doctor's meaning washed over him. "The bear-cows might have encountered the spider-wolves and learned that the spider-wolves liked eating their prey alive, and that they considered bear-cows prey?"

"It is something we must consider," Dr. Nasr said. "We don't know. But it is a possibility. We don't *know* that these bear-cows didn't deal with predators like that on their own world before they achieved dominance. We don't know whether or not they've encountered other species who like the taste of bear-cow. Humans do not usually consider themselves prey, Admiral. But when we do get that feeling, that we are nothing but something's next meal, it is a very horrifying feeling. I wondered at first why a sentient species would develop the means of shutting down its own vital functions, of willing itself to die. But these bear-cows are prey. They have always been prey. They may have developed the means to will themselves to death at the same time as they developed intelligence. I can imagine the physical pain of being eaten, but I cannot imagine the mental pain of *knowing* I am being eaten.

Under such circumstances, the ability to cease suffering would be a welcome option."

A buzz sounded in Dr. Nasr's office, and he jerked in reaction. "My surgery. Admiral, I must go."

"All right, Doctor. Make sure the remaining five bear-cows are kept sedated, kept unconscious."

Dr. Nasr paused in midreach to end the call. "You realize that we know so little of their physiology, of how they react to medications, that we might easily kill them by trying to keep them sedated."

"I understand, Doctor." *Damned if we do and damned if we don't.* "Unless we want the other five to kill themselves, or die of other causes, I don't see any alternative at this point."

Geary sat brooding after the call ended. What could he do with the bear-cows? An attempted humanitarian gesture had turned into a need to keep them in a state of living death to keep them from actually dying. Would letting them die be the humane thing to do?

He realized that he was thinking of them as bear-cows again, not as Kicks, after speaking with the scientists and the doctor. But no matter what they were called, the same problems remained.

And the talk with Dr. Nasr about Commander Benan hadn't exactly been comforting, either.

He had no doubt that someone, or more likely a number of important someones, had convinced themselves that the use of mental blocks in a few cases was a justified and humane way to handle knowledge too explosive to risk its ending up in the wrong hands.

But at least one someone who knew about Benan's involvement in Brass Prince hadn't been blocked, and had been able to use their knowledge to blackmail Rione. Furthermore, everything pointed to that someone being a very high-ranking individual in the fleet or the government.

It was long past time to shine some light on an ugly shadow. He could ask Lieutenant Iger about proper security procedures, and would undoubtedly be told that proper procedures required Geary to say nothing to anyone though he did wonder if even the intelligence officer knew about this particular thing. No. He wouldn't do that. "Don't ask the question if you don't want to know the answer," a chief had advised him when he was just an ensign. It felt like that conversation had taken place a hundred years ago.

Actually, he realized, it had taken place a hundred years ago. But it would take a lot longer than that for him to forget that particular wise advice.

When I get back to Alliance space, there will be changes made, and people like Commander Benan will be helped. I'll tell anyone I need to in order for that to happen. Security is not a license for people in authority to hide tactics they would never openly admit to using.

The next morning, he was stopping by *Dauntless*'s bridge, trying to look rested and confident while he checked on the latest status of everything. He could have done those same checks from inside his stateroom, but leaders had to get out among their people, had to show that they were engaged and involved.

"I hope to hear today that we've got clearance to head home through spider-wolf-controlled territory," he told Tanya.

"Good," she replied. "Before you make any agreements with

them, though, Lieutenant Yuon has something to tell you." Desjani gestured to her combat systems watch-stander.

Lieutenant Yuon blinked, stood a bit straighter, then nodded toward his display. "Admiral, Captain Desjani asked us to take a real good look at the jump points in this star system. There wasn't anything we hadn't seen already at the one we arrived at, but we eventually found something at each of the other ones."

Geary saw new symbols appear on his display, glowing red with familiar danger markers. "Mines?"

"A mine, Admiral. Just one. At each jump exit. Hidden by some really impressive stealth technology. A really *big* mine."

That made no sense at all. One really big mine? Geary bent a puzzled look on Desjani.

She waved toward Yuon again. "Make your report, Lieutenant."

"Yes, Captain. I had the sensors report everything on the mines, but nothing unusual registered. So then I had them scan the areas right around the mines for anything unusual. And eventually the fleet's sensors spotted some space-time distortion."

"Space-time distortion? Around a mine? How could—? Wait a minute. Space-time distortion. Isn't that what happens close to a hypernet gate?"

Desjani mimed applause. "You got it. Or rather, Lieutenant Yuon got it."

"They're weaponized versions of the gates, Admiral," Yuon explained eagerly. "No transportation capability, just a means to set off incredibly powerful bursts of energy."

"What do the weapons engineers say about this?"

"We asked Captain Smythe," Desjani said. "His people first

denied that you could put that sort of thing in something the size of those mines, big as they are, then conceded that really good engineers might be able to do it."

"Really good engineers," Geary repeated. "Like the spider-wolves."

"And that," Desjani concluded, "is why the bear-cows haven't just waltzed through this star system and jumped onward. If anybody tries to use one of those jump points without spider-wolf permission, it's boom boom out go the lights. I thought you should know that."

"Thanks. And thank you, Lieutenant Yuon. That was an impressive piece of research and analysis."

Yuon beamed, and Lieutenant Castries raised a congratulatory fist toward him.

"Just remember when dealing with these guys," Desjani said, "that they have tricks up their sleeves. And they have more sleeves than we do. How do we know what they're thinking?"

"The civilian experts believe that the spider-wolves think in patterns, and that they see us as having a role in keeping that pattern stable. As if we help anchor the pattern."

Desjani raised her eyebrows skeptically. "A stable pattern? You mean, like, everything?"

"Yeah. Everything. Life. The universe."

"How can they think that's stable? There's nothing stable about life, the universe, or anything else. Everything is always changing. They can't believe that some pattern exists and never alters as long as it is anchored well enough."

"No," Geary said. "They said something about the pattern

changing but remaining. It can change. But to them, reality is that pattern."

"Hmmph." Her skepticism was clear enough. "I'm not saying they're bear-cows, or enigmas, but they're still aliens."

"You don't have to remind me of that."

Her reply was interrupted by an incoming call from Rione, with Charban visible in the background. "The spider-wolves are willing to let us transit their territory," Rione told Geary slightly breathlessly.

"Thank the living stars. How soon—"

"There's more." The corners of her mouth bent upward in a triumphant smile. "They have a hypernet. They will use some of their ships to escort us through it to some location much, much closer to human territory."

Geary stared, unable to believe their luck. "That's absolutely wonderful. When—"

"There's more," Rione broke in again. "They have two conditions. The first condition is that one of their ships, carrying a diplomatic delegation, accompany us home."

"Agreed," Geary said immediately.

"Such an agreement would allow the spider-wolves to know exactly where human space is located, Admiral."

"I suspect they already had an idea of that if their border with the enigmas runs that close to Pele. Maybe they've never actually come into contact with us, but they must have picked up some indications of another race confronting the enigmas in that region. What's the other condition?"

"They want something from us," Charban said.

"What?"

"That's the problem. We can't figure out what it is they want."

"But—Some piece of information? Do they want the superbattleship we captured from the bear-cows?"

"No," Charban insisted. "It is definitely not the superbattleship. It is not information. It is a thing. Something related to engineering."

"Engineering? A race of master engineers wants something related to engineering from us?" Geary questioned.

"Yes. They seem to want it badly. The offer to let us use their hypernet came while we were trying to figure out what they wanted. Apparently, they thought we were bargaining as opposed to being confused."

"Whatever works. But we still don't know what it is?"

"No!" Charban's frustration grew more visible. "As best I can translate the pictograms and words they are using, it is something like 'universal fixing substance.'"

"Universal fixing substance?" Geary asked. "We have a universal fixing substance?"

Charban spread his hands in exasperation. "*They* think we do. And they want it from us."

"But why do they think that? What did we do to make them think we had some universal fixing substance?"

"I can't determine the answer to that given our very limited communications. From their persistence, and their certainty, I would guess that they thought we had demonstrated the use of such a thing."

Geary looked around the bridge. "What do we have that fits that name?"

Everyone looked as if they were thinking intently. No one offered any suggestions.

"Glue?" Lieutenant Yuon finally suggested.

That made as much sense as anything. "Glue?" Geary echoed to Charban.

"No, Admiral. I thought of that and offered a tube of adhesive. They said no, then asked for the universal fixing substance again."

"Admiral, ask the engineers," Desjani said. "Captain Smythe and his people. If anyone would know anything about that, it would be the engineers on the auxiliaries."

"If any of the engineers know about some universal fixing substance," Geary said, "and never mentioned it to me, there's going to be hell to pay."

But Smythe, already worn from the days of work getting repairs done, only stared back at Geary with a blank expression. "Universal fixing substance?"

"Right. What have we got that fits that description?"

"Nothing. That's like... universal solvent. Nice to have, but no one has ever actually come up with one. Well, actually, a universal solvent would be very bad to have because you couldn't make a container to hold it—"

"Captain Smythe," Geary broke in, "the spider-wolves are certain we have it."

"*I* don't have it."

"Please notify all of your engineers that we need it and ask them what they think could be it."

"Very well, Admiral. But I'll be frank that I wouldn't hold my breath expecting anyone in this fleet to produce something that can fix anything."

Geary waited until Smythe had ended the call, then sent out a message to every ship asking them if any could identify whatever it was the aliens wanted.

Then he waited, with growing impatience. With every second, the enigma retaliatory force was getting closer to Midway, but all he could do was sit here. He made another call. "Captain Smythe, have you figured out how to move that superbattleship yet?"

"Uh, yes, Admiral," Smythe replied, only momentarily fazed by the new topic. "We'll use the battleships."

"Battleships? Plural?"

"Yes." Smythe perked up at the chance to discuss something any engineer would see as sexy. "Four of them. *Relentless*, *Reprisal*, *Superb*, and *Splendid*. They were shot up fairly badly, but their propulsion systems remain in fine shape. We'll mate them to the superbattleship, link their propulsion controls through a coordination unit, and use them to haul the superbattleship home."

"Those are going to be four very unhappy battleships," Desjani murmured.

"What else have we got that can haul around that much mass?" Geary asked her. "Besides, they'll also serve as defenders of that thing. Since we blew away every weapon on the superbattleship, our own battleships' weapons will have to do the job of making sure no one destroys it. Have we heard any answers on the universal fixing substance yet?"

"Not since the last time you asked," she replied.

"The question went to every ship?"

"Via the command circuit, yes, Admiral. You sent it."

Something about that made Geary pause, trying to catch an elusive thought. "Command circuit."

"That's what you used," Desjani said, eyeing him defensively.

"Which goes to the commanding officers of all the ships in the fleet."

"Yes... It always has."

What was it? What idea was flitting just out of reach? "Who would they ask? On their ships?"

"Members of their crew." Desjani shrugged. "Their officers, I suppose."

"Their officers. You asked the officers on *Dauntless*?"

"Yes, Admiral." She seemed curious as well as defensive now. "Are we going somewhere with this?"

"I don't—" Going somewhere? The old joke. If junior officers are confused about where to go next, they should ask the senior enlisted, who will be happy to tell the junior officers where to go. "I'm an idiot."

Desjani raised an eyebrow at him. "Are you speaking purely on a professional basis? Because on a personal basis, I resent that."

"Tanya, when you need to know something, how to do something, who do you go to? Who gets things done?"

She looked puzzled, then smiled. "The chiefs."

"The chiefs. The senior enlisted. Why the hell haven't we asked them what they think this universal fixing substance is?"

"Because we're both idiots. That's the first place I should have asked." Desjani tapped her internal comm controls. "This is the captain speaking. All chief petty officers are to muster in the chief's mess immediately. Notify me when all are present."

It took perhaps five minutes, then Desjani passed the question to her assembled senior enlisted corps. "Now we wait, Admiral."

She had scarcely finished speaking when the image of Master Chief Gioninni appeared on the bridge. "Captain? You really want to know what universal fixing substance could refer to?"

"I take it you have an idea?" Desjani replied.

"Yes, Captain. As soon as you said it I looked at Senior Chief Tarrini and she looked at me and we both said 'duct tape.'"

11

"Duct tape?" Desjani stared at Gioninni.

"Duct tape," Gioninni repeated.

"Duct tape," she told Geary.

"I heard." Geary considered the idea, outrageous though it seemed. How could a race of expert engineers be impressed by something as simple and as ancient as duct tape? "What do the other chiefs think?"

"They agreed," Gioninni said.

Geary called Captain Smythe, who had a frazzled expression as he answered for the third time. "Yes, Admiral? I'm afraid my staff has yet to produce any answer."

"I've been given one, Captain Smythe. Do you think the answer could be duct tape?"

Smythe's expression shifted comically as his jaw dropped and his eyes widened. "Oh, damn. Where—A chief figured it out. Right?"

"Right. Where could the aliens have been so impressed with duct tape? When could they have seen us use it?"

"Did your emissaries talking to them—No, wait. Have they been aboard any of our ships?"

"No," Geary said.

"They were aboard that escape pod," Gioninni suggested.

"Escape pod?" An instant later he remembered. "The damaged escape pod from *Balestra*. Two of them boarded it."

"They did?" Smythe asked. "Is there a working record of that? That pod's systems were pretty messed up as I recall."

"There's the record of a comm call I made to them," Geary said, gesturing to Desjani, who turned back to point to her communications watch, who in turn frantically ran searches.

"Got it!" the watch-stander announced. "Coming up now."

Another image popped into existence between the images of Gioninni and Smythe. Geary once again saw the interior of the damaged escape pod, Chief Madigan near the comm panel, the two spider-wolves sealed in their space armor at the air lock. "We can't tell what they're looking at," Geary said.

"No," Smythe agreed, "but we can see, and they could see, the sailors in that pod using duct tape. Patching the hull, repairing that panel, first aid on that injured sailor. Does it really work on sucking chest wounds?"

"Yes, sir," Master Chief Gioninni said.

Desjani nodded. "Fixing electronics, fixing hull material, fixing human bodies. That's pretty universal, I guess."

"That's why every escape pod has a couple of rolls of duct tape on it," Master Chief Gioninni pointed out. "We've got to inventory the stuff on a monthly basis because otherwise people sneak into the pods and carry off the duct tape to sell it or use it on their ships."

"Sell it?" Desjani asked, her expression as she looked at Gioninni turning dangerous.

"Not on this ship, Captain," Gioninni said. "Some folks get that idea sometimes, but they always get shown the error of their ways by older and wiser heads. Selling the duct tape out of escape pods would be like selling... oh, the parachutes out of aerospace craft. If you need that stuff, you're really going to need it, so we make sure no one messes with it."

"Don't we have duct tape as part of our standard supplies?" Desjani demanded, mollified but still a little suspicious.

"Sure, Captain, but you can never have too much duct tape."

Geary heard laughter, then realized it was coming from him. "Humanity's gift to the universe. Duct tape."

"We wouldn't have made it to the stars without duct tape, Admiral," Gioninni said.

"We also wouldn't have made it without chiefs."

Gioninni grinned. "Yes, sir. Uh, if I may be so bold, Admiral, why did we need to know what these particular aliens call our duct tape?"

"They want it," Desjani said.

The master chief stopped moving for just a moment, then nodded. "How badly do they want it, Captain? We might be able to work out a real nice deal."

Geary tried not to smile back at the master chief. "Do you happen to know anyone who's good at working out deals. Master Chief Gioninni?"

"I might have a little expertise in that particular area, Admiral," Gioninni said with every appearance of modesty. "Not that I do much wheeling and dealing myself, you understand. But sometimes you have to work out swaps or trades, and if the other party really wants or needs whatever you have to trade, it can provide some very nice benefits."

"You do indeed, Master Chief," Desjani agreed. "However, this particular deal is already done. We give them our duct tape, and they let us use their hypernet to get home. I don't think anyone wants to risk messing up that deal, and we can't afford to cheat or swindle the only bunch of aliens who don't appear to be set on wiping us out."

"I would never cheat or swindle anyone, Captain!" Gioninni declared piously, somehow also projecting shock at the very idea. "I'm the soul of fairness and honesty."

"So I've heard. From you. Thank you, Master Chief. We'll let the emissaries know that you are available to assist in the deal-making." After Gioninni's image vanished, Desjani looked at Geary. "Where do you suppose those spider-wolves would put Master Chief Gioninni in their pattern?"

"Let's not find out. General Charban? Emissary Rione? We've identified the mystery substance. Captain Smythe, get going on hitching those four battleships to the superbattleship. How long will it take?"

Smythe scratched his cheek as he thought. "Two days, Admiral."

"Make it one."

"The impossible takes a little longer, Admiral. I can push for a day and a half. I won't promise anything less than that."

"All right." Geary had never forgotten the old lament he had heard from the first enlisted sailors he had commanded. *Why is there never enough time to do it right but always enough time to do it over?* The simple logic of that had stuck with him, especially when experience proved the truth of it.

After that call ended, Geary sat looking steadily at his display for a second. "All units, be advised we intend getting under way for the next jump point in one and a half days. Ensure that you are fully ready to move at that time."

Smythe must have gotten right to work on the towing arrangement for the captured warship because the commanding officer of *Reprisal* called within minutes. "Admiral, with all due respect, I have to protest the use of my ship as a tug!"

"I understand your concerns, Captain," Geary said with all of the diplomacy he possessed. According to Rione, that wasn't much, but hopefully it would be enough. "I made this decision based upon the performance of *Reprisal* in the recent engagement. It is critically important that we get this alien ship safely home, and I know *Reprisal* can be trusted to make certain that happens no matter what threats we encounter. You will be the last and strongest line of defense for that superbattleship."

Reprisal's commanding officer hesitated. "It's... a position of honor?"

"Very much so." He truly wasn't lying. If push came to shove, it would be very comforting to know that ships as steady as those four battleships were his last bastions defending the bear-cow superbattleship.

Within the next several minutes, he repeated the same reassurances to the commanding officers of *Relentless*, *Superb*, and *Splendid*, then called *Dreadnaught*, *Orion*, *Dependable*, and *Conqueror* to let them know they would have the honor of operating as close-in escorts for their sister ships and the captured warship.

"Jane," he said to his grandniece. "You'll be commander of the close-in escorts for the superbattleship. You have to protect it."

Captain Jane Geary nodded in reply. "I understand, Admiral."

"You did a good job here. No one will ever doubt your courage, your initiative, or your ability."

"Thank you, Admiral."

And there it rested (again), Jane Geary hiding behind professional courtesy to avoid discussing anything personal.

It took almost half a day more before the emissaries reported back in. "We have a deal," Rione said. "I will caution you again about your decision to allow spider-wolf ships to accompany us back."

"Ships? I thought it was one ship."

"That was due to a misinterpretation on the part of General Charban and myself," Rione explained. She didn't seem too upset by the misinterpretation, but perhaps she was simply too worn-out by the negotiations to care at this point. "They actually want to send six ships."

"Six ships." Geary rubbed his chin as he thought about that. An alien flotilla brought into human space? But, on the other hand, he didn't know what kinds of risks they might face on the way back. If a single spider-wolf ship came with them, and something happened to it, how could they ever explain that to the spider-wolves back here?

"Those six ships will escort us through spider-wolf space," Charban added. "They will accompany us through the spider-wolf hypernet. Then they will stay with us as we head for home."

"Do they already know where we're going?"

"They know we want to get to the star Midway, Admiral. We had to tell them that in order to discuss their permission to go through their space."

Could he say no? Absolutely not. And the more he thought about it, the more he liked the idea of having multiple spider-wolf ships along to look after each other. "Very well. I agree. Do they have the duct tape yet?"

"No," Rione said. "We will hand that over, in person." She must have noticed Geary's reaction. "The spider-wolves insist on actually meeting with us to exchange our 'gift' to them in exchange for their promises. That involves some sort of embrace, I think."

"Embrace? For the love of your ancestors, Victoria—"

"I'm not looking forward to it, but any woman has had unpleasant dating experiences," Rione said. "I'll just pretend this is another blind date set up by misguided friends when I was still single. A loose hug at the end, perhaps a ghost of a peck on the cheek, a vague assurance to call at some future, undefined time, and I'm home free."

"We will both be there," General Charban said. "We'll need a shuttle to meet one of their shuttle equivalents. The two of us as passengers, and two of them. We'll meet in the air locks."

"Can their air locks mate with ours?" Geary asked.

"They don't seem to consider that a problem, Admiral."

"How much duct tape do you need?"

"Emissary Rione thought we should offer them a full case."

A full case of duct tape in a fleet that had been away from home for too long and lately frantically patching damage. Geary turned to Desjani, who was apparently fighting down a case of the giggles. "What's so funny?"

"Nothing, Admiral." But her eyes slid toward Rione's image for a moment before Desjani focused back on him.

Of course. Rione, her old rival, would have to embrace a spider-wolf. "You're evil sometimes," he whispered to her. "Do you have a spare case of duct tape aboard?" he asked in a normal voice.

"A full case, untouched? Probably not," Desjani replied as if unconcerned. "When do you need it?"

"Now."

"All right." Desjani looked to her communications watch-stander. "Have Master Chief Gioninni call up here again. The Alliance fleet is in need of his special talents."

Half an hour later, a shuttle left *Dauntless*, carrying the pilot and a Marine guard sealed into the flight deck and Rione and Charban in the passenger area, Charban holding a full, unopened case labeled alliance fleet issue, tape, duct, multipurpose, twenty count (not for use on ducts). *Dauntless*'s supply officer had just finished telling Captain Desjani that an exhaustive search had confirmed that there were no unopened cases of duct tape aboard. Desjani had not informed her supply officer that fifteen minutes earlier, Master Chief Gioninni, with such a case under one arm, had appeared on the hangar deck where General Charban awaited him.

As the shuttle lifted from *Dauntless*'s hangar deck and headed out toward the spider-wolf formation, a small shape detached itself from one of the spider-wolf ships and came zipping toward a rendezvous. "Even their shuttles are hot rods," Desjani remarked.

"You're in an awfully good mood," Geary replied.

"It's a nice day, Admiral."

"You mean it's a day when Victoria Rione has to embrace a spider-wolf."

"Is that what's going to happen?" Desjani asked in a surprised tone that didn't sound remotely authentic. "What do you suppose those spider-wolves are going to do when they read that duct tape can't fix ducts? They think it can fix anything, but the only thing it can't fix is what it's named for."

"They can't read our language."

"That's true. At least now we know that the next time the pattern of the universe frays a little, the spider-wolves will be able to patch it up with duct tape."

"You do realize," Geary said, "that Victoria Rione is going to be in all of the histories? She will be the first human known to have made physical contact with a friendly alien species."

Desjani shrugged. "The Marines made physical contact with an awful lot of bear-cows."

"Not friendly, and I don't think anyone can sort out who first made contact in that fight anyway."

"There are the enigmas—"

"Given the mysteries surrounding when they first encountered humans and where, the identity of the first human the enigmas met will probably remain eternally unknown except perhaps to the enigmas themselves. And, definitely, not friendly."

The human shuttle and the spider-wolf craft came together, the human pilot making a special effort to pilot her shuttle just as smoothly and surely as the spider-wolf craft moved. Geary had a good view of the shuttle passenger area in the video feed being sent to him, and he watched both Charban and Rione for signs of nerves. Remarkably, they appeared perfectly calm.

The two vessels came alongside each other, and the shuttle pilot glanced out from her own video feed. "At dead stop relative to alien craft. Awaiting further instructions."

"This is Admiral Geary. Let's wait and see what they do."

"Yes, sir."

He had external views from the shuttle as well, and now the one focused on the smooth egg shape that was the spider-wolf spacecraft showed an oval tube extending toward the human shuttle.

"It feels right," Desjani commented. "That oval shape. The proportions, I mean. It's like these spider-wolves share the same fondness we have for that Golden Mean thing."

The tube came to rest against the side of the shuttle, and warning lights flashed before the pilot's seat. "We've got hull contact. I'm not sure what's happening." Her voice stayed steady.

"Are they all on drugs?" Geary asked. "Why aren't any of them nervous?"

"I picked the pilot, Admiral," Desjani replied. "She's as sound as they come. You'll have to ask the emissaries if they took anything."

"Pressure outside the air lock," the pilot announced. "About point nine five standard. Composition of gases is within acceptable standards for humans to breathe. I can't confirm this, but that flexible tube that joined us to the alien ship seems to have become rigid now."

How had the spider-wolf tube formed an airtight seal against the shuttle hull? And how had it then become a rigid tube rather than the flexing object that had reached out toward the shuttle?

Rione and Charban had both heard the pilot's report, and now Charban moved to the air lock. He turned to salute the video feed, smiling crookedly. "Here we go."

Rione came up beside him as the inner air lock hatch cycled open, then the outer hatch. Geary saw her inhale deeply as the alien atmosphere mixed with that inside the shuttle. "Spicy," she announced to no one in particular. "Not too sharp or pungent. Almost pleasant."

"Maybe they smell good," Geary speculated.

"It sounds like they smell better than we do, anyway," Desjani replied. "Present company excepted, of course."

He wondered what he was supposed to feel as they waited for the spider-wolves to appear. Finally, humanity was making contact with another intelligence. The enigmas refused to really converse with humans, only making threats and demands, and the bear-cows had refused to communicate at all. But the spider-wolves were intelligent and willing to talk. For the first time, humans would learn how a different intelligence viewed the universe the two species shared. In time, the crude methods used to exchange information would be refined, the two peoples would learn each other's language, and—

The spider-wolves would still be incredibly hard to look at, Geary concluded as two of them came into view inside the oval tube, which was wide enough for them to stand side by side.

He had seen spider-wolves in armor inside *Balestra*'s escape pod, but armor could exaggerate many things. For the first time, seeing these spider-wolves wearing nothing but their brilliant silklike garments, he could be sure of the size. Not short like the bear-cows, but not as tall as humans, either. Perhaps a meter and a half in height, the spider-wolves were wider than humans because of the way their arms protruded outward and the middle of their abdomens swelled to the sides.

Charban offered the case of duct tape to them. "For our friends," he said. "One of humanity's greatest secrets and discoveries, but we freely share it with your species in the spirit of friendship and understanding."

Somehow, the case of duct tape didn't seem quite worthy of the language surrounding its transfer to the spider-wolves. One of the aliens extended four arms, the claws closing on the case and holding it with what struck Geary as great care, as if an immensely valuable item was being grasped.

The other spider-wolf faced Rione, who stood with a certain tenseness that he found oddly familiar. Not in her... but... Perhaps it was Rione's earlier use of the analogy of a date that triggered his memory of his own youthful dates, the unsuccessful ones where, during the good-bye, his date had stood so. It hadn't taken too many such experiences before he realized that slightly tense posture foretold an offered cheek instead of lips for a good-night kiss and a loose-armed "hug" with no body contact.

Did the spider-wolf feel the same way? Its four claw-tipped arms rose, swinging around slowly, to barely touch Rione, then its hideous head dipped forward just enough to barely graze her forehead as she lowered her head to mimic his gesture.

The spider-wolf dropped its "embrace" quickly and Geary saw colors shift on its face and upper abdomen. A rose shade, then something bluish, and finally a purple that spread and stayed. He and others had joked that humans might be as repulsive to the spider-wolves as the spider-wolves were to humans. If he read the reactions of this spider-wolf properly, that guess might well be right.

Desjani laughed, the sound short and soft. "She's got guts. I hate that woman, but she's brave. How long are they going to have to stay in quarantine?"

"That'll be up to medical after they get back and get examined."

"Damn." Desjani's voice had changed, low and intense now. "It's really hitting me. This is a moment the human race has looked forward to, dreamed about, feared, for who knows how many thousands of years. And now it's happening, and we're here to watch it."

"Pretty awesome, isn't it?" Geary said.

"Am I still being evil if I hope that I can see the spider-wolf delegation we take back with us embracing the politicians on the Alliance grand council?"

"No." He had a vision of Senator Suva in the embrace of a spider-wolf and smiled. "I wouldn't mind seeing that myself."

The first spider-wolf was speaking in the high-pitched, rapid buzz of the alien language. Its arms waved in what looked like carefully made gestures, ending folded across the front of its body, the claws clicking several times before the creature bowed toward Charban and Rione. It gestured again, this time pointing in the direction of one of the jump points, then pointed back to the humans with all four arms.

Charban hesitated, then slowly brought his arm up in a salute, lowered it, and backed away.

Rione spread her hands, smiling, and nodded to the spider-wolves before she stepped back as well.

The spider-wolves both backed down the oval tube, vanishing from Geary's view.

"Now what?" Rione asked Charban.

"We close the hatch, I suppose." General Charban cycled the outer and the inner air lock hatches closed, then stood with uncertainty obvious in his stance.

The pilot had been staring at her own video feed of the passenger area, but she now reacted to an alert on the panel before her. "Atmosphere outside the air lock is dropping very rapidly. Down, down, gone. Whatever was in contact with the shuttle hull is also gone."

"Bring it home," Geary ordered. "Follow quarantine procedures for all personnel and the shuttle."

"I understand, Admiral. Returning to *Dauntless* now."

The two small craft separated, each heading back to its own kind.

The moment was over, yet as Geary watched the returning shuttle, he thought that the pattern the spider-wolves spoke of had been altered in ways that no amount of duct tape could ever return to its former state.

The shuttle was just arriving at *Dauntless* when the spider-wolf craft zipped into a larger ship, which promptly turned and headed for another jump point than the one the humans had been told to proceed toward. Nearly simultaneously, one of the curving arms of the spider-wolf formation unraveled as six spider-wolf ships broke free and cut forward to a point between the Alliance fleet and the designated jump point.

"Our escorts, I presume," Geary commented, as the six spider-wolf ships slid to a halt relative to the human warships. He called down to the civilian experts, knowing they would have been watching everything, and found a cross-looking Dr. Shwartz answering. "Is anything wrong?"

Shwartz took a deep breath before answering. "I am sorry for being unprofessional, Admiral, but do you have any idea how hard it was to watch that meeting and not be able to participate?"

"I regret that, Doctor, but the spider-wolves said only two human representatives, and both Emissary Rione and General Charban were specifically designated by the Alliance government as our leads for contact with alien species. I couldn't choose anyone over them without a very good reason."

"Yes, I know," Shwartz said. "That's why I admitted to being unprofessional. But, still… all my life I dreamed of that moment, Admiral, and I freely admit that in my dreams, I was the one greeting the aliens firsthand."

"A lot of people dreamed that dream, Doctor. You got to see it happen." Shwartz grinned. "Our two emissaries are going to be busy for a while being run through every health test our medical doctors can dream up. Our escort through spider-wolf space has already moved into position, but we won't be ready to go for another twelve hours. Can you and Dr. Setin contact the spider-wolves and let them know that?"

"Twelve hours?" Dr. Shwartz questioned. "Twelve is easy. Hours, well, that will take some work. I will get my comrades on it, though I should warn you that they are sulking worse than I am at the moment."

"Good luck, Dr. Shwartz."

She smiled again. "Thank you, Admiral."

He signed off, then noticed Desjani glowering in her seat. "What?"

"We're having a problem with Commander Benan down at the quarantine site," Desjani grumbled.

"What's the problem?"

"He's insisting on seeing her. The docs say no. I'm about to have him arrested."

Geary tensed, then relaxed himself. "He wants to see her? In person, or just communication?"

She replied with an annoyed look. "Let me check... All right. He says he wants to see her image, talk to her. The docs want to work in peace."

"Give Commander Benan comm access to his wife," Geary ordered.

Desjani's expression this time was startled. "Excuse *me*, sir."

"What?"

"You used your 'command voice.' You don't have to use your command voice with me. You know that." She hit a control. "Commander Benan has authorization for comms with his wife. Video and audio. I don't care. Just make it happen. Tell the medical staff that the admiral ordered it, and if they don't like it, they can debate the matter with him."

"I'm sorry, Tanya," Geary said. "Commander Benan's actions, his lack of self-control, are the result of something that was done to him."

"I know," she shot back. "The Syndics——"

"And the Alliance. I told you that."

"Fine. You didn't tell me *what* was done." Her gaze challenged him.

"It's very highly classified, Tanya. If I tell you, it could cause difficulties for you."

"Difficulties?" She laughed. "Oh, mercy, no! Difficulties? Whatever would I do without my guardian and protector to keep difficulties from me?"

"All right," Geary admitted. "That did sound a little condescending—"

"Duh."

"—but it's not as if you don't already have enough to worry about."

Desjani snorted derisively. "Speaking of things I need to worry about, we both agree that Commander Benan is an accident waiting to happen. Since he is on *my* ship, and if he flies off the handle it will imperil *my* ship, perhaps it would be a good idea to let me know exactly what's going on aboard *my* ship so that I can help control the situation."

"You've got a point, even if you are driving it home with a jackhammer. Once we reenter jump space, I'll tell you."

Her eyebrows went up. "You can't tell me in real space?"

"I just think I'll be too busy," Geary said. "Speaking of which..." He put in a call to Captain Smythe.

"It's still twelve more hours," Smythe announced before Geary could say anything. "Not a minute less."

"Our escorts are waiting," Geary pointed out.

"Unless our escorts intend helping to haul along that monstrosity you call a superbattleship, I suggest they continue waiting until I've gotten rigging the tow job done properly."

"That wasn't actually why I called. There's an update on *Orion*."

"Oh." Captain Smythe nodded. "She's been hit too hard, too often. The repair patches are what's holding *Orion* together more than anything now."

"Is she or is she not capable of facing combat? This update hedges and avoids giving a straight answer."

The senior engineer frowned, checking his own readout. "It looks straightforward to me. Points in the structure where stress has accumulated, areas of the hull where armor is judged weak, cumulative effects of multiple repairs on systems... What is the problem, Admiral?"

"It doesn't tell me whether or not *Orion* is still combat capable," Geary repeated.

"That's not our call to make, Admiral. We tell you what state the ship is in. You decide how and when to risk it. *Orion* has not exceeded any of the measures by which a ship is definitely declared unsafe or unable to carry out its basic functions. But it has a great many measures by which the ship is marginal. Another volley from the Kicks at *Orion* in that last engagement, and we would very likely have been salvaging pieces of her after the battle. I didn't pick her as one of the battleships for towing the captured bear-cow ship because I was worried about *Orion*'s ability to survive the extra stress on her structure."

Smythe was right, unfortunately. This was a case where Geary couldn't defer to the judgment of the engineers. He would have to make the call himself. "Very well, Captain Smythe." He paused, unable to resist his next words. "It's still twelve hours?"

"It's only eleven hours and fifty-seven minutes now, Admiral."

Geary called Commander Shen, seeing him in one of the passageways of *Orion*, where Shen had answered on the nearest comm panel. "How is your ship, Captain?" Geary asked bluntly.

"She's been in better condition." Shen looked around. "I could not ask for a better crew, nor a harder working crew, but there's been a lot to do."

"Do you consider *Orion* to be combat capable?"

Shen paused, eyes hooded as he considered his reply, his usual dissatisfied expression no clue to his thoughts. "*Orion* is not front-line capable," he finally said. "She can fight. We have our shields back on maximum, and about one-third of our weapons operational."

"I saw that," Geary said. "A remarkable achievement given the damage that *Orion* has sustained in the last two fights."

"Thank you, sir. However, we have numerous patches on our hull armor, and two-thirds of our weapons are *not* operational." Shen looked around again, viewing those of his crew who were in sight. "We are understrength as a result of battle casualties even though we have received a number of replacements who are former members of the crew of *Invincible*. They have rendered good service even though most seem to consider reassignment to a battleship from a battle cruiser to be the equivalent of being banished to the third ring of hell."

"Your primary assignment will be defense of the captured super-battleship. Do you feel that *Orion* can provide that service?"

"I have no doubt of it, Admiral."

"Then I will continue to list *Orion* as combat capable. Please let your crew know that they have the most important assignment in the fleet. We must get that superbattleship home in one piece. I am entrusting it to *Orion* because I know *Orion* can do the job."

Was that a ghost of a smile breaking through the rigid strata of Shen's usual sourness? "I will ensure that my crew is aware of what you have said, Admiral."

As he ended that call, Geary noticed Desjani gazing somberly straight ahead. "What's the matter?"

She looked over at him. "Shen and I are old friends. Shipmates. I don't want to see him die, too. I've lost too many shipmates over the years."

"Why do you think—?"

"I know him, Admiral, and you're beginning to know him. You know he meant what he said. Shen will defend that captured superbattleship to the last even though *Orion* is coming apart at the seams. And I know why you wanted him and *Orion* to be on that job despite the material condition of *Orion*."

He watched her, a tight feeling inside him. "Why?"

She leaned close, inside his privacy field so no one else on the bridge could hear what she said, her eyes on his. "Because," Desjani said in a low voice, "you're worried that Captain Jane Geary will take *Dreadnaught* off on another glorious charge, leaving the superbattleship undefended, and you know that this time Shen won't follow her, and if he doesn't follow *Dreadnaught* with *Orion*, then *Dependable* and *Conqueror* will also stay with that superbattleship. Commander Shen and *Orion* are your insurance against Jane Geary's seeking glory again."

He wanted to tell her that she was wrong, that he would not risk Shen and *Orion* that way, but in his heart he knew that he could not deny Desjani's words.

12

"All units, come port zero two zero degrees, down four degrees, and accelerate to point one light speed at time four zero." The First Fleet of the Alliance, battered but once again ready to face whatever awaited it, headed for the jump point designated by the spider-wolves. Ahead of the human fleet, the six spider-wolf ships that would accompany it easily maintained a distance exactly one light-minute ahead.

They would be transiting through spider-wolf space, not fighting their way through, so Geary had arranged the fleet in a simple, vast elliptical formation, relatively compact, nonthreatening, and one of the more graceful formations he could have chosen from. The assemblage of human ships still looked crude judged against the spider-wolf formation, as if a barely organized band of barbarians had stumbled into the midst of a formal dance, but it didn't look as bad in comparison as some of the other choices would have. In the center of the ellipse of human warships, protected alongside the assault transports and the auxiliaries, four battleships mated to the captured superbattleship strained to pull it along with the fleet.

As they moved across the outer span of the star system, the main spider-wolf formation, still watching the jump point leading to the bear-cow star Pandora, slid past to their right. The beautiful whorls and patterns of the spider-wolf formation changed as the view from the human ships altered, the curves seeming to swirl and melt in upon themselves.

"Four and a half light-hours to the jump point. Forty-five hours' travel time if you want to keep to point one light speed," Desjani announced.

"It wouldn't be worth the cost in fuel cells to speed up, then slow down again for the jump," Geary said. "Not for the small amount of time we'd gain. And getting the captured superbattleship up to speed or slowing it down again is not fast or easy to do."

"Is the hypernet gate at the next star?"

"Our emissaries and our experts aren't sure," Geary replied. He watched his display, trying to relax the tension inside him as he waited for problems to pop up. But no propulsion units failed, no maneuvering difficulties appeared, and no pieces came off any of the ships. *It doesn't take all that much to make me happy these days. A century ago, when I was in a peacetime fleet with ships made to last at least several decades, I never could have imagined being thrilled to see none of my ships break when we started a simple movement.* "If the hypernet gate isn't at the next star, we'll be able to use the additional time in transit and jump space for more repair work."

"You've gotten very good at rationalizing things," Desjani said.

"I don't have any choice. We need to get to Midway before the enigmas do, but we can only get there so fast." He had seriously considered leaving the bear-cow superbattleship with a strong escort to follow on behind while he took the rest of the fleet ahead on a dash to Midway. But General Charban had expressed serious doubts that he could get across to the spider-wolves that the human fleet wanted to split and pass through their space in two separate movements. And there was no telling what might await them at any star system they would have to jump through to reach human space after using the spider-wolf hypernet. What if one of those star systems was occupied by the enigmas? What would the enigmas do when they saw a bear-cow warship being towed along by the human fleet? Probably something drastic.

But nothing had gone wrong yet, and as Geary sat there watching everything happen without a hitch, he realized how incredibly worn-out he was after the last several days of unrelenting work. The effects of the rest day he had ordered hadn't lasted all that long, probably because he hadn't really had much chance to rest. "I'm going to get some sleep."

He walked down to his stateroom, feeling the mixture of tension, relief, and happiness among the crew members he passed. Happiness to be on the way home again. Relief to be under way. Tension over what they might find along the way home.

Senior Chief Tarrini smiled as she saluted Geary. "Are there any more questions you need answered, Admiral?"

Geary almost said no, then paused. "Yes, Senior Chief. I've heard the sailors using a word I haven't heard before."

"Well, now, Admiral, you know sailors—"

"It's not that kind of word, Senior Chief. At least I don't think so.

Do you know what 'Bub' means?"

"'Bub'?" Tarrini asked.

"Yes, and I can tell by the way you asked me that you do know what it means."

The senior chief nodded. "It's short for Big Ugly Bugs, Admiral. Or Butt-Ugly Bugs. It's what the sailors are starting to call the, uh…"

"The spider-wolves." Geary let his unhappiness show. "They're our allies, Senior Chief. They fought alongside us, they took losses fighting alongside us, and they're helping us get home quickly."

"Yes, sir, Admiral," Tarrini agreed. "But you know sailors. To them, those guys are Bubs. Though I think some Marines might have actually coined the term. You know how Marines are."

Geary looked around, exasperated. "I also know what would happen if I ordered the fleet not to use the term 'Bub.'"

"Every sailor would be using it as much as possible," Senior Chief Tarrini said. "And the Marines would be using it even more."

"Do you have something against Marines, Senior Chief?"

"Hell, no, Admiral. I was married to a Marine for a while, before he moved on to take another objective, as they say. I hardly ever think about that bas—I mean, that individual, sir."

"I'll take your word for it." Geary looked the senior chief in the eye. "Do me a favor. Spread the word that I have heard the term 'Bub,' and I don't like it. It makes me unhappy to know people are using it."

"Certainly, Admiral." Senior Chief Tarrini saluted him again. "Everyone will know you'd rather they not use that term. If anything can keep it under control, that will. But it won't go away. You know sailors."

"I do, yes, Senior Chief. Thank you."

For the rest of his walk, Geary found the strength to look unconcerned and ready for anything as he returned salutes, then slumped against his hatch once safely inside his stateroom. He dropped down on his bunk without undressing, finally feeling that he could justify some time asleep.

His comm panel buzzed relentlessly.

Geary finally roused enough to hit the hold control, knowing that if it were a real emergency, he would be getting a different alert from the device. He took enough time to get his uniform in halfway-decent shape before answering.

Captain Smythe's beaming face seemed oddly incongruous. "Good afternoon, Admiral. I have good news."

"That would be welcome." Geary sat down, rubbing his face with both hands.

"Our engineers have extensively analyzed the systems failures that occurred when preparing for the battle here. They have concluded that the spike in failures was caused by the extra stresses on already-weak systems during the power ramp-ups."

"I thought we already knew that."

"We did." Smythe's smile grew smug. "But, Admiral, here's what we didn't know. We blew out the weakest system components. That means we had a spike then, but it also means we will now have a period of relatively low failures. Those components most prone to failure have failed. Those components that didn't fail will probably last a little longer before going bad."

Geary ran that through his head once, then one more time to

make sure he had understood it. "You're telling me that the next time we go into battle we shouldn't have a sudden cascade of failures on numerous ships."

"As long as that battle isn't too far in the future. If it is within the next month or so, you'll be fine."

"That *is* good news."

"You don't have to sound so surprised, Admiral."

Realizing that he was smiling, Geary pushed his luck. "Does this mean we'll have a chance to get a little ahead on the repair and replacement work?"

Smythe shook his head. "No, sir. We're so far behind the curve on that one that we're in danger of being rear-ended by ourselves. We will continue to get done what we can, but there will be many more system failures before we can get so many internal systems rebuilt on so many ships."

"I understand."

"It would help," Smythe added, "if we didn't have to spend quite so much time repairing battle damage."

"I'll see what I can do to avoid further battle damage, Captain Smythe." Geary tried to think. There was something else... "Has Lieutenant Jamenson discovered anything else regarding that topic she was researching?"

"Researching? Oh, that. I'm afraid she's been as busy as the rest of us lately, Admiral. As a matter of fact, she's on *Orion* right now as part of the tiger team overseeing the tow linkages to the BKS."

"The BKS?" Geary asked, squinting as he tried to recall what such an acronym could stand for.

"The Big Kick Ship," Smythe explained.

I have to come up with an official name for that thing, Geary thought. "Very well, Captain Smythe. Thank you for the good news."

Once Smythe's image had gone, Geary cast a longing look at his bunk. But the last conversation had brought up other matters that he had to check on. He called Admiral Lagemann on the captured bear-cow superbattleship.

Lagemann answered fairly quickly, grinning at Geary. The other admiral gestured around him. "Greetings from the bridge of my command, Admiral Geary."

"Have we confirmed that's the bridge?"

"We're pretty sure it is," Lagemann said. "The Kicks have some interesting variations in design philosophy from normal human practice." He ran one hand just above his head. "They also don't build their overheads as high as we do. My prize crew is suffering an inordinate number of blows to the head whenever we move around. We're all developing posture problems."

"How much space have you got?" Geary asked.

"This bridge. Some adjoining compartments. The engineers rigged temporary portable life support for these areas. If we go outside those areas, we need to be suited up because the atmosphere in the rest of the ship has become as foul as the air in a port-side bar." Lagemann indicated some panels propped before him. "They've also run some sensor and comm cables and linked up a basic network for us so we can see what's going on outside."

"Does any of the bear-cow stuff still work?"

"We don't know." Lagemann reached toward one of ship's control consoles but stopped short of touching anything. "The engineers got everything shut down and have strongly advised against trying to power up any of the Kick systems again. They're worried that some self-destruct routine might have been triggered by the Kicks but hung up or locked up before activating. If we restarted a system, that might clear such a glitch, with very unfortunate consequences."

Geary breathed a silent prayer of thanks that someone had thought of that. "How is everything else over there?"

"We have Marine sleeping gear and Marine rations," Lagemann said. "The sleeping gear isn't bad at all."

"What about the rations?"

"They're better than fleet battle rations, though that doesn't mean much."

"No. It doesn't."

Lagemann grinned. "We're a bit cramped and a bit uncomfortable, but we've all seen worse conditions. As for me, I am in command of by far the largest warship to ever be part of the Alliance fleet. I'm good."

"Let me know if conditions aboard deteriorate or if you run into anything or discover anything that you think I should know about."

"Have you talked to Angela Meloch or Bran Ezeigwe on *Mistral*?" Lagemann asked.

"Very briefly. Admiral Meloch and General Ezeigwe have been told that they have a clear channel to call me with anything they think I need to know."

"Then you're in good hands." Lagemann reached out again, this time gently running his fingers across the edge of a bear-cow control console. "The malcontents on *Mistral* and *Typhoon* won't let go of the past. They want to be who they once were, they want to fulfill the roles they once dreamed of living during the war. I told them before I left, 'That's all gone. You can't rewrite what has happened. But you can find new dreams, and those are all around us.' Many of them seemed chastised by that, and by events in the past few months. Had you taken us home right after we were liberated, the homecoming would have been very interesting and very lively. But now that things have had time to soak in, now that we've all had time to absorb the changes, you have a lot less to worry about from that quarter." Lagemann smiled with simple joy. "An alien spacecraft, Admiral Geary. Something built by an intelligence different than our own. It's simply awesome."

"It is," Geary agreed. "With everything that's going on, I can lose sight of that. When we get that ship home, and the spider-wolf delegation with it, we're going to learn answers to things we've been wondering about ever since our first ancestor gazed up at the stars for the first time."

"Will we like those answers? I have to wonder."

"Like them or not, we'll have to deal with them."

As they finally approached the jump point nearly two days later, Geary found his gaze straying repeatedly to the other jump point from which they had arrived in this star system. He kept wondering if more bear-cows would appear, a second wave of attackers intent on wiping out the new predators who had appeared on the Kick's doorstep.

Then his eyes would go to hundreds of small markers on his display, each with its own vector aimed inward toward the star. Hundreds of dead from this fleet, on their final journey toward the fires of the star, to be consumed there and eventually reborn as another part of the universe. "Light, then dark, then light," he murmured the words. "The dark is just an interval."

Desjani heard, turning a somber gaze his way. "The dark does not last," she said, the proper response from the ritual. Then her voice changed. "Are we certain that the spider-wolves won't desecrate any of our dead? It will be months before they reach the star."

"Our emissaries and our experts are all positive that the spider-wolves understand how important we consider the safe journeys of our dead to be," Geary answered. "Just as insurance, we provided the spider-wolves with full scans and biological information about our species. There's nothing the spider-wolves could learn from those bodies that we haven't already given them."

"Have the spider-wolves given us all that stuff about them?"

"Not yet."

"Politicians and civilians," Desjani grumbled disdainfully.

"Coming up on jump point in five minutes," Lieutenant Castries said.

Geary activated his comms. "All units, this is Admiral Geary. We are not expecting hostilities at the next star and must not act in a threatening manner inside space controlled by the spider-wolves. No evasive maneuver will be preplanned for execution upon exit from jump, and no weapons are to be powered up when we leave jump. However, all shields are to be at maximum and all personnel are to be prepared for anything. All units jump as scheduled."

The moment of jump came, the stars vanishing and human bodies and minds twisting at the shift from somewhere to somewhere else.

There would be some time for rest in jump space, but not a great deal. While in jump space, the engineers on the auxiliaries could no longer travel to and perform work on other ships, but they could spend that time manufacturing new spare parts and replacement equipment, both of which were in very high demand, as well as new fuel cells and new missiles to replace those expended. The crews of the other ships would, in most cases, be busy with extra internal maintenance and repairs.

Geary sat looking at a display showing the outside view. The dull gray of jump space spread on all sides, an infinity of nothing. It was possible to go outside on a ship's hull while in jump space. It was possible to do work on the exterior of a ship in jump space. But if anything, human or equipment, lost physical contact with the ship for even an instant, it was gone. It was still in jump space, but somewhere else. Just like the ships that made up this fleet, which were all in jump space together, all traveling from one jump point to the same new jump point, but which could not see or interact with each other except for some very simple and basic messages that could be exchanged.

The difference was that those ships all had the means to leave jump space when they reached their destination. Anyone who lost contact with a ship did not.

As a result of that, no work was done by humans on the outside of ships in jump space. In emergencies, robots might be employed, but with the expectation that those robots would very likely be lost forever.

Was that what the mysterious lights of jump space were? Frantic distress flares from someone or something eternally caught in nothing? Geary almost shivered at the thought. The common belief that those lights had some mystical significance was much more comforting and easier to live with.

Also comforting was the knowledge that no external threat could reach them in jump space. For now, he could truly focus on other issues for a while.

"I'm going to be down in my stateroom," he told Desjani. "Do we have any of those VIP wraps left?"

"Not that I've discovered," she replied.

"Maybe I'll eat a meal with the crew and get a feel for morale."

"Morale on my ship is fine, Admiral," Desjani said. "I haven't had to have anyone flogged to improve their morale for days now."

"That's good to hear, Captain."

The walk to a dining compartment did feel almost relaxing, the crew obviously feeling as relieved as Geary to be going away from the bear-cows and toward home. He talked with some of the crew as he ate, asking about their home worlds. Most were from Kosatka, and some had been there during the brief but memorable few days he and Tanya had spent on that planet for what had passed as a honeymoon. "I didn't buy one drink during those days," one sailor told Geary. "I'd walk into a bar in uniform, and they'd see *Dauntless* on my ship badge, and that was all there was to it."

"I got two marriage proposals," another crew member said. "I told both of them I was okay with it but that my husband probably wouldn't go along."

As the laughter from that died down, the questions turned to other matters. Usually with an admiral within reach, sailors would ask about living conditions and food and time off and working conditions, but this time the questions were about bigger issues. The thousands of Marines who had been aboard the bear-cow superbattleship had spread their stories far and wide, so everyone knew a lot about the creatures. But that still left some serious concerns. "Are we going back there, Admiral, to where the Kicks live?"

Geary shook his head firmly. "No." He could see the crew members around him relaxing immediately at his unambiguous reply. "Any human ship going there for the foreseeable future would have to be fully automated. I'm not going to risk another human life dealing with the bear-cows."

"Why are we bringing that huge ship with us, sir?" another sailor asked. "It's slowing us down, isn't it?"

"A bit," Geary admitted. "But it's incredibly valuable. It's a treasure trove of bear-cow technology. Maybe when we have time to analyze everything back in Alliance space, they won't find anything amazing on it, just different ways of doing what we can already do. But maybe they'll find things we never knew we could do."

A veteran systems technician nodded. "Something really revolutionary that we never thought of. How do you measure how much that could be worth?"

"Exactly. And, if nothing there is beyond what we can already do, that at least tells us the limits of what the bear-cows can do."

That earned him more nods, then one sailor proffered her data unit where a picture was displayed. "Admiral, is this really what the B—the things that helped us look like?"

It was a good representation of a spider-wolf, probably taken from one of the messages the spider-wolves had sent to the fleet as a whole when it had arrived at Honor. But although the sailor had shown the sense not to call them Bubs to Geary's face, the term obviously was still in use. "Yes. That's what they look like.

Unattractive as sin, aren't they?" Geary asked, trying to disarm the inevitable reactions. "That's on the outside. On the inside, they seem to have a lot more in common with us than the bear-cows or the enigmas."

"Some of them tried to help a pod off of *Balestra*," another crewman noted.

"That makes them better than Syndics, too," someone else remarked.

The laughter this time was a bit nervous. "The bottom line," Geary said as convincingly as he could, "is that they did fight alongside us, and they did attempt to aid us in other ways. They're letting us use their hypernet to get home a lot faster than we could otherwise. You judge someone by how they act, not by how they look."

"Tell that to my chief at the next uniform inspection, Admiral!"

"Yeah, Admiral, can I quote you on that?"

Geary laughed, standing up and waving away the eager, joking requests. "I'm only an admiral. I can lead chiefs, but I can't push them around. Besides, according to Captain Desjani, you're the best sailors in the fleet. Why would I need to ask for special treatment for you?"

He left the dining compartment feeling better, but the sailors' questions had brought to life some of his own concerns. Once Geary reached his stateroom, he put in a call to another officer aboard *Dauntless*, asking him to drop by as soon as possible.

"Admiral." General Charban, at least, was enjoying some rest.

With the ships isolated in jump space, he was no longer being called upon to try to communicate with the spider-wolves on a constant basis. "You wanted to see me?" he asked as he entered Geary's stateroom.

"Yes." Geary waved Charban to a seat. "I was afraid you'd already passed out for a while."

"After all those days I had to stay awake to deal with negotiations, my metabolism will take a few more hours to slow down again to the point where I can sleep," Charban said as he sat. "I could slam it down with some different meds, but I prefer to let my body handle getting back to normal a little more naturally."

"A wise move," Geary said. "I wanted a candid appraisal from you, without any pressure from anyone else being present. You've had as much contact with the spider-wolves as anyone has so far."

"Emissary Rione is actually the only one to have had 'contact,'" Charban pointed out. "Though that distinction didn't seem to mean much to the fleet medical personnel who inflicted such a wide array of tests and examinations on both of us. In preparation for that meeting with the spider-wolves, I had read a number of accounts of supposed encounters with alien species in the far past. Those old stories often claimed the aliens used probes and other uncomfortable forms of physical inspection. In fact, the spider-wolves were very courteous. It was our own doctors who probed away with considerable enthusiasm."

"I'm sorry about that." Geary sat down opposite Charban. "General, I want to know any impressions you have of the spider-wolves that have not appeared in formal reporting."

"Impressions, Admiral? As to what? I can speak for hours about different matters, but it would help if I knew exactly what you're interested in."

"Can we trust them?" Geary saw Charban taken aback by the question. "Yes, they fought alongside us against the bear-cows. But what about now? Jump space is not a big trust issue. We know where we're going. I don't have a gut feeling that we need fear any kind of trap or ambush from the spider-wolves there. But we'll be entering their hypernet, dependent on them as to where we come out."

"I see." Charban gave Geary a wry look. "Admiral, have you ever met the sorts of people who strike you as dangerous because they're unpredictable? You know the kind. It's not just that they're capable of doing things but that they might strike out at any time at anyone. Or they might do something totally unexpected."

He nodded, an image of Jane Geary flashing into his mind, followed by that of Commander Benan. But he wouldn't say either name aloud.

"But," Charban continued, "there are other sorts of people, like General Carabali, who are dangerous because of their capabilities, but in a very targeted way. General Carabali will only strike after carefully considering options and deciding this target must be hit in this way."

"Sure," Geary agreed. "I've met both types."

"The spider-wolves strike me as being fundamentally of that second nature. They can be very deadly, but they always calculate their strikes. They always act to support their goals, and those goals and plans are well thought out. This pattern thing that the civilian experts came up with, for example. Just thinking in terms of that, in terms of how one action will impact not only those things around it but also anything that might somehow be tied to it, requires acting in a well-planned way. You or I might act in that fashion because we believe it is smart. The spider-wolves, I am convinced, act that way because they feel they must."

Geary sat thinking about that for a while, Charban waiting patiently. "That's scary, isn't it?" Geary finally said. "An intelligent species that feels an obligation to think out its actions, to consider consequences. That makes them smarter than us."

"Smarter? Perhaps. It depends on how you define 'smarts.'" Charban shook his head. "Do they take chances? I don't think so. Not as we would define it. What about leaps of faith? Unlikely, I am guessing. Spontaneous moves? Sudden inspirations driving immediate actions? No. I don't think so. It's all planned out carefully, thought out carefully."

"Engineers," Geary said. "Really good engineers. They do the planning before they act. They don't build something they don't expect to work. We could probably outreact them."

"Or at least confuse them." Charban hunched forward, his eyes on Geary's. "But here's what I think is the most important part of my assessment. Admiral, would a race that always plans ahead, that doesn't like to deal with unanticipated or uncontrollable events or consequences, a race that wants to be sure of what will happen, would such a species *ever* begin a war by choice?"

That one was easy. "No."

"No," Charban repeated. "War is chaos. War is unpredictable. I heard a story once about an ancient king who asked an infallible oracle about what would happen if he invaded a neighboring kingdom, and the oracle answered that if he did that, a mighty kingdom would fall. Assuming that guaranteed victory, he invaded, only to be utterly crushed, his own kingdom destroyed. He hadn't considered the possibility that the oracle's answer meant that his kingdom would be the one to fall."

"Unforeseen circumstances," Geary said.

"Right. If humans were a rational species, we would take heed of such examples from our history, and no one would start a war. But some humans always convince themselves that 'this time' it will be different and that they can confidently predict the outcome. Why did the Syndic Executive Council start the war with the Alliance a century ago when they should have realized that even with enigma help they couldn't have won? Even then it should have been obvious that a bloody stalemate was inevitable. But we humans find ways to fool ourselves. I don't believe that the spider-wolves think like that. On the contrary, their bias to avoid the unpredictable might prevent them from ever being aggressive against their neighbors."

Geary nodded. "But self-defense is another matter. Failure to have sufficient defenses would produce an outcome they don't want, or introduce uncertainty into whether or not someone would attack."

"Yes. Which is all a very convoluted way of answering your initial question. Yes, I believe we can trust the spider-wolves. I am certain that they don't want to start a war with us. If we started a war with them, they would fight back with all of the cleverness and skill they possess. But they won't begin a war with us. They don't know what that would do to the pattern."

It all fit together. "Self-interest."

"I beg your pardon?"

"Self-interest," Geary explained. "How is every nonhuman intelligent species acting? In what they believe to be their own self-interest. The enigmas are convinced that hiding anything about themselves is vitally important, so they'll do anything to keep us from learning anything. The bear-cows think we want to eat them, so they'll do anything to stop us from doing that. And the spider-wolves think we can help anchor their pattern if we work together, or seriously disrupt it if we fought. The one thing they all have in common is the pursuit of what they have decided is their own self-interest."

General Charban sat back, considering that. "Humans, too. Why are we here? Because we considered it important to know whether the enigmas could be dealt with short of war and to learn how powerful they were. It was in our self-interest to risk this fleet on such a mission."

"The self-interest of humanity as a whole, you mean," Geary said, hearing the acid in his tone.

"Just so," Charban agreed. "This mission isn't the sort of thing that promotes the self-interests of the humans in the crews. Perhaps we're not so different in that respect from the enigmas or the bear-cows. Humanity is just as willing to sacrifice some of its own number in the name of the greater good. I'm going to pass your idea on to our civilian experts if that's all right with you. It might offer a place, a concept, where we can make emotional contact with even the most alien of species."

"Good." Geary held out a restraining hand as Charban began to rise. "About the civilian experts…"

"I think we can trust them, Admiral," Charban joked, then noticed Geary's reaction. "Are you concerned about that?"

"I don't know. I've been picking up some different impressions from them lately. Those I contact regularly I mean. I rarely deal directly with any of them but Dr. Setin and Dr. Shwartz now."

"I see." Charban relaxed in his seat again. "I've been working with all of them. You know there have always been three factions among our civilian experts? One small faction was convinced before we met a single alien intelligence that it would be a fight to the death between our species. Remarkably, that faction sees everything we've learned as supporting that argument. Another small faction started out believing that the universe would greet us with open arms of peace and friendship. They also remain unshaken in their position, blaming any contact problems on our own blunders."

"The blunders of the military, you mean," Geary said dryly.

"Of course. Then there's the biggest faction, who to varying degrees like to wait to see the evidence before they decide what the evidence means. I've been frankly surprised to see so many of that sort with us, but that is due, I think, to the efforts of Dr. Setin in influencing who accompanied us." Charban fell silent for a moment. "That group was badly shaken by the enigmas and the bear-cows. The evidence seemed to support the crowd that claimed the universe hates us. The discovery and interaction with the spider-wolves has been incredibly important in restoring their faith in the universe and in this mission."

"You believe everything is all right there, then? There's nothing I need to worry about?"

"I didn't say that, Admiral." Charban's smile held no humor. "Soon after we return to Alliance space, academic and popular journals will be full of articles penned by our experts in which they will describe how very badly the military and some of the other civilian experts handled just about everything, and how only the presence of the authors of said articles prevented total and complete disaster."

"I see that academia hasn't changed in the last century," Geary said.

"No. Of course not." Charban thought, his eyes on the star display. "Dr. Setin has been one of your strongest supporters among the civilian experts. But he was badly shaken by the slaughter aboard that bear-cow superbattleship. I think he understands that you had no choice but to order such an action, and that we did all we could to get the bear-cow crew to surrender rather than fight to the death, but, emotionally, he has had great difficulty with those events. Still, he's a good man with a good mind. I believe he will come around."

"And Dr. Shwartz?"

"You have no firmer ally among them, Admiral. You have given her not one, not two, but three intelligent nonhuman species to study. The circumstances involving some of those meetings haven't been what we wished, but Dr. Shwartz is that rare sort of academic who realizes the difference between the universe in which theories live and the universe as it really exists."

"Thank you, General," Geary said. "Please go now and let your metabolism wind down so you can rest."

The next three and a half days in jump space were quiet. Geary noticed that Desjani kept her crew working but also allowed an unusually large amount of downtime, so everyone could take a break.

He did his own best to relax despite gnawing worries about how close the enigmas were to Midway and whether or not the spider-wolves might yet decide that humans were too unpredictable to make worthwhile friends or allies.

Geary was back on the bridge of *Dauntless* when the fleet popped out of jump into a star system that humans would have considered prime. Twelve planets orbiting a star whose nuclear furnace appeared as stable as stars got, one of those planets orbiting just under eight light-minutes from the star in the perfect zone for life as humans knew it, while two more planets swung around each other and the star at nine light-minutes out. Those planets were a bit cool and must have some impressive tidal effects, but were otherwise not bad at all. Off to one side and two light-hours away, what could only be a hypernet gate loomed.

"Nice," Desjani approved, her eyes still searching for threats. The star system was filled with spider-wolf ships, all of which appeared to use the same beautifully streamlined shape but the vast majority of which were on paths indicating they were taking merchant ship–type tracks between planets.

Aside from the six spider-wolf warships accompanying the human fleet, only two other spider-wolf ships were at the jump point.

Geary shook his head. "We know they sent some ships ahead to tell them that we were coming, but still I expected some stronger force to be on guard here, even if disguised as an honor guard of some sort. Can you imagine letting a fleet of alien warships just waltz through your territory?"

"Don't forget those stealthy megamines the spider-wolves had at Honor," Desjani pointed out. "They might have stuff hidden around here that would make us really unhappy really fast if we did the wrong thing."

"Your warning is noted and appreciated," Geary replied. She was right. Just because he couldn't see spider-wolf precautions didn't mean there weren't any. "Emissary Rione, General Charban, please contact our friends the spider-wolves and find out if we're just supposed to transit directly to the hypernet gate."

Virtual windows were appearing around Geary. Dr. Setin, Lieutenant Iger, Captain Smythe... all begging for an extended opportunity to examine everything that could be learned in this spider-wolf-occupied star system. Geary cut them all off, grateful again for the fleet commander override, then answered everyone at once. "We are contacting the spider-wolves to ask them what path we should follow through this star system. We will have to abide by their wishes. Every sensor in this fleet, every means of collection, is sucking up every bit of data it possibly can, and we will continue to vacuum up information as long as we are in this star system. That's all I can promise."

Desjani pointed to her display. "Our escorts are heading for the gate. Do we follow?"

"Yes." It might take the emissaries a while to reestablish contact, so he had best stick to the safest course until then. Geary brought the fleet around in the wake of the six spider-wolf ships, grateful to see how smoothly even the four battleships linked to the captured bear-cow ship carried out the maneuver.

"They're watching us, too, you know," Desjani commented, as the fleet steadied out on a vector following the spider-wolf escort.

"I know." He was watching the two spider-wolf ships that had met them here. Without warning, both of those ships accelerated into the human formation, gliding and weaving between human ships with the grace and ease of dolphins racing through an underwater obstacle course.

"They're heading for the LCCO," Desjani said, her voice tense.

"The LCCO?"

"Large Clumsy Captured Object."

"The Kick superbattleship," Geary realized. He hit his comm controls. "All units, this is Admiral Geary, do not interfere with or engage any spider-wolf ships. No weapons use is authorized except by my direct order. Do not lock fire control systems on any spider-wolf craft." The two spider-wolf ships slowed, coming almost to a stop relative to the superbattleship and the four Alliance battleships towing it, even though all of those ships were traveling through space at point one light speed. Moving with almost dainty precision, the spider-wolf ships split up, coursing along close above the hull of the former Kick ship in a long and careful examination that was still under way when Rione called Geary.

"The spider-wolves want permission to send someone aboard the captured bear-cow ship."

13

Geary glared at Rione. "Are you certain they just want to visit? They don't want to take control of it, or take things off it?"

"I am certain, Admiral. They want to look around."

Desjani was looking upward, pretending not to have heard. Well, this was entirely up to him. "All right. Tell them they can send some teams aboard," Geary told Rione before tapping another control. "Admiral Lagemann, are you prepared for visitors?"

It took another half an hour before one of the spider-wolf ships slipped next to one of the air locks human engineers had installed where the Marines had blasted their way inside the bear-cow superbattleship. By then, a reception committee was waiting, including Admiral Lagemann, the senior Marine aboard the captured ship, and some of the engineers in the prize crew. Even though all of the humans were in survival suits or battle armor, and the spider-wolves were themselves encased in their own armor, the spider-wolves still offered greetings that consisted of cautious "air hugs" that avoided actual physical contact with the humans.

Looking over the human party, Geary saw one of them identified as Lieutenant Jamenson, though, of course, he couldn't see her bright green hair under her survival-suit helmet.

He called the head engineer on *Tanuki*. "Captain Smythe, I thought Lieutenant Jamenson was on *Orion*."

"She was, Admiral. I directed her to do an individual movement between ships so she could be part of the welcoming committee."

"Why?"

Smythe grinned. "First of all, to see how the spider-wolves would react to a human whose physical appearance doesn't fit the, uh, pattern that they are used to. That will only work if they go into an area where Lieutenant Jamenson can remove her helmet, of course. But it also occurred to me that Lieutenant Jamenson's particular talents might be useful as she watched the spider-wolves in action. Perhaps she'll see something the rest of us miss."

"Two inspired ideas, Captain. Thank you."

Desjani looked skeptical. "That's the lieutenant who confuses things, right? I mean, on purpose she can confuse things."

"Right," Geary confirmed.

"And this helps with the spider-wolves how?"

"It's the flip side of that which could prove useful," Geary explained. "Lieutenant Jamenson can also spot information that is related but buried among lots of other data."

"You mean like patterns?"

"Sort of."

"Maybe she is a good choice, then." Desjani settled back in her seat, touching her internal comm controls as she did so. "We have a little more than nineteen hours of travel time to the hypernet gate," she told her crew. "Let's get cracking on external hull work."

The spider-wolves spent six hours aboard the captured bear-cow warship, focusing attention on areas like the control and engineering spaces while the human fleet focused their attention on what the spider-wolves were examining. Lieutenant Jamenson did get the opportunity to open her helmet at one point, but if her green hair surprised the spider-wolves as much as it did the average human, no one could tell.

Data poured in from fleet sensors examining the inhabited worlds. Grateful that he didn't have to analyze threat activity, Geary left most of that to the civilian experts and Lieutenant Iger's intelligence people. Occasionally, he would view areas of the planets that had come into view of the fleet's full-spectrum sensors, seeing cities and towns that spread widely and seemed thinly occupied by human standards. The spider-wolves had plenty of population here, but they must prefer spreading out rather than concentrating into dense urban centers. Unlike in the bear-cow star system, the planets here had a wide variety of vegetation and a lot of it even within the spider-wolf cities.

Four hours after the spider-wolf team had left the captured bear-cow ship to another round of air hugs and with ten hours remaining before the human fleet reached the hypernet gate, Rione called Geary in his stateroom. "I need to brief you on a few things."

"All right. Go ahead."

"In person."

He sighed. Late at night. Rione in his cabin. Admiral Timbale had warned him that people would be watching for any signs of unprofessional behavior by either him or Desjani. "Madam Emissary—"

"Commander Benan can escort me." She said it ironically, as if they were sharing a joke.

Naturally Commander Benan, her husband, wouldn't be thrilled by this, either. "All right," Geary said.

She showed up in only a few minutes, Commander Benan walking stiffly beside her as she entered. Once inside, he looked around, narrowed-eyed as if searching for dangers, then saluted with a rigid arm before pivoting and walking out of the stateroom to stand by the hatch as it closed.

Geary waited until the hatch had sealed before speaking. "How is he doing?"

"Better since that talk you had with him."

"At least now we know what the root of his problem is and at least now I know how you're being blackmailed."

She didn't answer for a while. "Without confirming the last part of your statement, it's unfortunate that neither piece of information offers much in the way of immediate benefit," Rione finally said.

"Yes. You're right about that. But you say Commander Benan is more stable now?"

"I said he was better." Rione walked to a chair and sat down, her gaze now on the star display. "More stable? A little. He's still dangerous."

"Be careful."

"I'm always careful. Let me inform you of things I have learned from conversations with some of the spider-wolves while General Charban and the civilian experts talked with others."

Geary sat down opposite her. "Were you talking to the one in charge? How senior in rank are the spider-wolves who have been talking to us?" The question had kept occurring to him but never when he was speaking to anyone who could answer it.

"I don't know. We don't know." Rione spread her hands, palms up. "Whatever organizational structure the spider-wolves use is too complicated or too odd for us to grasp as of yet. One of those experts, that Dr. Shwartz, thinks the organizational diagram itself may resemble a web. She could be right. Whatever way they are arranged in rank, we haven't been able to figure it out even though it seems clear enough to the spider-wolves.

"Now, there are things I have been told that you must know. I do not know how much of this should be known to others in this fleet, which is why I am briefing you in this manner." Rione spoke briskly but matter-of-factly. "First off, the spider-wolves have informed me in a manner that cannot be misunderstood that when we encounter enigmas, they will not aid in any attack on the enigmas; nor will they help defend us against the enigmas. They will defend themselves, but they will not otherwise engage in hostilities."

"You're certain of that?"

"Absolutely. We're on our own when it comes to hostilities with the enigmas."

"Has General Charban discussed with you his feelings about the spider-wolves and war?"

"Yes." Rione shook her head. "It's a possible explanation, but we don't know it's true. All I know is that they will not fight the enigmas except to save themselves."

"At least they told us," Geary said. "Do you think there might be a nonaggression pact between the enigmas and the spider-wolves?"

She started to reply, stopped as a thought hit her, then gave him a slight smile. "Because if there were such an agreement between the enigmas and another species, it might hold out hope that we could reach such a pact with the enigmas?"

"Yes."

"I don't know. I'll see what I can find out." Rione tapped the controls on the star display, leaning in as she did so that she was close to Geary.

Even though they didn't touch, he felt her closeness, memories coming unbidden of times they had been together in this stateroom before he and Tanya had known their own feelings for each other.

He gave Rione no sign that he had felt that, remembered those things, and she also did not react at all, her voice remaining composed and unemotional. "We're going to come out of the spider-wolf hypernet at this star. It has a human designation but no name. The Syndics didn't get that far when they were pushing into that region more than a century ago. From that star we will jump a short distance to this star. Again, no name from human sources, but when the spider-wolves spoke of it, they used the same symbol as they used for the star Honor even though this is a different type of star."

Geary looked steadily at the display as he thought. "A symbol, a label, not for the star type, but for something else? They had a defensive force at Honor, guarding against the bear-cows. Does that star serve a similar purpose against the enigmas? That symbol might mean fortress or stronghold, or something like that."

"It might." Rione pointed again. "From that star, we jump to this one, which the Syndics named Hua and may have reached before the enigmas knocked them back to Midway. I don't think the Syndics got that far, though, because the spider-wolves indicated that Hua is an enigma strongpoint of some kind. They signified some danger there."

"Hopefully not an enigma hypernet gate," Geary said. "I don't want to have to run that kind of gauntlet again." His own hand went out, tracing a path on the display. "And Hua is within jump range of Pele."

"And from Pele we get to Midway," Rione finished.

"Thank you. That's all very important—"

"There's one thing more." She held out her data pad, revealing that it was displaying the symbol used by Syndicate Worlds' ships to identify themselves. "I showed this to the spider-wolves I was talking to. They recognized it."

Geary stared at the symbol. "You're sure?"

"They told me they recognized it."

"The spider-wolves know about the Syndics? They've had contact with the Syndicate Worlds?"

"I don't think so. I think the Syndics are just as oblivious to the existence of the spider-wolves as we were. But here is the thing, Admiral. I asked them what this symbol represented, and they used the symbols for 'enemy of your people.'"

"How could they—" Geary's stare shifted to Rione. "The border with the Alliance is a very long distance from here. There haven't been any Alliance ships in the region of Syndic space nearest here for at least a century except for our fleet. There certainly haven't been any battles fought anywhere near that region. How the hell could they know that we were fighting a war with the Syndics?"

"That's a very good question, Admiral." Rione rested her chin on one hand, looking pensive. "We have learned that the enigmas had been spying on us long before we knew the enigmas existed. Perhaps…"

"The spider-wolves have been in Alliance space?" He forced himself to consider the idea.

"The enigmas planted worms in our sensor systems that hid them from us," Rione said. "Could the spider-wolves have done the same?"

"If they have, they're using yet another totally different principle. We've scrubbed those systems using everything we could dream up and found nothing else."

"Have you ever heard of something like a spider-wolf ship being spotted in Alliance space?"

He searched his memory, finding nothing specific. "There are always false sightings. We call them that. Sensors say there's something there. We take another look, and maybe that next look doesn't see anything. Or we send a ship to investigate. Sometimes it finds something that was just hard to spot." That had been how the Alliance fleet had found him, frozen in survival sleep in a damaged escape pod, its beacon inoperative and its power levels failing, so low they barely showed up on the latest fleet sensors. If they hadn't spotted him then, if they hadn't recognized that this wasn't just another piece of lifeless debris, if a destroyer hadn't taken a good look around and found him… Geary tried to banish the memory of the ice that had once filled him. "Usually, most of the time, whatever gets sent to investigate finds nothing. That's called a false sighting."

"What causes them?" Rione asked.

"Every system has glitches. Gremlins. Loose electrons. The name varies, but it means that something that isn't there shows up as being there, or something that isn't happening shows as happening, or something sticks where nothing should be able to stick. The same sort of tick that impacts everything that uses electronics and coding. That's why we have human overrides on all of our systems."

She nodded. "I did a little research before coming down here. There have been examples of such 'false sightings' all through human history, dating back to Old Earth. Most were easily explained. The others were dismissed. But if we knew such things happened, then it would too easily explain events that might not all actually be the result of glitches or gremlins. If the spider-wolves have decent stealth technology—"

"They have excellent stealth technology." He thought of the mines at Honor.

"Then, Admiral, we must conclude the real possibility that while humanity tended to its own issues and bemoaned a universe empty of other minds like ours, more than one set of such minds may have been snooping around to learn what they could of us."

He dug his palms into his eyes. "But why wouldn't the spider-wolves have contacted us? We know why the enigmas didn't. Why not the spider-wolves?"

"I don't know."

"What would they have done if our colonies, our exploration, had reached their boundaries before this?"

"Perhaps just what they did with us," Rione said. "For whatever reason, they waited for us to get to them. The reason or reasons must have made sense to them. In practice, the enigmas were along the paths that humanity was expanding through in that region, so the enigmas blocked human contact with the spider-wolves."

Geary sat looking at the display, trying to think. "If the spider-wolves know that the Syndics are our enemies, *were* our enemies, why do they think that we're so eager to get to Midway before the enigmas?"

Rione smiled again. "The spider-wolves believe that we are helping our brother-enemies against our not-brother-enemies. They appear to be extremely impressed by that." She stood up. "I shouldn't spend too long in here."

"I understand." He stood as well, but as Rione turned to go Geary spoke again. "Victoria, I'm going to help him. I know what needs to be done, and I will make sure it is done when we get back to Alliance space."

She watched him, then slowly nodded once. "Let us hope that he lives that long."

Rione had barely been gone for a minute before Geary's comm panel buzzed again with a familiar pattern. "Oh, you're still up?" Desjani asked.

"As if you didn't know. Are you calling to find out why Emissary Rione was here?"

"Was she?"

"Yes. Briefing me on items she has learned from the spider-wolves." Items that Desjani needed to know as well. "Since I've already fed the gossip-beast enough tonight, I'll let you know about it all tomorrow."

"Thank you, Admiral." Desjani gave him a curious look. "Whatever it is seems to have impressed you. Is it something we have to worry about?"

"I don't know. For tonight, let's just say that for some time now, humanity has been congratulating itself on how much we knew about the universe. And all that time it seems the universe has been laughing at us and making faces behind our back."

He didn't know why he had expected the spider-wolf hypernet gate to look different from the ones humans and enigmas had constructed, but he had. And in that, Geary wasn't disappointed. The spider-wolves had crafted the tethers in ways that evoked the webs Dr. Shwartz kept using as metaphors. To Geary, the spider-wolf hypernet gate looked not only like a great feat of engineering (just as human hypernet gates did), but also like a work of art. Nonetheless, it was still a hypernet gate.

"I don't like hypernets," Geary mumbled just loud enough for Desjani to hear. He didn't want to share his feelings with everyone on the bridge.

She looked up from checking the status of *Dauntless* to ensure her ship was ready for the transit. "Why not?"

"It feels unnatural."

"Compared to what? Jump space?"

He glowered at her. "You know what I mean."

"No, I don't," Desjani replied. "Seriously. If you want to travel from one star to another, you can't do it in less than decades without doing something weird. Personally, I think hypernet space isn't as weird as jump space."

He didn't reply, feeling grumpy. Rione's information was weighing on his mind, worries about Midway kept rising to the surface, the lack of solid information about what the enigmas had at Hua meant he had to worry about that—

"The spider-wolves want to know if we're ready," General Charban said.

Geary ran his eyes down the fleet status readouts. It could be better. A lot better. Too much damage, not enough time or resources for all of the repairs that needed to be done. But they were ready to go. "Yes. The fleet is ready. Will the spider-wolves give us a countdown?"

"I'm not certain," Charban said after passing on Geary's reply using the coordination circuit. The words had barely left his mouth when the universe twitched and the stars disappeared, leaving only darkness around *Dauntless*. "Correction. The answer is no, they will not provide a countdown."

"Thank you, General." Geary looked at the different kind of nothing that surrounded ships during hypernet transits. A bubble of nothing, Desjani had called it, in which the ships were suspended. According to physicists, they didn't actually go anywhere, but at the other hypernet gate they would drop out into normal space a very long ways from where they had entered the gate here.

"Four days, the spider-wolves said," Charban reminded Geary.

"We're going a long ways," Desjani commented. "Did I tell you that the longer the trip in hypernet space, the less time it takes?"

"Yes, you did." He remembered that moment vividly, waiting to go into the fleet conference room on *Dauntless* for the first time to assume command of a trapped fleet. It had been the first time he'd really met Tanya, and she had frightened him with her expressions of faith in his ability to save them all.

She had been right, but he still thought that luck had played far too large a part in that.

Maybe it was being in hyperspace, which—being nowhere—shouldn't cause any discomfort but still did as far as Geary was concerned. Maybe it was the many unknowns he had to face. Maybe something had reminded him of past trials.

In the middle of the ship's night he woke up, sweating heavily, his eyes on the overhead reassuring him that it was intact. The clamor of alarms, the crash of explosions, and the screams of the dying still echoed in his head, but his stateroom was quiet with the hush that came during nights, even when those nights were artificial on ships far from any planet.

Geary sat up in the dark, rubbing his face with both hands, feet on the deck to reassure him with the solidity of the ship and the countless small vibrations transmitted through *Dauntless*, which told him that the ship lived.

"Admiral?" Desjani's face was on his comm screen, her hair disheveled from sleep, her eyes still focusing as she came fully awake.

In hypernet space, like jump space, even a battle cruiser commander could try to get a decent night's sleep.

He took a deep breath before answering. "What is it?"

"'What is it?' You called me."

"No, I didn't."

She frowned. "I can call up comm system records if you want. Maybe you hit the hot button to call me in your sleep, but you hit it."

Feeling guilty, Geary looked at the controls ranked beneath the screen at his bunk. He could have accidentally hit the one that went direct to Tanya, especially since it was the closest one to where he might have flailed an arm while fighting battles in his sleep. "I'm sorry. It was just an accident."

Instead of ringing off, she studied him. "You look like hell."

"Thank you."

"Nightmare?"

"Yes."

She just waited, watching him with the patience of a cat standing sentry at a mousehole, ready to be there all the rest of the night if necessary.

"There was a battle," Geary said. "That's all. The usual."

"The usual?" Tanya sighed. "You're not the only one to get flashbacks. And I know about the nightmares about *Merlon*, remember? One of them woke me on our honeymoon. Was this just reliving *Merlon*'s last moments?"

He could have said yes, but she probably would have known he wasn't being honest. "Partly. It was mixed in with other stuff." She was still waiting. "I have these dreams sometimes. I'm on the bridge of *Dauntless*, or *Merlon*, and I'm in command of a fleet, and I'm not paying attention for a moment, just for a tiny moment, and all of a sudden enemies are there, right on top of us. Overwhelming numbers of them. I send orders, but they're late, and they're wrong, and ships get destroyed. Ships are being destroyed on all sides, and the ship I'm on is getting hit hard, and I know it's the end because I know how that feels when a ship has lost, and it's all my fault."

"All right," Tanya said. "Been there, though not the fleet commander part. Have you been getting stress therapy?"

"Yeah." He felt a little better just from talking to her, though that had also brought back vividly the images of destruction from his nightmare. "They make it easier. They don't make it go away."

She laughed, low and soft and bitter. "You think I don't know that? I've been fighting longer than you have, sailor."

"I was hoping the treatments had gotten better in the century of the war."

"They've had plenty of guinea pigs to practice on," Desjani said with dry and dark humor. "But, no. Humans are complicated. When something goes wrong in our heads, recalibrating is not easy or simple. The docs these days can help us keep going when by all rights we should be unable to function, but they're human, too, not gods. Stress and trauma are two of the never-ending benefits of military life, just like bad food, too little sleep, lousy living accommodations, and long separations from our families."

He smiled wryly. "With benefits like that, you wonder why they have to pay us, too."

"It is a puzzlement. Feel better?"

"Yeah," Geary said.

"Liar. What else is there?"

He ran one hand through his hair. "In the nightmare, I saw you... die. Tanya, I swear that I don't know what I'd do if—"

"If I died?" She said it in a hard and blunt way. "If that happens, you will suck it up and keep on doing your duty and living your life."

He stared at her. "You think it would be that easy?"

"No, but that's not the point. Do you think I'd want a memorial that consisted of a ruined man? 'Yeah, that's Black Jack. He used to be a hero before she died and destroyed him.' Oh, yes. That's what I want everyone thinking about me when I'm gone."

"Tanya—"

"No," she interrupted again. "Not negotiable. If it comes to that, you will *live* the rest of your life. You will find happiness again, and you will continue to do the things you must do and should do. Is that clear?"

"Very clear," Geary said. "Will you do the same?"

"What, if you die? The legendary, idolized hero of the Alliance? I'll probably write a tell-all memoir and make more money than I can count. Don't forget that my uncle is not only a literary agent, but he has yet to be caught doing anything unethical. *Sleeping with Black Jack.* How's that for a title?"

He felt himself smiling. "Can you at least avoid calling me Black Jack while you're making your money by selling the story of our time together?"

Tanya shook her head. "Nope. I'm sure marketing will insist on it. I can just imagine the kind of book cover they'll insist on. Some really heroic pose by you doing something you never did, probably. Maybe in battle armor. With a gun."

"Like that would ever happen. So if I die, you'll just write a memoir?"

"No. I'll probably get a cat, too." She peered at him. "Now do you feel better?"

"Yes, Tanya, I do. Thanks. Are you going back to sleep now?"

"I'll try." Her expression went serious. "See the docs in the morning to find out if you need any extra therapy or stuff. This junk isn't easy to live with."

"I will," Geary promised.

After his comm screen blanked, he lay down again, looking upward, wondering where he would be if he were facing all of this alone.

The unnamed spider-wolf-occupied star system at the other end of the hypernet journey wasn't the paradise the other star system had been, but it still offered a more-than-decent collection of planets and resources as well as plenty of spider-wolf towns on the single inhabited planet. Geary and the rest of the fleet didn't see much of that star system and what it held, though, since the jump point the six escorting spider-wolf ships headed for was barely a light-hour from the hypernet gate. His lingering worries that the spider-wolves might take them somewhere else far from the promised destination dissipated as the fleet's sensors scanned the heavens and confirmed that the stars were in the right places for them to be where they had expected to be.

Though Rione, Charban, and the civilian experts waited expectantly for communications from the spider-wolves, nothing came from either local sources or the escorts until the fleet was almost at the jump point.

"They want to know if we're ready," Charban said.

"We're ready," Geary replied, grateful that this time he would control when his ships jumped.

After the jump, Desjani eyed the gray emptiness around them. "The next star should be easy. The one after that might have trouble."

"And the one after that *will* have trouble," Geary said.

* * *

Geary wasn't too surprised when they arrived at what he thought of as the spider-wolf fortress star to find the same massive and stealthy mines lurking near every jump point, as well as another gorgeous formation of spider-wolf warships positioned where they could block any force coming from either of the other two jump points here. "Whatever the spider-wolves think of the enigmas, they clearly don't trust them."

"Look at this." Desjani tapped the readings from the star with her forefinger, then indicated what the sensors were reporting of the four planets in this star system. "The star is showing erratic output. Something has disrupted it. And those planets have been swept hard by something more than once."

"An erratic star could have thrown off some outbursts..." Geary studied the readings. "But that star isn't the right type to be naturally erratic, and its rotation isn't unusually fast."

"Where have we seen this kind of thing before?" Desjani asked, her voice sounding chill and distant.

"Kalixa," Geary said. "And Lakota. Though Lakota wasn't as bad as this."

"They've used those mines here." Desjani swung her hand across her display, studying it intently. "More than once. The enigmas must have tried to push through here repeatedly."

"I wonder what this place was like before that."

Rione had come forward from the observation seat, staring ahead of her. "What happened here?"

"Hypernet gate—scale mines," Desjani answered shortly, rattled enough to speak directly to Rione.

Geary nodded to reinforce her words. "The spider-wolves play for keeps when it comes to defending their space."

Rione shuddered, closing her eyes. "How fortunate that the spider-wolves decided we were friends."

You could almost feel the emotions on the bridge, the withdrawing within everyone from any sense of connection or trust in the spider-wolves. The Bubs. Any species that would routinely employ such weapons...

"Hold on." General Charban had stepped forward as well, his intent gaze on the bridge displays. "What tactics would the spider-wolves use? Am I right, Admiral, that their ships here could simply withdraw toward a jump point, then leave as the mine was detonated to destroy all enemies in the star system behind them?"

Geary met Desjani's eyes and saw the agreement there. "Yes. The spider-wolf ships are fast enough to make that tactic work against any enemy we know of."

"Then, if we hadn't been there at Honor," Charban continued, "the spider-wolves could have done that. They didn't need to fight the bear-cows. They could have gone to a jump point and waited until the bear-cows either got too far away from any other jump point to escape the blast, or the bear-cows gave up and went home. But the spider-wolves didn't do that. They stayed and fought because we were there. They assisted us and took losses even though their own tactics wouldn't have risked any of their ships or people."

"You're right." Geary had been feeling a growing horror of the spider-wolves for using such weapons, but Charban's idea countered that. "They chose to help us fight the bear-cows. Hell, they could have withdrawn and wiped out all of us, humans and bear-cows."

Desjani blew out a long breath. "I am really glad I didn't realize that at the time. Things were interesting enough as it was while we were fighting the Kicks."

Low, harsh laughter came from Rione. "I have been worried. I have been concerned about what the Syndicate Worlds' government might do. Would they try to launch attacks on the spider-wolves? I do not think I have to worry anymore."

"Not about what might happen to the spider-wolves," Geary agreed. "But we still have to worry. These defenses, and the fact that they've been used more than once, argue that the enigma presence at Hua is very strong."

Desjani pointed ahead. "Our escort is heading straight for the jump point to Hua. They don't seem to be worried."

"Good for them." Geary gave the orders to his fleet to follow in the wake of the six spider-wolf ships.

It took three days to cross almost the full width of the star system and reach the jump point for Hua, three days spent viewing the awful aftermath of repeated subnova bursts of energy from the spider-wolf mines. Repair and resupply work went on within and among the human warships, but with a somber determination rendered grim by the devastated star system around them. Shuttles crisscrossed through the fleet, bearing fuel cells, parts, weapons, and personnel.

"The stocks of raw materials on all of my auxiliaries are growing very low," Captain Smythe reported. "There aren't a lot of loose asteroids in this star system, so restocking with local resources isn't much of an option."

"I don't think we would want raw materials from here in any event," Geary said. Fleet tracking systems had identified quite a few distant asteroids that must have once orbited this star but had been blown outward by the repeated mine detonations and were now dispersing into the dark between stars. Some of those asteroids might once have been moons about the surviving planets. The smaller asteroids must have been pulverized into dust by the same explosions. "Captain Smythe, we're getting close to Midway. We can get new supplies there. Until then, I am actually grateful that your auxiliaries are carrying a lot less mass. That will make them relatively more nimble if we face a fight at Hua or Pele or Midway."

"No one really uses the words 'nimble' and 'auxiliaries' in the same sentence," Smythe pointed out. "Admiral, my reports have listed the steady decline in raw materials stockpiles on the auxiliaries. I know you have been kept aware of that. However, I must insist now on pointing out how perilously low levels of raw materials have become. According to my projections, *Witch* will run out of critical materials before we reach the jump point for Hua. Her personnel can still make repairs using what parts they have, but they will be unable to manufacture new components or new fuel cells or weapons. By the time we reach Pele, assuming we charge right through Hua, *Jinn*, *Alchemist*, and *Cyclops* will also be out of critical materials, and stockpiles on *Titan*, *Tanuki*, *Kupua*, and *Domovoi* will be within days of exhaustion."

"Captain Smythe, I appreciate the seriousness of the supply situation," Geary said. "I do not believe that we will have any prospect of getting raw materials at Hua. The enigma presence there will make that star system too perilous for mining operations. If we weren't heading for Midway as quickly as feasible, then I would agree to stop at Pele in order to mine asteroids for more raw materials. But speed is of the essence now. We need to get to Midway in time to prevent the enigmas from devastating that star system."

"That's your call, Admiral," Captain Smythe said, his customary cheery nature markedly subdued. "I have done my duty by ensuring that you know the consequences of your decision."

"Thank you, Captain. Your engineers have done a remarkable job. I will be having a fleet conference this afternoon and will ensure that everyone is aware of the state of your supplies."

Geary sat, looking at nothing for a while after Captain Smythe's image departed. Being forced to acquire raw materials from Syndic sources, to acquire *anything* from Syndic sources, was a bad position to be in. The only good thing about it was that the Syndic CEO he had dealt with at Midway had given the impression of being… he couldn't say trustworthy, not when it came to a Syndic CEO. That would be ridiculous. But CEO Gwen Iceni had struck him as pragmatic enough to know how important good relations were and how important his fleet would be to the safety of her star system.

Though if the fleet got to Midway too late after the enigmas did, there might well be no Syndics at all left there to deal with.

14

"We have to be prepared to fight our way through Hua," Geary said to the assembled ship commanding officers of his fleet.

They looked back at him, some determined, some resigned at the prospect, none of them looking enthusiastic.

Captain Badaya had a dissatisfied expression as he glowered at the star display above the conference table. "Why can't the Bu— the spider-wolves tell us anything about the enigma defenses at Hua?" He turned his scowl, now accusing, toward where Emissary Rione and General Charban sat.

Rione gave Badaya back a look of bland authority. "It can be very challenging for humans to comprehend the meanings of even other humans who have different perspectives and experiences. Such as, say, military and civilians. We are still trying to establish basic concepts in communicating with the spider-wolves. We are far from their being able to enumerate information that specific."

"Captain Badaya," Charban said, his own tones using the familiar delivery of one officer speaking to another to subtly emphasize his comradeship with the military here, "if my assessments of the military nature of the spider-wolves are correct, they are not an aggressive species. Anyone who attacks them will quickly learn the error of their ways, as we can see from the state of this star system, which they use as a defensive barrier; but I am confident that they do not attack. That would mean that the enigmas, who have much more extensive experience with the spider-wolves than we do, would not feel the need for massive defenses at Hua. The enigmas would know that such defenses would be superfluous."

"They might have just picket forces?" Captain Bradamont suggested. "Sentries? Like lions facing off against sharks. The lions would know that if they go into the shark environment, they're going to get chewed up, but they wouldn't worry much about the sharks coming after them."

"They would still need some defenses," Captain Tulev pointed out. "Perhaps not major defenses, but something. Defenses are many times driven by perception of threat, not the reality, and we know that the enigmas personify the concept of paranoia."

Geary nodded. "We're assuming something in the way of strong defenses, but not something too tough for us to handle."

Captain Duellos was eyeing the display. "If our assessments are right, and the enigmas are sending a strong strike force against the Syndic-controlled star Midway, then they will have collected available ships for that mission. We should not encounter much in the way of enigma warships at Hua."

"Yes," Badaya agreed. "*If* the enigma fleet is on its way to Midway, it won't be waiting for us at Hua. But it would still be nice to know," he added with forced sarcasm and another glare toward Rione, "at least whether or not the enigmas had a hypernet gate at Hua!"

Charban shook his head. "The spider-wolves either won't or can't tell us that."

"As I told you earlier," Geary said, "the six spider-wolf ships with us will not aid in any action against the enigmas. They might consider providing that kind of information as being such aid. But that leaves us in no worse shape than we were when we sailed through enigma territory the first time. We'll arrive at Hua, see what's there, and head for Pele. We will plan an automated evasive maneuver for the fleet to use at Hua just in case the enigmas have a conventional minefield in place there."

Commander Neeson rapped his hand on the table as a thought struck him, the software obligingly adding in the sound even though he had actually hit a table on his own ship. "The enigmas have faster-than-light comms. When we go through Hua, they can warn their attack force headed for Midway that we're coming."

Badaya shrugged. "So then they'll wait for us at Pele, and we'll beat them there."

"If the enigmas want to fight at Pele, we'll fight them there," Geary agreed. "There's nothing we can do about the enigma ability to warn their attack force that we're on the way, but that does emphasize the need for us to move as fast as we can to get to Midway."

"Admiral," Captain Jane Geary said, "if we detached the captured superbattleship, we could make more speed."

Admiral Lagemann had been invited to the meeting this time, and many officers looked toward him, while others looked toward Geary.

"My ship is a pig," Lagemann agreed. "The engineers are not

ready to risk powering up the cores yet, and the main propulsion units are mangled, so we couldn't move even if we did have power. But we can defend ourselves if anyone tries to board us."

"Not very well," General Carabali objected. "You only have a company of Marines aboard. I'd like to at least double that."

"The temporary life support we rigged on the BKS can't handle that many extra bodies," Captain Smythe objected.

"Can your engineers add more life-support capability?" Geary asked.

"They could. I'd have to haul them off other high-priority tasks to do that."

"*My* engineers," Carabali said, "can break out portable landing-force life-support gear intended for operations on hostile surfaces. That can take care of the extra requirements."

Smythe frowned in thought. "Can I see the specifications on that gear, General? I don't doubt your assessment, but I'd like to know what we have in place."

"You wouldn't object, then?" Geary said.

"To using Marine equipment? No, Admiral. It's designed to be compatible with fleet equipment, and General Carabali's combat engineers know their trade."

"It's nice to hear a fleet engineer admit that," Carabali said. "If you approve this, Admiral, we'll have it done before the fleet leaves this star system. The captured ship will have embarked two companies of Marines reinforced with some heavy-weapons detachments. No one will take that ship from us without a very stiff fight and a very powerful boarding force."

Commander Shen looked slightly more dissatisfied than usual.

"I don't object to the idea of reinforcing the Marines aboard the captured ship, but anyone trying to land such a boarding force will face a very stiff fight before they get there. *Orion* and her sister ships will not be easily overcome."

"I for one will feel very secure with eight battleships and two companies of Marines between me and any threat," Admiral Lagemann commented. "And, of course, that superbattleship's armor will be between my prize crew and any threat as well."

"Good. Let's get that done," Geary ordered.

Jane Geary leaned forward. "Does that mean we're detaching that ship under escort?"

"No," Geary said firmly, "or at least not yet. That captured ship is of immense value. I'd have to detach half of the fleet to escort it, and until I have a better idea of what the enigmas have available in terms of warships, and whether we're going to meet them at Pele, I don't want to split the fleet."

"Not before we make it through Hua," Tulev agreed.

Geary was about to end the meeting when Desjani leaned close to him. "Ask Roberto Duellos to stay. You should talk with him."

He covered his surprise, nodding in reply, then gestured to Duellos to stand by before nodding to the rest of his ship commanders. "That is all. We'll be ready for a fight wherever the enigmas try to meet us."

Images of officers disappeared in a flurry, the apparent size of the compartment dwindling with each departure so that for a moment the illusion of contracting bulkheads actually felt threatening.

Rione and Charban, who, like Desjani, had been physically present, stood up, both wearing resigned expressions. "We'll get in touch with the spider-wolves again. Back to trying to understand strange ways of thinking," Charban commented.

"If you want to go into politics," Rione replied, "you have to get used to that. But it does get old at times. If you will excuse us, Admiral."

Desjani waited until they had left, and only she, Geary, and the virtual presence of Duellos remained. "I think you boys need a play-date."

"Excuse me?" Geary said.

"You've been talking to me a lot. A certain fleet commander should share his worries with someone besides a certain battle cruiser captain to ensure he gets more than one point of view. You know that Captain Duellos can be trusted with anything. And, Roberto, you've been talking to me about what's eating at you since you came back from leave, and I've been telling you to talk to Jack a bit. For the love of your ancestors, listen to me this time."

"Jack?" Duellos asked.

"You know who I mean. The *admiral*," Desjani added, giving comic emphasis to the rank. "Now excuse me so you can talk about me, too, if you need to."

Duellos grinned and bowed to her as Desjani left. "What did you do to deserve her?"

"I don't deserve her," Geary said. "I guess you and I have our orders."

"I have often thought that admirals should have a voice at hand ready and willing to inform them of their own fallibility," Duellos said. "In Tanya, you actually have such a voice."

"Which," Geary said, "sometimes gets pretty forceful when I

don't listen to her. What is Tanya worried about?"

"You and me, I suppose." Duellos turned to look back toward where the images of the other officers had sat. "And Jane Geary, though that one won't talk. She still appears to be champing at the bit for glory, however."

"I've noticed. Believe me." Geary sat down and gestured Duellos to a seat. "Relax. I guess this is a personal counseling session even though neither one of us requested it."

"That's what friends are for." Duellos sighed as he sat down, somehow looking older than Geary remembered from the last time he had seen him, a few days before.

"What's the matter?" Geary asked. "We're heading home."

"And I should be as happy as everyone else." Duellos shrugged, his expression reflecting uncertainty. "I went home during our brief period of celebration after the war. It felt odd."

"Odd?"

"You haven't been home to Glenlyon."

"No. You know what that would be like. Kosatka was bad enough."

Duellos nodded. "The hero out of legend coming home. I confess I went home not only expecting to have my family rejoicing but expecting to hear praise for all the fleet had done. 'Good job, Roberto.' That sort of thing. Nothing effusive. Just 'good job.' But the mood was very different, Admiral. Very different."

"I don't understand," Geary said.

"It's over." Duellos paused, thinking. "That's how it felt. It's over. Not, hurrah we won! Not, welcome the heroes home! But, it's over. There's a big training base on Catalan. It can handle twenty thousand inductees at a time. For the last century, Fort Cinque has taught countless draftees how to march and obey orders, with varying degrees of success. I went by it, Admiral. It was closed."

"They are shutting it down?" Geary asked, thinking that such a move made sense.

"No. What they did the day after they heard the war was over was to simply give every draftee there a ticket home. They hustled them out the gate that same day, then the instructors and the guards and the maintenance workers and everyone else followed, and before sunset the base commander left last and locked the gate behind him." Duellos looked at Geary, his expression hard to read. "For a century, tens of thousands of men and women went through that fort. It was a part of their lives, a part of history. And the day after they knew the war was over, it was simply shut down."

"Is that what they are doing with everything?" Geary asked.

"Pretty much. Bases being shut down everywhere, local defense forces mustered out as fast as the paperwork can go through, military-related contracts being canceled, equipment being mothballed or simply scrapped. It's not so much a demobilization or a downsizing of the military effort as it is a dismantling of everything." Duellos smiled bitterly. "We went to some gatherings, my wife and I. And those we met didn't ask what I'd done. They asked if I'd seen you. But otherwise they just said, 'What will you do now?' Now that the war was over, and fleet officers aren't needed."

Geary remembered the special forces troops he had met on Umbaru Station at Varandal, themselves wondering what they would do now that special forces troops weren't needed in anything like the numbers once required. It would have been different if the war had been much shorter, five or even ten years. Not long enough to have become a way of life for those engaged in it. But as Duellos had said, these were people whose entire lives had been about the war. "What do you want to do?"

"I don't know," Duellos said. "I'm a fleet officer. It's what I grew up expecting to be. It's all I've ever done. I expected to die at some distant star, battling the Syndics, or perhaps at some Alliance border star system, throwing back a Syndic offensive. If by some miracle I survived long enough to retire, I would go home and watch more men and women go off to war. It's been that way for a century. I didn't expect it to ever end. We had all stopped believing that it would ever end. But it did end." He raised a hand, fingers curled as if he held a glass, in a toast and salute to Geary. "And now they don't want fleet officers."

"Not as many fleet officers," Geary said, "but the need—"

"No, Admiral. They don't *want* fleet officers. They are sick of war, of sending off their young men and women to disappear into the maw of war, of broken bodies coming home, of the wealth of their world being consumed by war." Duellos shrugged again. "How can I blame them? And yet, now so many of us who always had a purpose no longer have that purpose."

What could he say? Geary looked down for a while, trying to find words, then back at Duellos. "How does your wife feel?"

"Grateful that I came home alive. Grateful that no more of our children will be sent off to die in an endless war. Perplexed at the melancholy with which I confronted a world changed beyond recognition, a world in which what I am became obsolete in the blink of an eye." Duellos shook his head, gloom showing. "It's been wearing on me. Peace is good. The cost of war is so terrible. But I know nothing of peace. I've been molded for war. I hate war. I hate the death, I hate knowing more will die, I hate being away from those I love, but... but it is what I know. Everyone back home wishes to put it all behind them as fast as possible, to forget it happened, but when they forget the awful things, they also forget the sacrifices, the deeds done by those they sent off to fight. They don't want to hear about that now. And I simply don't know what I am supposed to be now that what I am has ceased to be wanted."

Geary looked away, trying to think of what to say. "I'm sorry."

"It's not your fault, Admiral," Duellos said. "You did what you should do. You did what legend said you would." He paused and looked closely at Geary. "But the legend never said what Black Jack would do after he saved the day, did it?"

"I don't know. I never wanted to hear about the legend."

"Tanya and I have talked about it. It's something we never realized even though we grew up being told that legend. It never had a 'happily ever after' or anything like that. Black Jack would save us, then..." Duellos looked at Geary again. "It doesn't say. The story just ends. Now we face the reality. Is there still a need for Black Jack? How many people still want Black Jack?"

"I don't exactly want to be Black Jack, remember?" Geary replied. "And you know about the popular movements to make me run things back home, to take over the government and 'fix' it, whatever that means, or somehow miraculously root out all of the corruption and misdeeds that plague any form of government. People want that."

"Do they?" Duellos asked. "They say that, but what if you were actually given those tasks? How long would it take for the hero to develop feet of clay?"

"The hero has always had feet of clay," Geary replied. "It would be a relief for me if people stopped thinking I should step in and save the day. It wouldn't break my heart to just… just…"

He paused to order his thoughts. *To just what?*

"Roberto," Geary said slowly, "you know I wasn't thrilled to have to assume command of the fleet back when it was trapped by the Syndics. You know that I never liked the Black Jack legend. For some time, I consoled myself by thinking that I would get the fleet home, then I would go somewhere and… hide. Just go away, to somewhere where no one had ever heard of Black Jack. Winning the war wasn't my job just because the government had dreamed up some stupid myth about me being the hero to end all heroes."

"But you changed your mind," Duellos said, pretending to be examining the imaginary wine in the imaginary wineglass he was still pretending to hold.

"Tanya made me realize that I couldn't do that." Geary sat looking glumly downward for a moment. "I knew it couldn't happen. I had a job to do. But the government never really wanted Black Jack. You know that. They wanted the legend to help inspire the fleet and the people of the Alliance. But they didn't want a real person. Ever since I stepped into that legend, I've been someone that the people who created the legend want to get rid of."

Duellos eyed Geary, then actually pretended to set down the wineglass before leaning forward. "And here we are, you and me and a lot of other people who aren't needed or wanted anymore. What a coincidence that we should be sent deep into territory unknown to the human race, on a mission whose level of danger was very literally unable to be calculated."

"Yes. Isn't that a coincidence." Geary felt his lips pressing into a single tight line. "There's something I've been wanting to talk about."

"So Tanya advised me. Something about the government?"

"Among other things. Fleet headquarters. Hidden agendas. Plots. Plans. Hidden construction of new warships. And maybe other things, too." Geary blew out a long breath as he ordered his thoughts. "Let me tell you what I know, what are facts, and what I suspect."

"Fair enough." From somewhere in his own stateroom, Duellos had produced an actual wineglass and now took an appreciative sip. "Fact one?"

"Fact one. The Alliance government and fleet headquarters tried to makes us leave for this mission too quickly, before we were as fully supplied and ready as I wanted. I understand that sort of nonsense goes on all the time. Hurry up and wait. Do nothing for six months, then get told it all has to be done in a week. That's normal. This didn't feel normal."

"Everyone noticed," Duellos commented. "We know all too well the feeling of being rushed into action. It was one thing to do so when the Syndics were knocking at the door, and another to have that same crisis-mode preparation when no crisis was known to exist. But you were in command, so we accepted that something required such urgency." He took another sip of wine. "Fact two?"

"Fact two," Geary said. "At the last minute, and I do mean literally at almost the last minute, fleet headquarters tried to yank the majority of our auxiliary force capability out from under us. *Titan, Tanuki, Kupua*, and *Domovoi*. What shape would we now be in if all we had were the four smaller auxiliaries?"

"Not good," Duellos said. "How did we dodge that bullet? Did you simply disregard the order?"

"No. Admiral Timbale pointed out that the order was sent contrary to standard protocols and therefore required clarification. He sent off the request for clarification, and I took off with the four auxiliaries in question."

"It is important to do things properly," Duellos agreed. "Fact three?"

"Fact three. We were all told, I was personally told several times, that new construction of warships had been halted to save money. But there's substantial evidence that the government is secretly building a significant number of new warships."

Duellos stopped moving, his eyes on his wineglass, a frown slowly developing. "How strong is this evidence?"

"It's convincing to people who understand such matters." He didn't want to go into detail with Duellos about the evidence uncovered by Lieutenant Jamenson in hundreds of apparently unrelated contracts and reports.

"How many ships?" Duellos asked, skepticism clear.

"Twenty battleships, twenty battle cruisers, and an appropriate number of cruisers and destroyers to serve as escorts."

The pause this time was much longer before Duellos spoke. "I can see," he began, "why the government would want to keep that hidden from a war-weary public, but why mislead you on the matter?"

"That's a very good question though it may be related to fact four. Our warships are facing major life-span issues with their systems. None of them were designed to operate for more than three years."

"That is not a secret to anyone who was present at Honor," Duellos said. "I knew problems have been developing, but that was a real eye-opener."

"For all of us," Geary admitted. "I knew about the problem, I knew it would be getting worse before it got better, but I wasn't prepared for that sudden cascade of failures at Honor. We may face something similar at Midway, though Captain Smythe thinks the stress on our systems at Honor blew out everything close to failure, so we'll now have a period of relative reliability. Still, even with everything our auxiliaries can do, we're slowly losing ground on readiness." Should he tell Duellos the next thing?

"There's more," Duellos said with calm assurance.

"There is." Geary smiled ruefully. "Everyone tells me that I'm a lousy liar."

"You are. You're horrible at it. It's one of your more commendable features."

"All right, then. Those new ships that are being built? We have reason to suspect that they're being built to much higher standards than these ships were."

"Not implausible," Duellos said. "In fact, it is what one would expect if our ships were built to be expendable in wartime and these new ships are built to last a long time as part of a peacetime fleet. But… it does imply that people in authority know that you would face a serious and growing problem with reliability among your fleet. Is there a fact five?"

"There is." Geary waved toward the star display. "We were sent on a mission into unknown regions against a foe of unknown strength, yet specifically ordered to find the extent of the territory occupied by the aliens even though that could have been much more distant than it has proven to be."

"Using a fleet that authorities knew would be suffering escalating problems with the reliability of its systems," Duellos said. "And one from which fleet headquarters tried to yank half of your auxiliaries. This isn't forming a particularly pleasant picture."

"It gets worse. Fact six. On the way to that mission, we were diverted, engaged in a major distraction liberating the POWs at Dunai. Fact seven. Rione was ordered to stay on the same ship with me and Tanya even though those issuing those orders must have known how disruptive that could easily have been."

"Another distraction."

"Fact eight. The enigmas could easily have isolated us on the far side of Syndic space by collapsing the entire Syndic hypernet. We could still have made it home, but it would have taken a lot longer. We didn't think of that. Some of the Syndics did, though. That's why I traded with the authorities at Midway for the Syndic-developed fix that will protect a hypernet from being collapsed by remote command."

Duellos's eyes had narrowed, his expression hardening. "And someone on our side may have thought of it also?"

"Fact nine," Geary said. "Fleet headquarters also tried to yank everyone in this fleet with theoretical knowledge of the hypernet."

"Someone did think of it."

"It's hard to assume otherwise, isn't it?" Geary agreed. "Fact ten. Victoria Rione has not been acting normally."

"In all seriousness," Duellos said, "I would be hard put to know what 'acting normally' is for that Rione woman."

"Has Tanya been talking to you about her, too?"

"Constantly. At least I assume 'that woman' is Rione."

"Did Tanya tell you that Rione finally admitted to having secret orders? From a source or sources that Rione still can't name?"

"According to Tanya," Duellos said judiciously, "'that woman' is a greater threat to this fleet and the Alliance than the enigmas, the Kicks, and everything left to the Syndicate Worlds. But I have seen that former senator, former vice president of the Callas Republic, and current Emissary of the Alliance Victoria Rione has done us services in the past, and I do not underrate her intelligence. Why would she accept such orders?"

"Blackmail."

"Concerning you?" Duellos asked.

"No. That's no secret, and the relationship that Rione and I briefly had, not knowing her husband was still alive, is something that could only reflect on her honor."

"Someone else's honor then?" Duellos nodded. "I've heard a few things about Commander Benan from Tanya as well. There are some secrets there that Tanya would not share with even me."

"Unfortunately, that's true. The point is, someone wanted to force Rione to accompany this fleet and to take certain actions. I don't know, but firmly believe, that Rione has refrained from doing anything that would have harmed this fleet while technically adhering to the terms of those secret orders."

Duellos nodded again, his eyes on his wine. "Are there more facts?"

"No, just suppositions."

"Let me guess." Duellos's gaze went to the star display. "Someone wished this fleet, of questionable loyalty to the government, to be lost again. As well as the hero from the past, who had the bad form to show up alive. With the Syndicate Worlds falling apart and a formal peace in place, the Alliance no longer needs either and is building a new fleet already to defend itself. It will crew those ships with men and women who have not been under the personal command of Black Jack and therefore have no personal loyalty to him, and give the command of the new ships to some officer whose loyalty to the government is unquestioned."

"Not quite," Geary said. "Rione has dropped hints that this isn't some monolithic conspiracy, that in fact different factions are maneuvering to do different things, some of which ended up pushing me and this fleet in this direction."

"The practical difference being?"

"Some of those factions, some of those individuals, may be pursuing agendas in which loyalty to them is more important than loyalty to the government."

Duellos stopped moving, nothing showing on his face now, but his eyes focused on some train of thought. "You told me," he finally said, "that when you have met with the grand council of the Alliance, some of the senators appeared to be openly hostile to you, while others appeared to be working more subtly."

"And some appeared to be honest and dedicated," Geary said. "Senator Navarro, for example. But as Victoria Rione said, Senator Navarro has been worn-out by his former duties as head of the council and attacks by political enemies. I don't trust Senator Suva at all, and I know she played a role in our orders to go on this mission. I still don't know what cards Senator Sakai is playing. Those are just three examples."

"Factions," Duellos mused. "You know, the bits about pulling the auxiliaries from the fleet and trying to strip you of anyone with knowledge of how the hypernet works could just be the usual bureaucratic stupidity. The orders could have originated from different sources, both acting as regulations or 'the needs of the fleet' demanded in their tunnel-vision eyes. We are, after all, talking about fleet headquarters, an organization not famed for its ability to coordinate even within itself. As the old saying goes, never attribute to malice that which could be explained by stupidity. I wonder who first said that?"

"That has occurred to me," Geary admitted. "Under normal circumstances it's easy enough to think that the military bureaucracy is gunning for you, and these are worse than normal circumstances."

"Exactly. You've also seen enough of the sort of minds that inhabit the higher ranks at fleet headquarters. Many of them got to those positions by focusing their careers on advancement. People like you who have advanced by actually accomplishing things are a threat to those whose résumés are all about ticket-punching. They would seek to trip you up out of general principles even if no plot existed. Rush you out the door, deny you time to prepare... why, you might fail in your assigned mission, and wouldn't that be awful for those who see themselves as your rivals? Even if you didn't fail, at the very least your life would be made more difficult, and that would be some reward to those of vast egos and small minds."

Duellos thought again. "The new ships. Again, that makes sense. These ships have seen much hard use and, as you mentioned, were not designed for long service lives. It is not hard to see why new ones would not be built to provide an enduring defense for the Alliance. Indeed, you could argue that is the responsible course of action."

"You could," Geary admitted. "Why keep it secret?"

"If you assume the whole process has no dark undertones? Because, as we discussed earlier, for the average taxpayer in the Alliance, military expenditures have become that-which-shall-not-be-done. But even corruption could be relatively routine. Construction contracts for favored individuals, kickbacks to politicians from suppliers, bribes, all the usual." Duellos sat quiet, brooding.

"Do you think that's all that's involved?" Geary pressed.

"I think it is for some. If we are dealing with many different factions, many different individuals, then we are dealing with different motivations. Some may have approved the contracts and the secrecy out of nothing more than recognition that this was necessary for the defense of the Alliance and had to be done in a politically viable way. Others may have been motivated by greed. And others…" Duellos glanced at Geary. "Who gets command of these new ships? That will tell us much. Some officers, such as the late and mostly unlamented Admiral Bloch, were known to have political ambitions."

"He wanted to stage a coup!"

"Yes." Duellos shrugged. "We simply don't know enough. But when someone is named to command that new fleet, the identity of that officer will tell us a great deal, as will how they justify—" He stopped speaking abruptly, his mouth tightening.

"Justify what?" Geary asked.

Duellos fixed his eyes on Geary. "Justify not giving you that command. You are the best fleet combat commander the Alliance possesses by far. Your popular acclaim, your standing among the populace, is far higher than those of any other officer. How do they justify not giving you those ships?"

"You seem to have thought of an answer."

"I have. If Admiral Geary is not there, Admiral Geary cannot be given the command."

Geary sat back, raising hands clenched in frustration. "'Not there' can have a lot of possible reasons behind it."

"It can. But those who differ in their reasons for wanting Admiral Geary to not be there can agree on wanting him not to be there." Duellos nodded with satisfaction. "That is how I read this situation. Not a colossal conspiracy working surely to one end, but various parties with various agendas, many of which converged to send this fleet on this mission in this manner. It's not you against the government."

"Thank you," Geary said. "I've been wanting to come to that conclusion myself, but because I wanted it I distrusted my thinking. But you came to the same results I have. There are people out there trying to create trouble for me, and other people trying to pursue personal agendas of power or money, and some who are actually working toward the common good but might be tricked into supporting actions that further other goals. Now, how can I help you with your concerns?"

"There's no help for my angst," Duellos said. "I no longer belong where I once called home. I'll have to adjust."

"You'll always have a home in any force I command," Geary said.

"You have my thanks." Duellos stood and saluted solemnly. "Though not, perhaps, the thanks of my wife. I will return to duty now, Admiral."

After Duellos had left, Geary sat looking at the star display. *Not me against the government. But what if the government changes? What if some of the people Rione has warned me against move to take control, using some pretext or even claiming my backing to keep the people of the Alliance quiet?*

But then it won't be the government. Not really. Certainly not a government of the people of the Alliance.

How many people would see that and understand my actions if that happens?

He had been reading a bit more about that ancient place called Rome, on Old Earth, and what had happened when military leaders declared themselves rulers of that land, always justifying it with claims of incompetence or corruption or weakness on the part of the government. Sometimes those claims had been true. But, true or false, each time the legions marched, the government became less about the Senate and people of Rome and more about the leaders whose power rested on the sharpness of their swords. He could not let that happen to the Alliance.

15

It's just another star occupied by the enigmas, Geary told himself as the last minutes went by before they left jump to arrive at Hua. *We've gotten through any number of those, even when the enigmas knew we were coming. We'll get through this one.*

"At least the enigmas should be totally surprised at seeing us show up at Hua," Desjani commented in unconscious echo of Geary's thoughts. "They're probably still congratulating themselves over our imagined annihilation in Kick territory. You know there's going to be a hypernet gate here, right?"

"Yeah, I know that." It was a border star system for the enigmas, and as far as they could tell, the enigmas used the gates themselves as defensive weapons instead of crafting the same sort of mechanisms into supermines as the spider-wolves did.

His mind fuzzed as *Dauntless* left jump, the Alliance warships twisting in the preplanned evasion straight off to one side. But as Geary's mind cleared, he noticed the lack of immediate danger warnings from the sensor systems and saw his display remain comfortingly clear of any sign of minefields or enigma warships near the jump point.

"There it is," Desjani said. A hypernet gate, hanging menacingly three light-hours off to the side opposite where the fleet had turned. "Good choice on the direction we turned, Admiral."

"Thanks." Where were the jump points?

Then he realized that he didn't have to wait for the fleet's sensors to identify those locales in space. Just ahead of the fleet, the six spider-wolf ships were leaping forward, accelerating toward a point off to starboard. He gave the necessary orders to his fleet to move in the wake of their alien allies, increasing velocity as well to match their increase in speed. "Let's follow the spider-wolves."

"Did you ever expect to say that?" Desjani was eyeing her display. "Fixed defenses scattered around… space docks here and there… that looks like a big orbiting military base… warships here, here, and here."

"Definitely enigma warships," Geary agreed. There were only five of them, all showing the squat, turtlelike shapes that the enigmas used for warships, though in size they varied from human destroyers to something larger than a heavy cruiser but much smaller than a battleship.

"Except for that damned hypernet gate," Desjani concluded, "it's not nearly as many defenses as I would have expected for a star system facing an opponent like the spider-wolves. General Charban may have been right."

"Captain," Lieutenant Yuon called, "there appear to be substantial docking facilities for military ships in this star system. It looks like they normally have a lot more warships here."

Desjani nodded. "Good assessment, Lieutenant. They've stripped out the defensive forces here to help equip an attack force." She looked over at Geary. "And we know where that attack force is probably going. It must have looked like a real safe bet to the enigmas to draw down the defenses at Hua long enough to trash Midway. We're supposed to be dead meat at the hands of the Kicks, with maybe some torn-up remnants far away from here trying to limp home, and the spider-wolves don't bother their neighbors as long as their neighbors leave them alone."

"When things look that good, you always have to wonder what you've missed," Geary agreed. "And the enigmas missed the fact that we might not fulfill our assigned role in their plan."

"The hypernet gate is three light-hours behind us now," Desjani pointed out. "The main military facility is four and a half light-hours off to port, a lot closer to the star. How far away is that jump point?"

It took several more seconds before the displays popped up that information.

"One and three-quarters light-hours," Desjani said, the fingers of one hand flying as she ran the data through the fleet's maneuvering systems. "If we keep trying to match the speed of the spider-wolves, that means reaching point one five light speed before braking and... fifteen hours transit time."

The geometry was simple enough. In no more than four and a half hours, the enigmas at the main military base would learn of the human fleet's arrival. If one of the enigma warships used its faster-than-light comms before then, that margin of safety might be whittled down to two hours. If the main base sent a collapse command to the hypernet gate, it would take almost five and a half hours to reach the gate, then the resulting blast more than another three hours to reach the fleet as it moved away from the gate. "Thirteen hours before they could hit us."

"Make that as little as ten hours if any of those warships report in via faster-than-light comms," Desjani warned.

Geary looked over the star system as the fleet's sensors continued to fill in details. Not wealthy or heavily populated with planets but a reasonably well-off star system. One planet had the veiled cities and towns of the enigmas straddling the borders of land and some impressive oceans. "We don't have any idea what level of detail their faster-than-light comms can provide. Would they blow this away without confirming whatever their ship reported? Especially if they saw us heading straight for a jump point out of here instead of lingering at all or heading for somewhere within the star system?"

"Using human logic hasn't always worked well when it comes to enigmas," Desjani pointed out.

"Granted. But we know that the number of star systems available to them is limited because they've got us on one border, the bear-cows on another, and the spider-wolves facing them elsewhere. And in our travels through their space, we didn't find any enigma star systems that had suffered through the collapse of a gate. They can't be authorized to blow up star systems unless as a last resort."

A vulnerability period of anywhere from two to five hours. But nothing could be done about that except what he was already doing, getting to that next jump point and getting out of here as fast as the fleet could manage it.

He hadn't slept well in the day before they arrived, and now nothing could happen to threaten the fleet for hours. "Captain Desjani, I am going down to my stateroom to get some rest. I encourage you to stand down your crew for the next few hours as well."

Desjani frowned at him, pretending to be unaware of the desperate efforts of every crew member within sight to avoid looking hopeful. "Let my crew rest?"

"If you're comfortable with that." He knew how hard they had been working to get every system ready for arrival here, testing and repairing and tweaking to bring *Dauntless* to the highest possible combat readiness.

"Yes, Admiral, I am. They earned it. All hands, this is the Captain. Stand down from normal work routine for three hours. Normal workday routine is to resume at the end of that time." She released the general announcing system control and winked at Geary in such a way that no one else could see. "Enjoy your rest, Admiral. I'll be keeping an eye on things."

"Tanya, you should—"

"I got plenty of rest last night."

She was probably exaggerating wildly when she said "plenty," but he couldn't very well call her a liar in front of her crew.

He was actually back on the bridge after only two hours, noticing as he traveled from his stateroom that numerous members of the crew had also drifted back to duty stations earlier than required.

"What do you suppose they're thinking?" Desjani asked. "The enigmas, I mean. We show up here with six spider-wolf ships along for the ride, and towing a Kick superbattleship that's obviously seen better days."

"What I hope," Geary replied, "is that the enigmas are seeing we have new allies and that we not only beat the Kicks but acquired a very impressive souvenir from them." He wondered for a moment by what name the enigmas called the Kicks. "Either one of those things might have influenced the enigmas to seriously negotiate with us. Taken together, maybe they'll be enough to convince the enigmas not to mess with us anymore."

"It doesn't sound like you believe that, though," Desjani commented, sitting back in her seat, her eyes on her display.

"No." Geary felt the old sense of futility. "General Charban thinks the enigmas will have to be beaten badly at least one more time in order to get across that they can't defeat us militarily."

"How did that ground-forces general get so good at figuring out how alien species think?"

"I have no idea. And, yet, he's single," Geary couldn't help adding.

Desjani didn't turn her head, just cutting him a look from the corners of her eyes. "Women are not an alien species."

"Did I say that? Is anything important happening?"

"Aside from an admiral skating on thin ice? No. You would have been informed, sir." She indicated one of the enigma warships. "This guy is closest to us. He will see us first, anytime now, as a matter of fact, and when we see his reaction in a few hours, it may give us some indication of what the enigmas are going to do."

Geary rubbed his lower face with one hand, wishing he had some more definitive and timely information. *You would think I would be used to this kind of time lag in information by now.* He tapped an internal comm circuit. "Emissary Rione? General Charban? Have we heard anything from the spider-wolves?"

Dr. Shwartz answered. "I'm the only one here at the moment, Admiral. We haven't heard a thing."

"What have we sent them?"

"Upon our arrival here, we sent a message trying to ask the spider-wolves what they would do. It's still hard to format the pictograms and other symbols in ways that we know get across anything but the simplest concepts. About an hour ago, we sent another message, asking them if they knew what the enigmas would do. We asked them that before we left spider-wolf space, of course, but they didn't answer us then. We thought it wouldn't hurt to repeat the question."

"Not too friendly," Geary muttered.

Dr. Shwartz must have heard. "We don't know that we're getting across the right question, and we don't know their social protocols. If you ask a human something, and they don't know the answer, the polite thing for them to do is say, 'I don't know,' or something like that. For spider-wolves, the polite thing might be to say nothing if you can't provide a meaningful answer."

"But we don't know if that's how they do things."

"No, Admiral, we don't know." Dr. Shwartz shook her head ruefully. "It's much easier dealing with imaginary aliens. They somehow always come around to acting the way you want them to act. That's what all of us 'experts' found during our careers prior to this, that is.

"But the enigmas, the bear-cows, and the spider-wolves persist in doing things that don't fit the molds we're trying to create for them. Some of my colleagues are having a great deal of trouble with that. They keep trying to make the aliens fit the mold rather than the mold fit the aliens. I can't blame them for that. It's how we all worked for a long time."

"Do you think that's why General Charban is coming up with some of the insights he's having? Because he's not an expert with a lifetime of trying to figure out how an alien species would think to hinder his ability to see how these aliens really are?"

Shwartz looked startled, then thoughtful. "That is possible, Admiral. Would it be immodest of me to point out that I've also come up with a few insights?"

Geary smiled. "You have indeed, Doctor. I am grateful for your presence with us and will ensure that everyone back in Alliance space knows how much you have contributed to our mission."

She laughed. "At which point my colleagues will all develop legendary levels of hatred for me! Have you ever seen the knives come out among academics? I'm not sure that I should thank you. Well, I will. If the government decides to send a delegation to the spider-wolves, I hope my name will be considered as a participant."

"If I have any say in it, you'll be part of such a delegation."

There had still been nothing from the spider-wolves, whose ships had maintained a steady vector aimed at the jump point for Pele, when a reaction from the enigmas could finally be seen. "He's coming around," Desjani said. "Looks like… I'll bet you he's coming to an intercept with us or something a few light-minutes short of an intercept."

"A lookout," Geary said. "Coming to tail us so it can send out faster-than-light status updates and let the enigma bosses in this star system know much quicker what we're doing. The same thing the enigmas did when we went through their star systems earlier."

"That doesn't imply they're going to collapse the gate," Desjani pointed out.

"No. It implies the opposite, that they're going to watch us and make sure we leave as fast as we came."

"So they want us to go to Pele," Desjani added, dumping a cold pail of water over his growing sense of relief.

"If they do, they're going to be sorry when we get there."

The enigma tail was still closing on Geary's fleet when the spider-wolves reached the jump point and vanished. Fifteen minutes later the human warships jumped as well, the star system of Hua disappearing and the nothingness of jump space taking its place.

"Five days," Desjani commented. "Like Neeson said, if they've got a force heading for Midway, the enigmas at Hua will have told them we're on the way."

"I know. Five days." But this time he felt no dread of what might await them at Pele, just an eagerness to come to grips with the last obstacle between this fleet and human space.

They came out of the jump point from Hua with every nerve tense, every weapon ready, waiting to see what awaited them at Pele.

"They're here," Desjani said.

"Not for long," Geary replied.

The enigma flotilla was far off to the right of the Alliance vessels, nearly three light-hours from the place where the human fleet had arrived. The enigmas were heading toward the jump point for Midway at point one six light speed, away from Geary's warships, and were not much more than one hour's travel time away from being able to jump. Because the light from the arrival of the Alliance fleet would not get to them for more than three hours, the aliens would reach that jump point and jump for Midway before they knew the human fleet had arrived at Pele.

Though they might not care if their orders were to get to Midway and do damage before Geary's fleet could catch up.

"Two hundred twenty-two enigma warships," Desjani commented. "I guess that's all they could scrape up."

"Yes, I——" Geary stopped speaking as a memory came to the fore. "Three hundred thirty-three."

"What?"

"Those humans we rescued from the enigma prison asteroid. Their numbers had been kept constant at three hundred thirty-three. And now this enigma force consists of two hundred twenty-two ships."

She looked startled, then shrugged. "So they like repeating numbers."

"Apparently. I wonder why?"

"Does it matter?"

"In terms of understanding them, yes." He saw the disdain Desjani couldn't quite conceal at the idea of bothering to continue trying to understand the enigmas. "Tanya, the more I understand them, the more I can out-think them and predict what they're going to do. That enigma force is going to get to Midway quite a few hours before we can. I would love to be able to know what could divert and distract them once we get to Midway so that we have time to get the enigmas before they do too much damage."

"All right. I'll admit that's a good reason to continue trying to figure them out. But regardless of how they think, how many hours they have at Midway to play with before we show up is partly dependent on what we do." Desjani glanced at him, awaiting Geary's decision.

He knew what she was asking, and also knew that every sailor in the fleet was wondering the same thing right now. Would the fleet continue its pursuit together, slowed by the battleships, auxiliaries, assault transports, and the captured superbattleship? Given the numbers of the enigma warships, that would be the prudent thing to do, keeping all of his firepower at hand. But being prudent might well mean arriving too late for that firepower to make a difference. "Help me set this up, Tanya. I want to split the fleet. All of the battle cruisers, all of the light cruisers, and half of the destroyers in a fast pursuit force, and all of the battleships, heavy cruisers, and the remaining destroyers following on at best speed."

Her grin told him how much Desjani liked that plan before she faced her display, hands and fingers flying to help designate who went where.

Before doing the same, Geary called Captain Armus. "Captain, I'm going to be splitting the fleet and going on ahead with our fastest ships to try to disrupt the enigma attack on Midway. You will be in command of the rest of the fleet, and are to bring it on at the best speed you can manage to catch up with us at Midway. I'm going to need the firepower of those warships with you as soon as you can get them to me, but do not leave the captured superbattleship and the battleships towing it behind. Any questions?"

If Armus had been the sort of person to beam with delight, he would have done so now. Battleship commanders were looked down upon in this fleet as the steady but unremarkable type, with formation command positions almost always going to battle cruiser commanders. Geary had usually been forced to follow that same pattern since he was stuck with the ship commanders he had inherited, which meant that the battle cruiser commanders were more likely to be his best commanders. Unfortunately, some of them had also been among his worst commanders.

But rather than show any sign of celebration at an opportunity battleship commanders rarely received, Armus merely nodded with slow deliberation and then, almost as an afterthought, threw in a salute. "I understand, Admiral. Thank you for your confidence in me."

After the call ended, Desjani gave Geary another glance. "Armus? He and Jane Geary are toss-ups for that assignment in terms of seniority."

"I know." *I also know which one of them I can trust to stay with that superbattleship and its tow ships.*

He didn't say that out loud, but Tanya surely knew he was thinking it. She didn't object or argue, though.

"All units, this is Admiral Geary. I will be dividing the fleet. The fast pursuit force will proceed to Midway to engage the enigmas while the main body of the fleet follows. Formation orders will be going out momentarily."

"Done," Desjani said. "How's yours? Oh, hell, let me finish it."

"I had to talk to people," Geary said defensively.

"Yes. You're the admiral. Now that you've told me and everyone else what to do, let us help you do it."

Maneuvering problems that would have taxed the minds of humans and taken long hours to work out could be done in moments with the assistance of the automated systems. If the person doing the work also had a good intuitive grasp of maneuvering and what could most easily go where, it went even faster.

Desjani had a very good intuitive grasp of maneuvering.

"Check it," she asked him.

He did a quick sanity check of her work, knowing that small problems would be corrected automatically by the fleet's maneuvering systems. In terms of the big picture... "It looks great." Two more taps on the comm system, and the maneuvering orders were flying out to every ship in the fleet.

Geary had specified an oval formation for the pursuit force, with one broad side facing forward, and the designated ships raced to get into position. Lined up along the center were the battle cruisers, where he could easily redistribute them to anywhere else in the formation. After the losses of *Invincible* and *Brilliant* he had only fourteen left, and of those, *Illustrious* and *Incredible* had been chewed up at Honor. While they were technically combat capable again after a tremendous amount of repair work, Geary had to be careful what he did with those two.

Around the battle cruisers ranged the light cruisers, while the destroyers formed up on the outer edges as well as the front and back of the formation. "All units in pursuit force, immediate execute accelerate to point two five light speed."

The pursuit force began pulling away from the main body while the battleships, heavy cruisers, and destroyers were still getting into position in another oval, this one centered on the captured superbattleship, the assault transports and auxiliaries, and the battleships.

Geary realized that his pursuit force was rapidly gaining on the small spider-wolf formation, which had remained in the lead thus far. "General Charban, Emissary Rione, we need to notify the spider-wolf delegation that this force is heading back to Alliance space at high speed to engage the enigmas."

Rione answered. "That message may exceed our vocabulary, Admiral, but we'll do our best."

What else? Something behind him. Another call. "Admiral Lagemann."

Lagemann looked more than a little haggard but still cheerful. Given the rough living conditions on the captured ship, Geary was only surprised that the other admiral didn't look worse. "I'm going ahead. Captain Armus is in charge of the formation around your ship. He won't let anything through to you."

"Thank you, Admiral," Lagemann replied. "If something does get through, I've got an impressive force of Marines to defend my ship. I never imagined going into combat in something like this."

"We'll try to keep you out of combat."

"Well," Lagemann said, waving a hand around to indicate his surroundings, "if worse comes to worst, at least there's a lot of armor and a lot of mass between us and whoever is attacking. Did I tell you that I've christened my ship?"

"No," Geary said. "You gave it a name?"

"Yes. A fitting name. I'm tired of hearing my ship called BKS or LCCO or RBST or—"

"RBST?" Geary asked.

"Really Big Slow Target. I came up with a much better name." Lagemann grinned. "This is the latest *Invincible*, Admiral."

Lagemann might be pleased by the joke but Geary didn't think that Desjani or a lot of other sailors would be. "Are you sure that's a good idea?"

"Yes, I do. First, because it's so damned big and hard to destroy. Second, because it's already been defeated and captured once. It's already been proven not to be truly *Invincible*. Maybe the Kicks thought of it that way, but we showed them wrong." Lagemann smiled again. "So you see, naming it *Invincible* is our acknowledgment of their error in thinking they could construct a ship too big and too tough to be defeated."

In a strange way, that almost made sense. "You're assuming that the living stars appreciate irony."

"Good heavens, Admiral, look at the universe. If whatever created and oversees it doesn't appreciate irony, how else do you explain some of the things in the universe? How else do explain us, the human race?"

Admiral Lagemann had a point. "How does your crew feel about the name?" It wasn't a very big crew, especially compared to the size of the superbattleship, only about a hundred officers and sailors plus the Marines.

"Surprisingly accepting," Lagemann said. "Some of them are off of the last *Invincible*, and all of them like the idea of trying to break the curse of that name. And, of course, the Marines are all in favor of being a threat magnet."

"Really?" Geary asked.

"All right, the Marines aren't actually all that thrilled, but they still like the thickness of the armor on this thing. Excuse me, on the new *Invincible*."

"I'll say good luck, then, and we'll see you at Midway." Geary broke the connection, looking over at Desjani. "Did you hear any of that?"

She had a horrified expression on her face, which gradually shaded into mere disbelief. "He's willing to do that? He's crazier than Benan."

"If he calls that hulk *Invincible*, then the fleet can't name any new ships *Invincible*, right?"

Desjani's expression shifted to calculation. "Right. I think. And those superbattleships are very hard to kill." She gestured toward her display. Geary saw that Desjani had opened a large virtual window that showed a view of the bear-cow ship—the *Invincible*, he corrected himself. Close-up, he saw the same armored hull he had last viewed this way during the Marine assault. The impression of strength was overwhelming in that surface of metal and composites, in some places pitted and scored by hits and in most others smooth and bright so that the stars themselves seemed to reflect in the dark surface.

"How do you make armor that thick?" Geary wondered.

"I imagine that's one of the things our own engineers and scientists will try to learn," Desjani said. "It's not my thing. I like speed and agility as well as power. But even I look at that hull, the size of that ship, and think, 'Wow, that is cool.'"

"But it's not really invincible."

"No, of course not. But that Admiral Lagemann may be right. It's a way of saying, 'We get it, living stars. We know this name doesn't fit even this ship because we've proven that it doesn't.'"

They were interrupted by a call. Geary gazed into the solemn face of Dr. Nasr. "Two more of the bear-cows died during our transit here from Hua," the chief medical officer said. "As nearly as we can tell, they were oversedated, but that's not a certainty."

That left three living Kick prisoners. Geary looked away, feeling sick inside. "Why won't they let us save them?"

"We've discussed this, Admiral. To them, we're only saving them for a future meal with fresh meat."

"Doctor, I'd like your honest opinion. What's the right thing to do here?"

Nasr sighed. "Admiral, the guiding rule of my profession is not to harm. That sounds like a simple rule, but any doctor with any experience will tell you that it can lead to severe dilemmas if you take the rule seriously. We tried to do the right thing as we saw it, to treat the injuries of the wounded bear-cows and save their lives. And we did that not just out of self-interest but because we truly wanted a chance to establish communications with their species. But you know the saying about the road to hell. Our best intentions have created a situation where every option is bad.

"They're going to die, Admiral. We don't know enough about their metabolism, about their bodies. Either we will oversedate them, or we will undersedate them. A moment of consciousness, of awareness, and the bear-cows will end their own lives. Enough oversedation, and they'll die anyway."

Geary stared at the doctor. "You're telling me I should let them die?"

"No. I can't do that. What I am telling you is that they will die, the only question being when and where. You can order me to reduce sedation, or order me to increase it. Or tell me that we should continue to try to tread the narrow line to keep them going as long as possible."

"Doctor, I can't tell you to kill them. Will they suffer if we keep trying to do our best?"

"Suffer? No. They'll simply go from sedated to dead, or from sedated to aware to dead. I don't know if the dying process hurts, but from the readings we got on the one who killed himself and the autopsy, it doesn't seem to cause trauma. Instead, the body floods itself with chemicals and hormones that block pain and might well create delusions while they cause metabolic functions to very quickly shut down."

It sounded almost pleasant. No pain. Perhaps visions of whatever the dying creature most wanted to see. Comfort. But to deliberately cause even that to happen... "Maintain your efforts to keep them alive. Those are *our* rules. I admit that. But those are the only rules I can use."

"We allow an ending when all hope is gone and the patient rejects artificial intervention," Dr. Nasr pointed out.

"Hope is not gone," Geary said, wondering whether he believed that.

The doctor nodded. Geary never had been able to get the medical staff to grasp the idea of saluting superior officers. "There's one more issue, Admiral. The Syndicate Worlds' citizens we rescued from the enigmas. Have you made any decision as to their disposition?"

"No, Doctor, I haven't. I've just played divine judge once with those bear-cows. Do I have to do it again with the Syndics?"

"Yes, Admiral, you do. If you turn them over to Syndicate Worlds' authorities, you know what will happen to them. They will be treated like lab animals, worse even than what the enigmas did to those people."

Geary shook his head angrily. "If I take them back to the Alliance, they are liable to be treated the same way! Our researchers may make noises about respecting their dignity and humanity, but the end result will be the same." He pulled up a report he recalled seeing, scanning the information in it to confirm his memories. "Those Syndic citizens have been asked what they want, and all of them said that they want to go home."

"Do you want to go home, Admiral?"

"I—" Yes. *But my home no longer exists. It went away a long time ago. And if I went to where home used to be, I wouldn't have a moment of peace. Just like those poor three hundred thirty-three Syndics.* "I understand, Doctor. I really do. I promise you that I will take no action without carefully considering the well-being of those people."

"Thank you, Admiral. I can't ask for more than that."

Geary slumped back, tired of making hard decisions, especially when the right thing to do was far from clear.

"Admiral?" Desjani said in a soft voice.

"Yes?"

"While you were talking to the doctor, we got another high-priority message for you. Captain Jane Geary requests a meeting as soon as possible."

Oh, great. He had known that was coming, though, and with the battle cruisers drawing steadily away from the battleships, the longer he put this off, the bigger the time delays between ships would be and the longer a painful conversation would take. "I'll call her from my stateroom."

"Don't beat around the bush. Don't try to spare her feelings. Be as blunt and clear as possible. And for the love of our ancestors, don't tell her I gave you any of that advice."

He sat on the bridge for a few more minutes, watching the enigma attack force vanishing as it jumped for Midway. That had actually happened hours ago, but seeing the event take place as the light from it finally reached them still carried a sense of immediacy. "All right. I'm off to speak with my grandniece."

He double-checked the security settings on his comm software before calling *Dreadnaught*. Experience had taught him that security with comms was never absolute, but he still had to try to keep this conversation private.

The image of Jane Geary appeared in his stateroom. She didn't look happy, but then he hadn't expected her to. "Admiral, I must respectfully request the reasons for my being passed over to command the main body of the fleet."

He could take a personal tack in answering her, or he could reply with the same sort of professional smoke screen that Jane Geary had repeatedly thrown up to hide her own feelings. Despite Desjani's advice, he decided to open with that second option. "Captain Geary," he began in a formal voice, "I chose the officer who in my opinion was best suited to carry out the tasks the main body has been assigned."

"If this is about the rumors that you are favoring me, it is unfair to penalize me because others have spread such a false accusation, Admiral."

Geary had to pause before replying. *There are rumors that I'm giving Jane Geary special treatment? Why hasn't Tanya told me about them? But then, she might not have heard. Who would repeat that gossip to Tanya?*

And what's the basis for such rumors? I commended her after the battle at Honor, but who could object to that? "Captain Geary, I assure you that my decision did not take into any account such rumors." *Since I hadn't heard them, that's as true a statement as I've ever made.*

It was Jane Geary's turn to hesitate before speaking again. "Why am I not the officer best suited to command the main body?"

Did he tell her the truth? If he didn't, wouldn't he bear responsibility for anything she did? He could see in his mind's eye Tanya giving him a severe look. *Be as blunt and clear as possible.* "I'm going to be direct, Captain Geary. The commanding officer of *Dreadnaught* who I first met at Varandal would have received that assignment. She was aggressive and smart, she was dependable and capable. I could feel confident that I knew what she would do. In the time since we have left Varandal on this mission, I have grown increasingly less certain as to what you would do in any situation."

She paled, then reddened. "In what way have I failed my duties? Which mission have I failed to carry out? I heard no fault being given for my actions at Honor."

"It is impossible to fault your actions at Honor," Geary said. "As my commendation of you for that engagement stated, you acted in the highest and finest traditions of the Alliance fleet. *But*," he added as she started to speak, "I don't need to know whether or not one of my commanding officers can act heroically. It's my job to do my best to prevent anyone from having to do that. When my efforts fail, then someone may have to step up as you did. The problem,

Captain Geary, is that you have developed a pattern of wanting to act heroically even when that is not required. You *want* to be a hero. There are few things more dangerous to a ship, to a crew, to a fleet, than a commanding officer who wants to be a hero."

As Jane Geary stared at him, he could almost see the professional armor cracking and falling away. "You..." she struggled to say. "You are Black Jack. He—"

"I am not the figure of legend. Everything I have done is because it was required of me, because I had to do it, not because I sought it."

"That is not how everyone else sees it!" She didn't seem aware that she had yelled that.

"Everyone else doesn't know me. I have tried to get to know you, to establish a personal relationship, but—"

"Why didn't you go to Glenlyon? They were waiting for you. They got *me*. The grandniece who is only good enough to be a battleship captain. I got to hear endless orations about Black Jack, and about my heroic brother, who fought under *his* command!"

Geary shot to his feet, feeling anger working in him. "You fought under my command at Varandal, and you fought damned well. Jane, you did what was necessary at Honor. What worries me is that you do the same kind of things when they *aren't* necessary. Tell me the truth. When you acted at Honor, were you thinking about anything other than what needed to be done?"

Her jaw muscles stood out as she stared at him, then Jane Geary spoke in a strangled voice. "I was scared. All I was thinking was that this was the only way. I didn't think the use of kinetic projectiles would work, but I was desperate. And ever since then, while everybody tells me how brave I was to lead that charge, all I can think about is how scared I was. There. You wanted the truth. You have it. I'm no hero. I'm not even a good officer. When I faced that situation, I was terrified."

It was his turn to stare, then he laughed, seeing the shock on her face and the growing anger after it. "Jane... please... I'm not... Ancestors preserve us. What do you think courage is?"

"Being unafraid when you face danger! Everybody knows—"

"Then everybody is wrong." Geary sat down again, looking at her. "You were terrified? Do you have any idea how frightened I was at Grendel? My ship was shot to pieces under me, the only crew left on *Merlon* were me and the dead, the power core self-destruct had been activated, and I couldn't find a working escape pod."

"You couldn't find—? Nobody ever said that."

"Nobody else knows! Except Tanya Desjani. And now you. Jane, when I was a lot younger, my father told me something. We were talking about heroes. I remember that I'd been reading histories and saying how great these people were who hadn't been afraid when they faced great challenges. And my father laughed a lot harder than I just did; and then he said that courage wasn't the absence of fear. Courage, real bravery, is being afraid and doing what you need to do anyway. I didn't believe him. Not really." Geary took a deep breath. "Not until I was on *Merlon* and ordering the surviving crew to evacuate while I kept fighting the ship a little longer. Not until I was pulling myself along a passageway littered with wreckage and the dead, trying to find a way off of a crippled ship that was about to explode."

Jane Geary looked down at the deck. "People have told me that, too. I haven't believed them. I feel like a fraud."

"You're human, Jane. And a good officer when you're not trying to prove that you're a hero. You showed that when you charged the enemy at Honor, thinking only of the necessity of doing that despite how scared you were." Did she believe him? He couldn't tell.

When she finally spoke again, it was in a voice so low he could barely hear. "Was Michael scared?"

"When he used *Repulse* to hold off the Syndics so the rest of the fleet could get away? Yes."

"Why didn't you tell me that?"

Why hadn't he? He suddenly understood the reason why he had been reticent before this. "Because if you haven't been through something like that," Geary said slowly, "then telling someone that the person who did it was scared can sound like a criticism, a put-down, instead of what it really is—a testament to just how brave they actually were. Now, there are people who get so involved in what they must do, in doing this and that and the next thing, that they don't have time to be scared. Tanya Desjani is like that. They're brave, too, just in a different way because they submerge their fears long enough to get the job done. But feeling no fear? That would make machines the bravest things in the universe."

She thought about that for a while, then spoke in a firm voice. "What do I need to do?"

That one was easy. "Be the officer I first saw at Varandal. I don't need someone trying to prove that she's Black Jack. I need Jane Geary."

She looked up, meeting his eyes, then nodded. "I think I remember her. She was trying to prove something else, though. She was trying to prove who she wasn't."

"We all are trying to prove things. All of the time." Geary stepped closer, searching her eyes. "Jane, we need to get that superbattleship, the new *Invincible*, home. Your battleships are the last line of defense before the four battleships towing the new *Invincible*. Don't leave them hanging. They need you blocking any attacks that come at them."

Her arm came up in a slow salute. "If anything gets through, it won't be because I let them." After she ended the call, Geary stood looking at where his grandniece's image had been. Once again, he had ordered her to stand and die. After this talk, he felt confident she would do it, not because of his order but because of who she was. That wouldn't make him feel any less guilty if this time she did die carrying out his orders.

16

The battle cruisers and the rest of the pursuit force had gradually passed the six spider-wolf ships, so that now the alien craft were between the pursuit-force formation and the heavier main-body formation coming on behind. The gap between the two subformations of the human fleet grew steadily larger as the battle cruisers, light cruisers, and destroyers accelerated faster than the cumbersome battleships, auxiliaries, and assault transports could manage. Geary watched the status reports from the four battleships towing the former bear-cow superbattleship, seeing the stress readings in their hulls as *Relentless*, *Reprisal*, *Superb*, and *Splendid* strained to haul the massive *Invincible* at higher and higher velocities. Given enough time, even a small amount of thrust could do that, but they didn't have decades to spend on slow acceleration, and so the four battleships were putting all they had into the task.

Status reports everywhere showed problems. Not anywhere near the scale that had happened at Honor, but as the ships of the pursuit force had pushed their maneuvering and propulsion systems to the maximum, there had been spot failures in a score of ships. *Implacable* and *Intemperate* had each lost a main propulsion unit, which they were frantically working to bring back on line, while *Valiant* had suffered failures in half of her maneuvering thruster systems. All three battle cruisers had lagged behind their places in formation. They were accompanied by several light cruisers as well as ten destroyers that had also lost partial propulsion or maneuvering. Geary started to think that at least no ship had lost all propulsion, then hastily cut off the thought lest it somehow jinx the fleet.

Dragon and *Victorious* were keeping place in formation but dealing with fluctuating shield failures, while individual hell-lance batteries were failing here and there on dozens of ships.

The main-body formation under Captain Armus was suffering from scattered problems as well, but they had the auxiliaries with them as well as more time to fix the sudden system failures.

As Captain Smythe had predicted, not only *Witch* but also *Jinn* and *Goblin* were out of critical materials and now unable to manufacture new items. *Cyclops* had an inventory so low that it would probably report the same condition within a few hours. Their engineers were assisting the crews of other ships in repair work, but that was all they could do for now.

"It could be worse," Geary said. "We've got a few more hours for this formation to fix things before we enter jump, and then the transit time to Midway to do internal repairs."

"And the Kicks aren't still chasing us," Desjani added.

He couldn't help a brief smile, which faded as he reviewed the repair status of fleet ships again. Yes, they had time to work, but having the parts they needed was another matter. "I hope we're not running low on duct tape, too. I think we're going to need a lot of it."

He had wondered if something else would show up at Pele while the fleet was passing through, perhaps more enigma ships racing to join up with their main force. But once the enigmas had jumped, there was nothing at Pele but the two human subformations and the spider-wolf formation between them. The main-body formation had fallen well behind the pursuit formation by the time the battle cruisers and their escorts pivoted to begin braking down to point one light speed for the jump.

Geary felt the stress as *Dauntless*'s main propulsion units roared at maximum force to slow the ship. Tanya had cut the maneuver to the barest safety margins to shave a few more minutes off the time to jump. One of these days he would learn to double-check how many demands she was putting on propulsion units, ships' structures, and the inertial nullifiers.

But then she almost never exceeded danger margins. She got the ships real close to those margins but never right up to them. Usually.

"Almost there," Desjani noted over the complaints of the inertial nullifiers as they tried to keep ships from disintegrating and their crews from being pulped into jelly by the forces being used. "Spider-wolves are still hanging exactly ten light-minutes behind us."

"They want us jumping first into whatever the enigmas will have waiting at Midway," Geary replied. "Not that I can blame them."

He tapped his comm controls. "Captain Armus, we'll see you at Midway. I have no doubt that we'll need your firepower there. To the honor of our ancestors, Geary, out." He ended his message in the ceremonial manner because that felt right this time.

There wouldn't be enough time for the message to reach Armus and for Armus to send a reply in the fifteen minutes remaining until jump, so Geary tried to relax despite the force of deceleration. "All units in pursuit force, this is Admiral Geary. Be at full combat readiness when we arrive at Midway. The enigma force that we saw jump for Midway may be awaiting our arrival or may be striking at targets in that star system. Either way, we're going to teach them once again that attacking human-controlled space is a very bad idea. To the honor of our ancestors, Geary, out."

"Being awfully formal for fleet communications, aren't you, Admiral?" Desjani said.

"The next time I talk to them, we may be in the middle of a fight."

As the pursuit-force formation had braked, any ships still lagging had taken advantage of that to catch up, *Implacable*, *Intemperate*, and *Valiant* as well as assorted light cruisers and destroyers sliding into their positions relative to *Dauntless*. Velocity kept slowing as the distance to the jump point shrank.

Every ship reached point one light speed as the jump point loomed right ahead. "All units jump."

Geary forced himself to relax as the outside went gray and formless. "How is *Dauntless* doing?" he asked Desjani.

"You don't believe my status reports?"

"Of course I do. But I'd like your impressions, too."

Tanya shrugged. "Being flagship, we got priority on a lot of systems upgrades. Once the engineers got tied up fixing battle damage and repairing failed systems, the upgrades slowed down, but *Dauntless* is still in good shape. I can't promise nothing will drop out on us without warning, but it shouldn't be anything major."

"Good. I know I can always count on *Dauntless*." That was partly for the benefit of any crew members in earshot, who would pass on his statement to their shipmates, but also because he believed it was true. And because when he spoke of *Dauntless*, he also meant her commanding officer.

Desjani's smile showed that she knew that. "Thank you, Admiral."

"Ten minutes until we leave jump," Lieutenant Castries announced.

Desjani had her chin resting on one hand, the elbow propped on the arm of her seat. "Do you know what would be bizarre?" she asked Geary.

"I can think of a few things. What exactly are you thinking of?"

"Once again we're about to leave jump, and once again we're all hyped up, ready for action, knowing that there's either going to be trouble or there very well might be trouble. In this case, we know there will be, of course."

"And that's bizarre?"

"No," Desjani said. "That's our normal. It's always that way. What would be bizarre is if we were arriving at our destination, readying to leave jump, and we were all calm and relaxed and not worrying at all about what was there."

"You know, there's a lot of truth to that," Geary said. "I guess when we arrive at Varandal—" The look on her face stopped him in mid-sentence.

"You're not worried about what might be waiting for us when

we return to Alliance space?" Desjani asked. "Seriously? Political games? Orders from fleet headquarters? Demands that Black Jack start running things? Demands that Black Jack be arrested before he launches a coup? You're not worried about any of that?"

He ran through various possible replies before deciding on one. "Let's just say that I've been in denial and trying not to think about it."

"Must be nice."

"Yeah." He smiled. "But consider this, Captain Desjani. If we pull this off, if we get through everything we have to deal with before we reach Varandal again, whoever or whatever awaits us there will see us arrive with six ships full of spider-wolves and a captured Kick superbattleship."

She smiled, too. "Surprise! Not only did we make it back, but we brought friends. Yeah, that may well throw some carefully laid plans off track."

"Five minutes to arrival," Lieutenant Castries said.

Desjani's smile vanished. "Do you think the Syndics at Midway will be keeping the enigmas busy?"

"I don't know," Geary said, wishing that he could make a decent estimate. "It all depends on what they had in that star system and how smart they use what they've got. If they haven't had reinforcements, they won't have any chance against an enigma force that large. I'm not even sure whether they'll still be calling themselves Syndics. I got a strong feeling that the CEOs at Midway, some of them anyway, were less than firm in their loyalty to the Syndicate government."

"Loyal? Syndic CEOs? Did you actually use those words in the same sentence?" Desjani asked. "Do you trust that woman you talked to? What was her name?"

"Iceni. CEO Iceni. I can't say I trust her. I'm not crazy. But our interests may coincide, as Victoria Rione would say."

That earned him a scowl. "I'd appreciate it if you didn't quote that woman when talking to me."

"Sorry."

"One minute to arrival." Lieutenant Castries's voice remained even, professional, but the tension level on the bridge could still be felt to be rising.

"Time to get your head in the game," Desjani said to Geary.

"It's there."

"Shields at maximum," Lieutenant Yuon reported. "All weapons ready."

The last seconds counted down, his guts felt the familiar twist and his mind the familiar disorientation, and the gray of jump space was abruptly replaced by black filled with stars as they arrived at Midway.

The thing they feared most to hear, the blare of combat systems alarms warning of nearby enemies, did not come. The combat systems had been set to immediately begin pumping out shots at enigma ships if those were right on top of the jump point, but that didn't happen either. As Geary shook the jump-created confusion from his mind, he saw threat markers popping to life on his display, none of them close. The enemy wasn't waiting for them at the jump point, but the enigmas were indeed still here.

"What are they doing?" Desjani wondered.

"I don't know," Geary replied.

He had expected and feared that the enigmas would head straight for the hypernet gate, which was located just shy of six light-hours from this jump point, well around the curve of the star system. If the enigmas had pumped their velocity up to point two light speed or higher, they could have reached that hypernet gate in only thirty hours. Once near the gate, those two hundred and twenty-two enigma warships could collapse it in no time by destroying the "tethers" that suspended an energy matrix between them.

Or the enigmas could have headed for the primary inhabited world, now orbiting its star only four and a half light-hours away, to conduct a close-in orbital bombardment that would have annihilated the human presence there and rendered the planet uninhabitable.

Instead, the enigmas were sitting only thirty light-minutes from the jump point where Geary's fleet had arrived.

"They're waiting for us," Desjani said. "They knew we were coming, and they're waiting to hit us. Why didn't they try one of those ambushes like they did at Alihi?"

The answer came to him immediately. "Because they knew we were coming but didn't have a precise enough knowledge of when we'd arrive. The enigmas at Hua did send out an alert, a faster-than-light message that we were on our way back toward Midway. That told these enigmas roughly when we would get here but not precisely enough to stage one of those ambushes at the jump point."

That left another question, though, and Desjani zeroed in on it. "So if they knew they had some time, why haven't they run amuck here, destroying stuff or getting close enough to destroy something knowing that we couldn't get there in time to stop them?"

He looked from hypernet gate to inhabited world, from the inhabited world to the space-dock facility orbiting a gas giant one light-hour out from the star, from that facility to the Syndic flotillas elsewhere in the star system… *Where do I go? I have to try to save*—"Hell."

"Does that mean you figured out the answer to that question?" Desjani asked.

"Yes." He stabbed a finger at the display. "They want *us*, too. If they destroyed the hypernet gate, if they wiped out the human presence on the inhabited world and the orbital space dock, what reason would we have to stay and fight?"

"And they want us to stay and fight." She nodded, grim now. "So they left everything intact that we want to try to save. That means they won't just run, either. They mean to make sure not only that the front door is closed but also that we're disposed of so we can't go charging back into their territory. But the odds don't favor them that much. They must intend doing something to ensure we get wiped out. And then…" She frowned at her display. "Three Syndic flotillas. Do we have to worry about those Syndics? Are they going to help us? Are any of them going to fight us? Or will they just sit back and watch us and the enigmas fight, laughing as their enemies kill each other?"

"The one thing I don't think we need to worry about is the Syndics fighting us." The need for haste weighed on him now, but he also knew that it would take his fleet five hours to reach the enigma force at its current velocity. Far wiser to figure out the situation in this star system, then act.

Desjani shook her head. "That CEO in charge of their ships when we came through here last. What was her name? Kolani. She was tough and mean. She'd love to fight us, even if that only meant finishing off our wounded after the enigmas had crippled us."

Three Syndic flotillas—though all three were tiny compared to the Alliance and enigma forces. One battleship and two heavy cruisers at the orbital dock near the gas giant; another battleship along with six heavy cruisers, four light cruisers, and ten Hunter-Killers hovering near the hypernet gate; and two heavy cruisers, six light cruisers, and twelve HuKs on their way toward the gas giant on a vector that indicated they had come from near the inhabited planet.

"If the Syndics can gather all of their forces together, combine those three little flotillas—" Geary began.

"They'd have one little flotilla," Desjani said. "If you add up the forces coming from the planet and the ones at the gas giant, not counting that battleship, you'd have about what the Syndics had here last time we came through. It looks like it's been quiet here. Those guys near the hypernet gate must be reinforcements from the Syndic central government at Prime."

"It's not much," Geary conceded, "but two battleships can't be discounted." He had barely finished speaking when one of the threat markers on his display altered, changing its message. "Assessed non-operational? The battleship at the gas giant isn't in fighting condition?"

"That's what the fleet sensors say, Admiral," Lieutenant Yuon confirmed. "From analysis of the outer hull, it looks to be brand-new, but from everything the sensors can pick up in terms of activity and equipment, it's estimated to still be under construction."

"That would explain why it's at Midway's orbiting shipyard dock," Desjani said. "The two heavy cruisers must be with it as protection, then."

Lieutenant Iger's face appeared near Geary. "Admiral, we've intercepted a message that was sent to the orbital dock near the gas giant from the Syndicate Worlds' flotilla near the hypernet gate. We were close enough to the path of the transmission to grab it. The message identifies the commander of the flotilla near the gate as CEO Boyens."

"I guess they didn't shoot him," Desjani said, sounding slightly disappointed.

"More importantly," Iger continued, "is what the message said. We couldn't break it completely, but we can say with confidence that it was a demand to surrender."

It took Geary a moment to answer that. "Surrender? Was it aimed at the cruisers and battleship or the dock facility?"

"All of them, Admiral. We're certain of that."

"Who would be crazy enough to rebel with a battleship that wasn't operational?" Desjani wondered. "So that force heading toward them from the planet is on their way to deal with the rebels there, too."

"Perhaps not." Lieutenant Iger spoke quickly. "Fleet sensors have spotted some indications of damage in several of the cities on the primary world. There's repair work under way already, but the damage was extensive enough to still be apparent."

"Bombardment by the enigmas?" Geary asked. "No. There hasn't been enough time for a bombardment by that force to reach the inhabited world, hit, and repair work to begin."

"That's correct, sir. And there are no bombardment craters visible. It looks like the sort of damage that would be caused by serious ground fighting."

Ground fighting. Who had been fighting whom? "Is there a civil war under way here?"

"No, sir. We'd have seen signs of that kind of fighting right away. Whatever happened is past."

"Somebody won and somebody lost," Desjani observed. "If the ships at the gas giant and the orbital dock are rebels, maybe they won there and lost on the planet."

Iger was listening to someone with him and reading rapidly. "Admiral, there's a lot of very unusual signal traffic in this star system, messages that predate our arrival and the arrival of the enigmas. That message from the flotilla led by CEO Boyens is in regular Syndic format, but the locals *haven't* been using standard Syndic codes recently, though they still seem to be sticking to Syndic protocols. The news-media transmissions we're picking up talk about 'President' Iceni and 'General' Drakon as if those two are in charge here. From the videos, those are the same people we knew as CEO Iceni and CEO Drakon."

"Now we know who won," Geary told Desjani.

"'President' Iceni"? Desjani asked. "Like someone elected her? Who are they kidding?"

"Wasn't there another CEO on the planet?" Geary asked.

Lieutenant Iger answered. "Yes, sir. CEO Hardrad. I can't find any mention of him in any of the current message traffic. Iceni was in overall charge of the star system, Drakon was the military ground forces commander, and Hardrad was in charge of Syndic internal security in this star system."

Internal security. On a Syndicate Worlds' planet, that meant a lot more than simply police. It meant someone who kept the population under control. But if Hardrad was gone...

"Hold on," Geary said. "If the people running things here, Iceni and Drakon, revolted against the Syndics and got rid of Hardrad, then that flotilla with the working battleship in it, the one under Boyens's command, might not have been reinforcements at all."

Iger said something rapidly to someone beside him, got an answer, and nodded to Geary. "Yes, Admiral. That's a real possibility. That flotilla may have been sent here to bring a system in revolt back under control of the Syndic government on Prime."

"Do we *know* who owns the battleship that doesn't work?" Desjani asked.

"Yes, Captain," Iger replied. "From the communications patterns it is under the control of the authorities on the planet."

Desjani gasped a short laugh. "This isn't a three-way fight. It's a four-way fight. Us, the enigmas, the Syndics, and the rebels. All we have to do is figure out what the other three are going to do."

"I know what Boyens will do," Geary said, pointing to the Syndic flotilla near the hypernet gate. "When we had him aboard *Dauntless* as a prisoner, he struck me as being deliberate and calculating. He tried to figure out where each possible move would lead before he acted, and even then preferred to wait to see what others did before he committed himself to a course of action. He's almost certainly here with orders to subdue the rebels in this star system. Getting involved with fighting the enigmas might damage or destroy his own ships, making it harder or impossible to defeat the rebels. So he'll stand off from any fighting, stay near the hypernet gate, and wait for us to beat the enigmas. Once that is done, he'll move in on the rebels, who might have lost ships to the enigmas during the fight, and regain control of Midway. To Boyens, that will be a win-win solution."

"What about the rebels, Admiral?" Lieutenant Iger asked. "Wouldn't it be to their advantage to also avoid getting involved in the fight so they could conserve their forces for the eventual battle with Boyens's flotilla?"

Desjani snorted. "Let's you and him fight. Sounds like Syndics, all right. They'll just wait to see how much damage we and the enigmas do to each other."

"If we need them, the rebels will have to act with us," Geary said, drawing a skeptical look from Desjani. "If we lose, then they face not just Boyens, who wants to bring them back into the Syndic fold—"

"Which doubtless means busy firing squads for weeks and weeks," Desjani broke in.

"—but they also face the enigmas, who, as far as they know, want to wipe them out."

"That's a point," she conceded.

"They might also want our gratitude," Lieutenant Iger pointed out. "A reason for us to back them against the Syndicate Worlds' flotilla."

Geary sat back, thinking out options, while everyone waited. He could feel them trying not to watch him as the seconds ticked past. "We arrived twenty minutes ago. In ten more minutes, the enigma force will know we've arrived. They're here, they're waiting here, to destroy us. I fully expect that as soon as they see us, those enigmas will accelerate straight for us and bring us to battle."

Desjani nodded. "Agreed. So where do we go?"

"We go to meet them, Captain. Meet them and kick them back into their territory so hard they won't be able to stop skidding until they reach Pandora."

He knew those words would be repeated around the fleet, or at least the portion of it that had arrived at Midway, and, from the shouts already echoing through *Dauntless*, that they would be greeted with approval. "All units, this is Admiral Geary. Immediate execute, accelerate to point one five light speed."

Geary called General Charban. "General, that message you put together offering the enigmas an agreement in which we leave them alone, and they leave us alone. Broadcast it to that enigma force here. I don't expect them to take the offer, but I want to try."

Charban nodded in sad agreement. "I think they will need at least one more unmistakable lesson that force cannot achieve their goals with us. The message will be sent immediately, Admiral, and I will let you know the instant that I receive a reply, if any reply comes."

Geary reactivated the window where Lieutenant Iger waited. "Lieutenant, find out everything you can about the situation in this star system. Confirm who really is in charge, what they've been doing, and anything else that might influence my decisions on what I should do."

Iger saluted, his image vanishing.

As the main propulsion units on the battle cruisers, light cruisers, and destroyers of the pursuit force kicked in, Geary saw another large virtual window pop up next to him. The only thing visible inside the window was text, which to his quick glance looked a lot like an official document of some kind. A voice began reciting words as those same words were highlighted in the document. "Fleet regulations mandate that no ship is allowed to go under seventy percent fuel-cell level in the course of operations so as to ensure sufficient power reserves to cope with any outcome or contingency. Any unit reaching the seventy percent level must immediately—"

Geary finally found his fleet commander override and punched it. The voice stopped. Then it started again.

He hit override once more.

The voice made a third effort and Geary held down the override this time. Once certain that the subroutine installed in the fleet's systems by headquarters had been choked into a coma by this final effort, he checked the fleet status readouts, seeing that after the dash through Pele his destroyers were either at or rapidly approaching the seventy percent mark.

"Problem?" Desjani asked, her voice tense at the possibility that Geary's comms might be acting up again.

"Staff infection," Geary explained, using the standard fleet term for mandatory subroutines loaded into fleet systems to enforce headquarters rules and requirements. "The destroyers are getting down to seventy percent on fuel cells."

"Oh, no," Desjani said in a noticeably insincere way. "What will you do? Halt the battle? Ask the enigmas to hold off until we're ready to fight in accordance with fleet regulations?"

"No." Geary tapped his comm controls. "All units, this is Admiral Geary. I take full, personal responsibility for the fuel-cell levels on every ship of this fleet. You will continue operations under my express orders, here placed officially in the record."

"You can get court-martialed for that, you know," Desjani said.

"I've heard that."

Desjani's next statement was cut off by the appearance of Emissary Rione, striding down to stand next to Geary's seat on the side away from Desjani. "What are you going to do?" Rione asked.

"Defeat the enigmas," Geary said, his tone as short as his answer. "Which I think will be necessary."

"And then? CEO Boyens will surely ask your assistance in 'reestablishing order' within this star system."

"I can't stop him from asking," Geary said.

Rione glared at him. "Admiral, we *need* this star system. It is not only the gateway to enigma territory, but is also our only known connection to spider-wolf-controlled regions."

"Believe me, Madam Emissary, I am abundantly aware of that."

Geary drummed his fingers on one armrest. "Are you about to tell me I have to help Boyens and the Syndicate government reassert control here?"

"I am telling you, Admiral, that there is already a major fight under way in this star system, one that could inflict serious collateral damage on everything here. A battle between Syndic loyalists and the rebel forces controlling this star system could easily cause even more damage. We do *not* need a star system blown apart by civil war and destroyed in the name of saving it from the enigmas."

"Your concerns are noted, Madam Emissary," Geary said, keeping his own tone of voice cool this time. "I will endeavor to ensure that any destruction is limited to things, people, and places that are not of any particular concern to the Alliance."

Rione's expression became like stone, but when she leaned in close to talk to him, her voice held plenty of emotion. "Dammit, listen to me, *Black Jack*. You may think that you can do anything you want right now, but the truth is that a wrong step could destroy everything."

"I am very much aware of that," Geary replied, keeping his own voice low. "I am also aware that the surest way to bring about a real mutiny in this fleet is to order my ships to assist the Syndicate Worlds in regaining control here. Even if I didn't find that morally repugnant, my own fleet wouldn't follow such orders, not even from Black Jack."

She pointed a rigid finger at his display. "Have you wondered why Boyens is hanging around that hypernet gate, Admiral?"

"He's there so that if the enigmas crush the locals, Boyens and his flotilla can pretend to put up a gallant fight, then hyper out of here," Geary replied.

"That's an option, but Boyens knows that hypernet gate has a safe-fail mechanism on it. He knows he could cause it to collapse without risking his own flotilla, and he has a battleship with him to bring that about if we don't do as he wants."

That was an ugly possibility. The hypernet gate at Midway was a critical element in the importance of this star system to the Alliance. If the Syndics lost control of the star system, they would have no reason to let that gate remain intact. "I can—" What? Threaten to attack an official Syndicate Worlds' flotilla despite the peace treaty? Start the war again? How much enthusiasm would the war-weary populace of the Alliance have for that course of action?

"How do you know," Rione pressed him with her words, "that the enigmas will attack when they see what you have here? Isn't this a substantial force? More than they would want to face?"

"It's not that substantial," Geary said. "Not compared to them. A number of the warships in this force have also been battered in previous engagements, and the enigmas will be able to spot that damage. If they think—" He paused again as a new thought struck. "Captain Desjani, have we ever figured out just how much detail the enigmas can transmit using their faster-than-light communications?"

She shook her head, pointedly ignoring Rione's presence. "No. Basic information, as far as we know. I was talking to my comm officer about that, and he said that if the enigmas had routine, complex, faster-than-light communication, we should have been able to see signs of that by what wasn't visible to us when we went through their territory. We wouldn't see all of the routine message traffic flying between parts of star systems. But the comm traffic in enigma star systems was about at the level we would expect, which implies they can send some data, but not a lot, and still depend on regular light-speed comms for most traffic."

"Which would mean the enigmas here would know the Alliance fleet was coming but not necessarily how many ships that involved."

"They'd know—" Desjani grinned. "They'd know what showed up here. So the enigmas here might think the bear-cows got all of our battleships and heavy cruisers? That only our fastest ships got away?"

"Maybe. If the enigmas don't know the battleships and heavy cruisers are coming on behind, they'll be overconfident, thinking our strength has really been whittled down already. But if the enigmas do know our battleships and heavy cruisers are coming, they'll know they have to try to beat this formation before we get those reinforcements," Geary added.

"Which will encourage the enigmas to attack as quickly as possible," Desjani concluded.

Rione had listened, and now her gaze was withdrawn, her expression intent as she thought. "The enigmas here might or might not know about the captured bear-cow warship, and might or might not know about the six spider-wolf ships coming here. But the Syndicate forces and the rebellious forces will not know either of those things."

Geary smiled. "Do you think they might throw off CEO Boyens's calculations?"

"They might well, Admiral. The importance of getting that information to the government on Prime might override any plan by Boyens to blackmail us by threatening the hypernet gate. Still, try not to destroy too much of this star system."

"I'll do my best, Madam Emissary."

Desjani had lost her smile as she looked at Geary. "Hey, Admiral, have you considered what the enigmas might do when they see that Kick superbattleship? Because that superbattleship doesn't work any more than one of those Syndic battleships does. Right now it's only military function is RBRSRIT."

"RBRSRIT?" Geary asked.

"Really Big Really Slow Really Inviting Target."

"I'll keep that in mind. At least our superbattleship that doesn't work isn't here yet. And don't forget, even though dreaming up new acronyms to describe that ship seems to have become everyone's favorite hobby in the fleet, she's called *Invincible* now."

"I still don't feel good about that."

The enigmas should have seen them coming at around half an hour after the Alliance fleet arrived at the jump point. Then the enigmas would very likely have begun accelerating toward the Alliance ships, while Geary had already pushed up his own velocity as he headed right for an intercept with the enigmas. On a display showing large reaches of the star system, the track of the Alliance fleet was a vast curve, heading in toward the star and the place where the enigma formation had awaited them.

The distance between the two forces should be closing rapidly, unless the enigmas had defied all expectations and instead charged in another direction. If the enigmas moved straight for the hypernet gate, they could still collapse it before Geary's pursuit force could get there.

Geary tried to look unconcerned as the last minutes elapsed before they should see the enigma reaction to their arrival. Much farther away, none of the Syndicate or rebel forces in this star system would see anything for almost another hour.

His display updated in a flurry of new information as the light from the enigma reaction finally reached the fleet. Desjani's lips drew back in a fierce grin. "Here they come. Just as predicted."

The enigmas were accelerating along a vector clearly aimed to meet Geary's forces, the alien ships showing off their impressive maneuverability as they increased speed at a rate the human ships couldn't match.

The estimated time to intercept kept updating, scrolling downward fast as the velocity of the enigma ships kept increasing.

Then there came a sudden shift, the alien ships ceasing their acceleration. "They saw us come up to point one five light speed," Desjani said. "So they stopped at… point one six light speed. If we both hold that, we'll meet in sixty-five minutes. Nobody's going to get any hits if we pass each other at that velocity, though."

Geary nodded, knowing he would have to reduce the velocity of his ships at some point before that intercept so his fire control systems would have a decent chance of scoring hits on the enigmas. The enigmas would also slow down to give themselves good shots so—

Would they?

That's what human warships would do. But he wasn't dealing with human warships, human commanders, human tactics.

Geary watched the enigmas coming, fast and on a direct intercept with the Alliance formation, an ugly certainty growing in him. They had seen something of enigma tactics in the long journey through enigma space. They knew what the enigmas would do. Straight, stand-up fights weren't how the enigmas liked doing things. It wasn't that they lacked courage or feared death. They just did things differently than humans might choose to do them. And one of the things the enigmas had done was… "They're going to ram."

17

"What?" Desjani's stare centered on him.

"They're going to ram," Geary repeated, feeling totally confident in that assessment. "If they order fourteen of their warships to ram, one each for our battle cruisers, they'll take out the core of our fighting force and a big chunk of our firepower in a single pass. The remaining enigma warships could easily handle our surviving light cruisers and destroyers, then mop up the Syndics here before dropping that hypernet gate on their way out. I will take any odds you want to name that they are planning on doing that."

Her eyes shifted rapidly as they went from point to point on her display, then Desjani almost snarled her reply. "You're right. It makes perfect sense to them. We saw them ram that asteroid, and we know they're willing to sacrifice their own people for any number of reasons. If we went in on a straight firing run, they'd have a real good chance of getting at least a glancing hit on our ships with one of theirs, and at the speeds we'd be moving, that would be all it took. But how will we know that's what they intend? If we just evade, we'll lose every chance to engage them."

"We watch to see if they slow down," Geary said. "If they don't brake their velocity down so they'd have a decent chance of scoring hits on a firing pass, it will tell us they want to score a different kind of hit."

"At those kinds of velocities, that's a tough shot even with a weapon the size of a warship," Desjani muttered, running some simulations. "Hmmm. If they assign two ships to ram each battle cruiser, their odds of success go way the hell up. But... a pretty much head-on pass... it's doable. Oh, hell. That's why they took up the position they did, so that when we came at them, it would be a head-on firing pass, which would greatly increase their odds of scoring a hit with a ramming tactic."

An hour could seem like a long time. When a strong force of alien warships was charging right down your throat, quite possibly with intent to take out your biggest ships using the surest and ugliest method available, it felt like far too short a period in which to think of an effective countertactic. After Geary had spent several frustrating minutes coming up with nothing, Desjani turned to look at him.

"Are you going to share with me your brilliant plan for handling this situation?"

"I will as soon as I come up with one," Geary muttered.

Her next words surprised him.

"You know, Admiral, we don't have to hit them hard on this pass. We don't have to hit them at all."

Geary swiveled his head to stare at her. "Are you feeling all right, Tanya?"

"I'm fine. Maybe a bit too much exposure to thinking when it comes to tactics, but otherwise fine." Desjani pointed to her display. "We dropped into this star system thinking we would have to hit the enigmas as hard as we could as fast as we could because we thought the enigmas would be destroying everything. The enigmas aren't doing that, though, because they want that stuff intact to keep us here so we have to fight. But I realized that we're still thinking we have to hit hard and fast even though the situation is much different than we expected. They're coming to us. We're a long ways from anything in this star system that the enigmas might target. At the rates we're both going, the main-body formation coming in behind us will arrive shortly before the enigmas pass through us, but the enigmas won't see that arrival until they've already gone past us, putting them between our two formations. *Then* we can go after them hard."

Geary felt like hitting himself. "That's right. I've still been thinking that time was critical, but right now time is on our side. We don't have to risk a high-threat firing pass this time. Captain Desjani, have I told you how very valuable you are to me?"

"Not often enough."

"I'll try to correct that." He looked at the situation with new eyes. "How do you see the enigmas trying to pull off ramming even though this fleet has a history of last-moment maneuvers to concentrate our force against one portion of the enemy formation? How are they going to know where to direct the ramming ships?"

"It's pretty simple," she said, sounding a trifle smug. "Look." Her display lit up with representations of Geary's force and the enigmas rushing toward each other. "They've seen us fight. They know you'll likely alter course at the last moment to hit just part of their formation with everything we've got. In order to do that, we'd need to be within a certain range of them, no matter which direction we dodge." She entered more data and a flattened cone spread out from the future location of Geary's force, surrounding the enemy formation. "We'd have to be somewhere on that cone. If I was running the show for the enigmas, I'd be watching for the first twitch of movement onto a new vector by us, and the instant I saw the direction of that vector, I would know where on this cone we were aiming to be.

"For example." Desjani entered one number, and the cone was replaced by a single vector. "See? Easy. *If* you're maneuverable enough to change your own vector fast enough to manage a new intercept at that point. Human ships aren't that maneuverable. Enigma ships are."

"And if I don't dodge, it just makes their solution simpler," Geary said. "I'm glad you're not running the show for the enigmas."

"Damn straight. So, what are you going to do?"

"Use your cone. How much farther do we have to deviate from course to hit whichever enigmas try to hit us, and still be safe from an intercept aimed at somewhere on that cone?"

"That depends which way you go." She raised one eyebrow at him. "You usually choose up and to the right."

"So you told me." He paused to think. "Let's seem to make it easy for them. We'll go up and to the right. Farther up, though."

"It might mean a clean miss on that firing run," Desjani cautioned.

"As a certain battle cruiser commander pointed out, we can afford that," Geary replied.

Rione was back. "Admiral, the spider-wolves have arrived in this star system."

"Good."

"How will we keep the enigmas from destroying them?"

That complicated things.

Desjani spoke as if saying thoughts out loud to Geary. "At least we don't have to worry about the spider-wolves. They're not quite as fast as the enigmas, but they seem to be slightly more maneuverable. Unless they want to fight the enigmas, they should be able to avoid any attempt to engage them."

Geary nodded and looked at Rione. "What she said."

"Thank you... Admiral." She looked forward at his display. "I understand that there have been some political changes here."

"It looks like it though we don't know the extent yet. Feel free to talk to Lieutenant Iger about it. His people are trying to sort out the changes."

Rione recognized a dismissal when she heard one. "I'll let you go back to focusing on your battle, Admiral."

"Half an hour to contact," Lieutenant Castries reported.

"Let's slow it down as if we intend a regular firing pass," Geary said. "All units in pursuit formation, reduce velocity to point one light speed at time one five."

A few minutes later, *Dauntless* and the other ships surrounding her pivoted around so their main propulsion units faced forward and began braking their velocity down to the speed Geary had ordered.

By the time that had been done, and the warships had brought their bows forward again to face the oncoming enigmas, only five minutes remained until contact.

Geary checked everything else on his display, wanting to make sure he didn't focus solely on the enigmas and miss important developments elsewhere in the star system. The spider-wolves had accelerated upward, apparently seeking an orbit out of the direct path of the combatants. The main body of Geary's fleet should have arrived at the jump point a few minutes ago, but the light from that event had not reached them yet. The Syndics here, as well as the rebels who used to be Syndics, would within the next hour begin seeing Geary's pursuit force, but so far none of those three flotillas had spotted the arrival of the Alliance warships or altered their previous vectors.

"The enigmas haven't reduced their velocity," Desjani said.

"Captain?" Lieutenant Yuon reported. "Our combined engagement speed with the enigmas will be point two six light speed. Combat systems accuracy will be significantly impacted. Recommend reducing speed."

"Thank you, Lieutenant. Not this time."

Geary nodded and then, confident of what to do and when to do it, activated his comms. "All units, at time four four come starboard seven degrees, up six degrees. Engage any enigma units that come within your weapons envelopes." He had already called up the battle cruiser captains, telling them to beware of ramming tactics, so now it was just a matter of letting physics call the shots.

At forty-four minutes past the hour, the pursuit-force formation rolled up and toward the star, drastically increasing the distance at which it would pass the enigma force if that did not also change course. Geary watched the enigmas, in the last seconds before contact, seeing them leap toward the path of the Alliance fleet. He felt a moment of fear even though his instincts told him that the enigma course change would fall short.

A moment too fast to really register on human senses, and they were past the enigmas. "All units, immediate execute, come up one eight five degrees, port zero eight degrees." As soon as the order was out of his mouth, Geary checked the fleet status display. "No hits."

"Not on us and not on them," Desjani agreed. "About what we expected. See these guys?" She pointed on her display to the tracks of more than a score of enigma warships that had veered wildly up toward the human formation before tearing past and angling down toward their own formation again. "Those were the rammers. They would have gone right through us if we'd been positioned for a normal firing run. You called it right, Admiral."

"We called it right," Geary corrected. His display lit up with symbols marking the arrival of the main body at the jump point as the light from that finally reached them. At first glance, before looking at the damage afflicting many of the battleships, the main body looked extremely dangerous, especially with the mass of *Invincible* bulking in the center of that formation. Humans had never built a warship that big, and now the Alliance had one.

The pursuit force was curving upward and over in a huge arc, heading back toward the jump point as the enigmas continued in that direction. But even though the enigmas had finally seen the main body as well, they now climbed up at a steep angle. "They're going for the—the spider-wolves," Lieutenant Castries said.

"They are indeed," Desjani agreed. "Watch this, ladies and gentlemen. I think the spider-wolves are going to put on a real how-to lesson in evasive maneuvers for us."

Geary halted the turn of his formation early, as it was reaching the crest of its arc up and over, steadying out so that the pursuit force was aiming for an intercept with the enigmas climbing toward the spider-wolves. He could not, for the moment, see how to bring the slower and still-distant main body into the action. "Captain Armus, proceed in-system and maneuver independently as you see fit."

"Whoa," Lieutenant Yuon gasped as the spider-wolf formation broke into six separate ships that began weaving around each other in a dance that spiraled ever higher above the plane of the star system. "What are they doing, Captain?"

"Distracting the bad guys," Desjani replied with a grin.

Geary nodded, feeling the same sense of satisfaction. The spider-wolves might not be willing to participate in fighting the enigmas, but they apparently had no reluctance to help lead the enigmas into a trap. "All units, engage at will."

The enigmas must have heard their own combat alerts sounding, frantic warnings that, while they had centered attention on the swirling flight of the spider-wolf ships, the human pursuit formation had come charging in from slightly above and behind. Enigma ships started to scatter, but too late, as the pursuit force buzz-sawed through the lower quarter of the enigma formation.

Geary felt *Dauntless* rocking slightly from a couple of hits as his force tore away from the enigmas again. He had to take a moment to see what the enigmas were doing this time and saw that the enigma commander had dropped his chase after the spider-wolves and swung the enemy formation around and to starboard, only to check that turn and weave back far to port. In the wake of the enigma fleet, disabled and destroyed ships tumbled out in all directions.

"Where the hell is he going?" Desjani asked.

"He's heading for the main body," Geary said. "They spotted *Invincible*."

"The thing really is a threat magnet."

"A magnet with some very nasty stings protecting it," Geary replied. He brought his fleet over to port as well, aiming to hit the front of the enigma formation this time as it tried to run past him toward the main body.

That left a moment to check on results of that last pass. Geary scanned enigma losses first, seeing that thirty-one ships had been knocked out of the battle. His own ships had taken some hits, too, but the big local firepower advantage they had enjoyed had meant he had only lost two light cruisers disabled and four destroyers out of the fight, one of them, *Musket*, being a total loss.

Even though his ships had taken relatively few hits, system failure reports rippled across Geary's display. Hell-lance batteries on some ships, fire control on others, here and there shields losing coverage. Another light cruiser was scrambling to get back to the formation, having apparently missed his last command, and wasn't reporting current status, so *Strike* had probably suffered a comm failure.

"If they aim to ram *Invincible*..." Desjani cautioned.

"Even her armor won't save her. I know." Geary tapped a combination of ships to talk to. "Captain Armus, and commanding officers of *Dreadnaught*, *Orion*, *Dependable*, *Conqueror*, *Relentless*, *Reprisal*, *Superb*, and *Splendid*. We assess that the enigmas intend to ram our capital ships, and that *Invincible* will be a focus for their attack on your formation. Watch for enigma ships on collision courses with yourselves and *Invincible*, and ensure neither they nor any large pieces of them get through. Captain Armus, you are to take necessary action to deal with enigma ramming tactics to the best of your ability and ensure that every ship in your formation is on guard for enemy ships aiming for collisions with battleships, auxiliaries, and assault transports."

The enigmas were accelerating again, trying to pull past the point where the path of Geary's pursuit force would swing through their formation. He watched the point of contact slide farther and farther back, wondering if the enigmas would manage to slip past completely.

"All units, hit them in the rear as we make contact. Watch for mines dropped in the wake of the enigma ships." Using mines that way would be a tactic of desperation but might still cripple some of Geary's ships if the enigmas got lucky.

The pursuit formation whipped up and across the back of the enigma formation, Alliance missiles and hell-lance fire slamming into the sterns of the enigma warships still accelerating toward the main body of the Alliance fleet. Geary, who had tried to hit the front of the enigma formation, realized that the relative motion, which had instead brought the formations together like this, had spared his own ships a lot of damage. The enigma ships were all stern-on to their attackers, unable to employ most of their weapons. The main propulsion of the enigma warships were also exposed to the Alliance fire, taking damage that might otherwise have been met by hull armor.

"All units immediate execute come starboard five zero degrees, down one zero degrees, accelerate to point one five light speed." As the pursuit swung back and down again, Geary realized that he couldn't catch the enigmas once more until after they had reached the main body. The enemy had used their superior acceleration to speed out of reach for now.

But in the wake of the enigma formation, another twenty-three enemy ships drifted, or had spun off out of control or had blown up into clouds of debris, and so far Alliance losses had been minimal.

Desjani shook her head. "Admiral, you're asking a lot of Captain Armus."

"I'm aware that Captain Armus is not distinguished by flexibility or quickness," Geary said, hearing the harshness in his voice. "But he is steady."

The spider-wolf ships had kept rising a little higher above the plane of the star system and the combatants, then leveled out heading toward the star and the inner planets. Their position would give them a box seat for the rest of the battle, taking them out of any risk of further contact with the enigmas.

The main body of the Alliance forces was almost directly ahead of Geary's pursuit force, between them the enigma formation, which was rapidly closing on the main body and slowly pulling away from Geary's ships.

"Contact between main body and enigma formation in twenty-five—" Lieutenant Castries's voice broke off. "Recalculating. Main body is braking."

"Braking?" Desjani asked in disbelieving tones. "They have so much trouble getting up to speed, and he's braking?"

Geary watched his display, understanding dawning. "You're thinking like a battle cruiser commander. Armus is a battleship captain. He wants the best opportunity to make the firepower of his battleships count, and that means getting the meeting velocity down to less than point two light speed."

"But when you're dealing with an enemy who wants to ram you—"

"Tanya, he can't dodge them. Not with those battleships and *Invincible*. And look what he's doing with the auxiliaries and the assault transports." Those ships had swung back, taking position behind a wall of combatants, which had compressed down, leaving relatively little space between them. "He knows he needs to blow away anything coming at him."

"This is way too much like the tactics you told us not to use. Head-to-head, firepower-versus-firepower, no finesse, no fancy maneuvering."

"There's a time and a place for everything, Tanya."

She started to say something else, then an expression of astonishment mixed with awe came over her. "You knew. You knew that you would need Armus now in just this way. How did you know?"

"I didn't know. It was a guess. A lucky guess."

"Sure." Desjani made a religious gesture of thanks. "You didn't feel any hints or inspiration. Sure."

He shook his head, not answering, knowing that the legend of Black Jack left little room for luck, instead attributing success to the favor of powers far beyond human.

Well, maybe that was another word for luck.

"Ten minutes to enigma contact with main body," Lieutenant Castries said.

The ships of the main body had stopped braking, turning to face the oncoming enemy bow on, where armor, shields, and weapons were thickest. Geary wanted to call the shots, literally call them, but the main body was too far away for that. He had to depend on Captain Armus's choosing the right moments to fire.

With the naked eye, he might have been able to see at best a curiously regular lattice of bright objects ahead, where the main body of the fleet came onward. On his display, Geary could see every ship plainly identified. Directly before *Invincible*, in a small diamond formation, *Dreadnaught*, *Orion*, *Dependable*, and *Conqueror* served as a shield for the captured Kick ship and the four battleships mated to it for towing. Watching them, Geary knew with a grim certainty that this time Jane Geary would hold her position just as doggedly as any bear-cow could.

The enigma formation had re-formed into a flat wedge, the broad side facing the center of Armus's force, as if aiming to slice the human formation in half.

Desjani's lips were moving in silent prayer, but her expression held confidence.

Geary kept his eyes on his display, knowing as the last minutes counted down that whatever had happened had already taken place. He would see it all too late to do anything but watch.

Bare moments before the two forces collided, specter missiles leaped from every human warship, racing to meet their targets as hell lances fired in terrible volleys; on the heels of the hell lances, masses of grapeshot filled space before the human warships.

The barrage had been perfectly coordinated. Missiles and hell lances struck almost simultaneously, followed within less than a second by the ball bearings of the grapeshot field. Instead of a series of hard blows, a single mighty blow struck all at once.

Geary heard someone on *Dauntless*'s bridge gasp as the region of space just before the main body of the fleet lit up with titanic bursts of energy, the enigma ships following behind the front of their formation running right into the debris and unleashed energy of the weapons and power cores detonating among the leading enigma ships.

More bursts of energy sparkled among the human warships as pieces of debris slammed into their shields and armor. *Dreadnaught* jerked under multiple hits flaring on her bow, *Orion* staggered, *Dependable* fell off under hammerblows to one side of her bow, and for one heart-stopping moment, *Conqueror* looked like she had exploded. Then, as the fleet's sensors peered beneath that flash of light, and status reports came in, Geary realized that a wave of dense but tiny debris had struck *Conqueror*'s shields, generating that terrifying outburst but not getting through to seriously damage the battleship.

More hits on *Superb*, and on *Splendid*, helplessly connected to *Invincible*. And then a huge blast as something substantial made it through and slammed into the immensely thick armor on *Invincible*'s bow.

As Armus's formation swept clear of the debris, it could be seen that *Invincible* now bore a substantial crater on her bow. But she was otherwise intact.

"I'll be damned," Desjani whispered. "I can't believe it survived that. An *Invincible* that lived up to the name."

The auxiliaries and assault transports were rushing ahead, or at least rushing as best they could, to be enfolded among the battleships again, while the heavy cruisers swiftly pivoted and faced the enigmas who had passed through their formation. The battleships began slowly swinging upward by the front edge of the formation, like a plate tilting up slowly to face in another direction, where the enigmas were now to be found.

The enigmas… Geary breathed a prayer of his own. Roughly one hundred and sixty enigma ships had met Armus's formation head-on. Fewer than eighty were still in motion, sweeping around behind the main body and—"What the hell."

"They're breaking up their formation," Desjani said.

In an instant, he knew why. "All units in the pursuit force, immediate execute you are free to maneuver. The enigma force is no longer concentrating on defeating our fleet and is instead scattering to get units past us so they can attack other targets in this star system. Operate independently to engage any enigma warship you can get within weapons range of. I repeat, all units in the pursuit force, maneuver independently now and get every enigma you can."

Desjani was already rapping out orders to jolt *Dauntless* onto a new vector aimed toward an intercept with a cluster of enigma warships that hadn't yet separated much. "I agree that they've given up on trying to take us out, but how do you know they aren't scattering to escape to the jump point?" she asked a moment later.

"If they wanted to run, they could have just kept going in formation. The reason for scattering like that is to make it damn near impossible for us to stop all of them from getting to targets like the hypernet gate. Not the complete victory they wanted, but it would still cost us something we want and need."

"If our main-body formation disperses, too—"

"No! Then some of the enigma ships might try for the assault transports and auxiliaries!"

On his display, the pursuit-force formation looked as if it, too, had exploded, ships hurtling outward on hundreds of vectors.

Geary swept his gaze across the rest of the display, taking in both the likely targets of the surviving enigmas and the three small Syndic or former Syndic flotillas. He hadn't called any of those possibly friendly/probably neutral forces yet, but now he punched in the right circuit for such a message. "All armed forces in the Midway Star System, this is Admiral Geary. The enigma ships have broken formation and will be heading for targets within this star system. We will stop all that we can, but you must also intercept and engage anything that gets past us. The enigmas will ram targets if all other methods of attack fail. Do not, repeat not, attempt to engage the six ovoid ships that accompanied my fleet. They are neutral in this fight and allies of humanity." That was perhaps strongly overstating the spider-wolf attitude toward humans, but now was no time to fine-tune adjectives.

"I welcome your assistance in defending this star system," Geary continued. "To the honor of our ancestors, Geary, out."

The widely dispersed and still-spreading force of enigma warships was expanding like a puff of dandelion seeds hit by a strong gust of wind, every ship bending toward a course heading toward the star and the human targets there. Opposite them, and slightly closer to the star, the ships of Geary's pursuit force had also burst outward, more numerous than the enigma vessels but with the harder task of stopping those who wanted to just get by them. Between them lay the main-body formation, and there Geary saw some hope. "The individual enigma ships can't go too close to our main body, or they'll get nailed by all the firepower there."

"It'll restrict the enigmas' maneuvering options and help us herd them a little," Desjani agreed, her expression intent. "I'm giving you two targets, Lieutenant Yuon. I want them both."

"Yes, Captain! Fire control systems are tracking the targets you've designated."

"Engage the targets as soon as they get close enough," Desjani ordered.

Geary couldn't keep track of everything anymore as his display filled with hundreds of vectors rising and dropping around the mass of the main-body formation, hunters and hunted twisting, evading, and pouncing as they flashed by each other. *Dauntless* lashed out as she tore past a much smaller enigma ship, pounding it badly enough that the alien craft broke in two. Moments later, a second enigma ship was engaged, this one tumbling away only partially under control as two Alliance destroyers chased after it.

"I have no idea of how things are going," Geary muttered, looking at the rat's-nest of intersecting and intertwining vectors, the reports of firing, the estimates of damage to enemy ships, and reports of damage to his own ships as the enigmas fought back.

"Keep an eye on this," Desjani suggested, as *Dauntless* swung down and over in a dive tight enough to generate groans of protest from the inertial nullifiers and the ship's structure. She pointed to a single number there. "Estimated number of enemy ships. As long as it keeps going down, we're doing okay."

His head jerked from momentum as *Dauntless* leveled out and surged after a third enigma warship, about the size of a heavy cruiser, which was dueling with a light cruiser and inflicting more damage than it was taking. "Tell engineering I need more thrust from main propulsion," Desjani ordered her bridge watch-standers.

"Engineering says we're already at one hundred and ten percent, Captain, and if we—"

"One hundred fifteen. *Now.*"

"Yes, Captain."

Seconds later, *Dauntless* surged from a bit more acceleration, closing the gap just enough. "Get him," Desjani ordered.

Specter missiles fired, racing toward the enigma ship, which belatedly realized that its battering of the light cruiser was not going unnoticed. The enigma tried to roll away, but two specters caught it, damaging its propulsion. *Dauntless* drew closer, hammering away with hell lances as the enigma ship fired frantically back.

"Our bow shields are almost down," Lieutenant Castries called out.

"I see," Desjani replied calmly. "They'll hold long enough."

One enigma shot got through, holing a storage compartment up forward, then the alien shields collapsed, and *Dauntless* poured a rain of hell-lance fire into the enemy.

Geary was barely aware of the enigma ship exploding under the punishment that *Dauntless* was inflicting; instead, he watched the whole situation and the number Desjani had pointed to. Even though their numbers were dwindling fast, the surviving enigma ships were breaking through and past the human warships.

"Thirty-five," he said as the Alliance ships steadied out in stern chases after the enigmas who had gotten clear and were heading for their targets. A moment later, several specters fired at extreme range got hits. "Thirty-four."

"Even the Syndics ought to be able to handle that," Desjani said, smiling. The smile disappeared as she studied the nearby situation. "Tell engineering to ease back to one hundred percent on main propulsion. We're going to have a long stern chase before we can catch up with any more enigmas."

"The Syndics don't have enough ships to cover all of the possible targets adequately," Geary said. "Have we ever heard from any of the Syndics?"

Desjani looked back at her comm watch, who nodded. "Something came in five minutes ago," the watch-stander reported. "Your standing instructions—"

"Are not to interrupt time-critical events for messages that are not time critical," Desjani finished. "You did the right thing. Who is this message from?"

"It came from the flotilla that has been transiting from the inhabited planet to the docks near the gas giant. The nearest one to us. It's addressed directly to Admiral Geary, Captain."

"Send it to me and Captain Desjani," Geary ordered.

An instant later, windows popped open before him and Desjani, showing a woman in Syndic uniform on the bridge of what was plainly a Syndic heavy cruiser. But her collar insignia were different than Syndic standard, and her words immediately contradicted the rest of her appearance. "This is Kommodor Marphissa on the heavy cruiser *Manticore* of the Midway Star System."

"Kommodor Marphissa on the heavy cruiser *Manticore*," Desjani repeated. "Military ranks and names for the ships? There have been a few changes around here. She didn't call herself a Syndic, either, but she still looks like a Syndic."

"I wonder what happened to CEO Kolani," Geary said.

"Probably something that we'd be better off not knowing." Desjani eyed the image of the kommodor suspiciously.

"Kolani struck me as being fiercely loyal to the Syndicate Worlds," Geary said, "which would explain why this Kommodor Marphissa is now in command rather than Kolani."

Kommodor Marphissa had paused for several seconds, as if anticipating that her audience would exchange comments, and now spoke with quiet assurance. "We welcome the assistance of the Alliance fleet under the command of Admiral Geary in defending the Midway Star System against *all* who threaten it."

Her emphasis on one word was impossible to miss. "All?" Desjani demanded. "All? That ex-Syndic bitch is trying to rope us into fighting their battles against the Syndic government. What makes her think we'll fall for that?"

"We are en route to the gas giant," Marphissa continued. "We will continue on that track until we either encounter enemy forces or are ordered to assist you. However, I already have standing orders that the fleet of Admiral Geary is always welcome at Midway. For the people! This is Kommodor Marphissa. Out."

Geary frowned in thought as the message ended. "Did you hear that?"

"Every word," Desjani said, her own voice sharp.

"I meant the end, where she said 'for the people.' I've heard that a lot from Syndic authorities, and it always gets said without any emphasis or emotion. Just 'for the people' spoken quickly and without feeling, as if the phrase didn't have any meaning."

Desjani shrugged. "Is that surprising? You know it's a joke. Nothing about the way the Syndicate Worlds has been and is run is really 'for the people.'"

"But the way that Kommodor said it, she really seemed to mean it," Geary insisted.

She replayed the end of the message, then nodded reluctantly. "All right. I see that. These people have revolted against the CEOs. Maybe they really are trying to be something other than Syndics. But the people at the top, Iceni and Drakon, are both former CEOs. Either they've changed their stripes, or this is all theater. I know where I'm placing my bets."

Geary sat back, looking at his display, where hundreds of individual Alliance warships chased after thirty-four enigma warships, every ship on a different path but all of the vectors arcing down toward either the inner star system or the hypernet gate. None of the vectors displayed intercept points, reflecting the reality that his ships couldn't catch those enigmas unless the enigmas altered their own courses or speeds. "Whoever these former Syndics are, they'd better fight smart. We can't stop those enigmas. They'll have to."

Alerts came to life on his display, highlighting a dozen enigma ships.

"They launched bombardment projectiles," Desjani said. "Aimed at the inhabited planet by the looks of the trajectories." She clenched a fist and pounded her seat arm softly but firmly. "Neither we nor the Syndics can stop those."

18

Dauntless was moving at close to point two light speed herself now, hurtling through space at almost sixty thousand kilometers per second, but even that was too slow to catch the enigma ships ahead of them. The bombardment the enigmas had launched was also unreachable.

They could only sit, knowing that they would spend the next couple of days watching the bombardment heading for its target and that they couldn't possibly stop it.

"Admiral, we're receiving a message from the inhabited planet."

Geary nodded despairingly. "They don't know what's coming at them yet. Let's see what 'President' Iceni has to say."

The image that appeared showed Iceni and a hard-looking man sitting behind an impressive desk of polished wood. He didn't look like an assistant but rather an equal.

Iceni no longer wore the dark blue suit that was standard wear for Syndicate Worlds' CEOs. Instead, her outfit suggested power and wealth without flaunting either. The man beside her wore an unfamiliar uniform that seemed to have been modified from Syndic designs. He didn't need that uniform to project an image of being military, though. Geary would have pegged him as such no matter what that man had worn.

"This is President Iceni of the independent star system of Midway." Iceni paused.

The man in uniform spoke crisply. "This is General Drakon, commanding officer of Midway's ground forces."

"We are happy to welcome the Alliance fleet back in our star system," Iceni continued. "Especially considering current circumstances and previous agreements between us. We will do our utmost to defend our star system against invaders, and ask only that you assist us in that task until the people of Midway are once again secure. Kommodor Marphissa, our senior warship commander, has been sent orders to follow your directions unless they conflict with her obligations to defend this star system.

"Be aware that the battleship located at our main military dockyards has functional propulsion but not working shields or weapons at this time, so it cannot be counted upon to assist in the defense of this star system.

"This is President Iceni, for the people, out."

Rione had appeared at Geary's elbow, bending a questioning expression his way. "Previous agreements?"

He nodded, trying not to look guilty. "Previous agreements," Geary said, as if that were natural and normal.

"Are we talking about more than the peace treaty made with the Syndicate Worlds' government? Additional agreements?"

"Why would you ask me that?"

Both Desjani and Rione were giving him hard looks now. He was abruptly aware that he was pinned between them. "Admiral, did you reach any other agreements with the authorities here at Midway?"

He nodded. "I agreed to help defend them against the enigmas, which was consistent with the peace treaty."

"That's all?" Rione pressed. "That kommodor also seemed to expect more from us than the peace treaty would necessarily require."

"Yes," Desjani said. "She did."

That was about as bad as it got, having Rione and Desjani agreeing with each other that he must have done something wrong.

"Did you say anything," Rione asked, "that this President Iceni could have twisted into a claim that Black Jack would defend them against their own government?"

"No. I did *not* promise that." They were watching him. "I did agree, for good reasons, not to publicly declare that I would not defend them against threats like that."

Desjani glowered at him. "I should never let you talk to women alone."

But Rione appeared thoughtful. "A vague commitment without real promises? I'm impressed, Admiral. We might be able to use that."

"Oh, wonderful!" Desjani said. "You've got *her* approval! Does that tell you just how wrong you are?"

Geary held out a restraining hand. "Later. I need to reply to those two. By the time they hear back from us, they'll have seen that we knocked out most of the enigma force but also that the enigma bombardment is already on its way toward them."

"That planet has a lot of water and not much land," Desjani commented, her expression gloomy once more. "Even if the enigma shots miss land targets, they'll kick up some nasty wave action that will swamp all of those islands. I'd tell them to try to evacuate everybody they can to orbit and get the rest to whatever high ground exists. But knowing Syndic CEOs, they'll probably just make sure they get clear so they can watch the citizens catch hell from some safe spot."

He almost asked Desjani how she could predict the results of a widespread planetary bombardment so well, then caught himself in time. The Alliance had adopted such tactics, had tried to destroy enemy morale as well as civilian targets by indiscriminate bombardment. That strategy had never worked in the past, it hadn't worked for the Alliance; but it had been followed for too long. And Desjani had been a fleet officer while those bombardments were conducted. It wasn't something they talked about, but he knew it had happened. It would be best not to comment on that now.

Instead, Geary focused on the last part of Desjani's assessment. "Iceni didn't run the last time the enigmas attacked, remember? She stayed on the planet even though before we showed up it looked like the enigmas were going to walk all over this star system. That's what she's like. What do you think of that Drakon character?"

Desjani made an irritated gesture. "He looked real. I mean, not like a CEO."

"That was my impression, too. He seems like a professional, like someone who wouldn't abandon his post."

"How did he get to be a CEO?"

"I don't know," Geary replied. "You're right that we can't forget that. But I'm going to assume the best of them because that can't hurt right now. All we can do is watch whatever they do."

Rione nodded somberly. "Will the planet be habitable after the bombardment hits?"

"That depends where the projectiles land," Geary said. He took a deep breath, blew it out slowly, tapped his comm controls, and started speaking.

"This is Admiral Geary. We have done our best to eliminate the enigma force, but some ships have gotten past us, and some of those have launched a bombardment aimed at your inhabited planet. We will continue our pursuit of the enigma ships but cannot stop the incoming bombardment. I urge you to take any possible measures to ensure the safety of your people. To the honor of our ancestors, Geary, out."

With nothing else to do after that but watch the paths of ships and bombardment projectiles heading toward their targets, Geary glumly studied the three Syndic or former Syndic flotillas, trying to figure out what he would do if he were the Syndic commander. "If they handled things right and coordinated the movements of those two heavy cruisers at the gas giant properly, they could force the enigmas to run a gauntlet to get to that battleship or the inhabited planet."

Desjani shook her head. "In theory, sure. But they're not that good."

"They need to be that good if they're going to survive. We can't stay here. Whatever the people here have left to defend them after we leave has to be able to fight smart, or they'll be overwhelmed."

"You can't teach them your ways of fighting," Desjani objected.

"Aside from the fact that we can't hang around this star system for months, teaching smart fighting tactics to Syndics would not sit well with anybody."

"It doesn't look like they are Syndics anymore."

"How do you judge that? Admiral, I agree anybody here has to fight better than the average Syndic CEO, but *you* can't teach them. The fleet and the government would raise hell if Black Jack himself offered his secrets to people who still wear Syndic uniforms, even if they call themselves something else."

Geary nodded, knowing that she was right but knowing that he was also right. How could he help the people here defend themselves?

That assumed that there would be anything left here worth defending, of course.

"Admiral?" General Charban had come onto the bridge and now pointed questioningly at the observer's display. "What are the spider-wolf ships doing?"

He hadn't bothered looking, not since the spider-wolves had swooped out of the fight. "They were above the plane of the star system and closer in to the star since they hadn't headed back to engage the enigmas like we did," Geary replied, searching his own display. "Now they're—What in the name of the living stars are they doing?"

Desjani gave him an alarmed look, herself focusing on the spider-wolves' position and movements. "They're… aiming for an intercept with the enigma bombardment," she said in disbelief. "According to our system, they can manage it since they were positioned closer to the inner star system than the enigma launch points and have better acceleration than we do."

"Why?" Geary demanded. "What's the point of intercepting a kinetic bombardment? The projectiles move too fast and are too small to get a decent fire control solution on them."

"For us," Desjani said, understanding growing in her eyes. "Admiral, the spider-wolf ships are faster than us and a lot more maneuverable. They were where they needed to be to intercept a bombardment launched from the enigma ships. If they can come in behind the kinetic projectiles, reducing the relative speed of the engagement, and maneuver into the right positions, our systems say that in theory they could at least score glancing hits and divert the paths of those rocks."

Rione was staring ahead, openmouthed with surprise. "They're intervening. They won't help us fight the enigmas, they won't help defend warships against the enigmas, but they are moving to try to defend our civilian population."

"You say the spider-wolves were where they needed to be to manage this intercept?" Charban asked Desjani. "It seems they intended to be able to do that if necessary."

Desjani looked frustrated. "Why do they have to be so damned ugly?"

"I am increasingly certain that they are asking the same thing of us," Charban replied with a smile. "They know that the people here are those who are, or were, our enemies, and it impressed them that we were willing to fight to defend them. Perhaps that action by us decided the spider-wolves to take their action. As different as we are, this is a point at which our understandings meet."

"It's strange," Geary said. "We seem to have a number of things in common with the spider-wolves, who are the most physically unlike us of the alien races we've encountered. The two other alien races, the enigmas and the bear-cows, may look a lot more like us but their mental processes are more alien than those of the spider-wolves."

"No one ever promised that the universe would be easy to understand," Charban said, "or that it would meet our expectations rather than challenging them."

"Nineteen minutes to intercept of the spider-wolves with that bombardment," Desjani said. "Look. The spider-wolf ships aren't locked into formation anymore. They're adjusting their vectors to come in behind different clusters of rocks launched by different enigma ships."

The resigned and disheartened waiting of a short time before had been replaced by tension. Geary watched the tracks of the spider-wolf ships and the rocks converging, curves sliding steadily close to contact, wondering if even the spider-wolves could handle a maneuvering problem that difficult.

"Beautiful," Desjani breathed, as the curving paths of the spider-wolf ships altered subtly. "Even their maneuvers are gorgeous."

"Our systems estimate that the spider-wolf ships will be within weapons range in two minutes," Lieutenant Yuon reported.

Geary checked the distance. Twelve light-minutes to where the spider-wolves and the kinetic bombardment would meet. Whatever the spider-wolves had accomplished might already be done, over before the human ships could even see the beginning.

The bridge had gone silent, everyone watching their displays. Geary realized that he was even breathing as quietly as he could, as if any sound could disrupt events occurring far distant from him. Human instincts, born of hunters in the ancient past and on a world unimaginably far away, still subconsciously dictating actions among the stars.

"How long until we know?" Rione asked, peering at her display, her voice, low as it was, still resounding to break the spell of silence on the bridge.

"Another three minutes until we might see something," Lieutenant Yuon replied.

They were a very, very long three minutes, then several gasps sounded simultaneously as the first actions were seen. "Look at that!" Desjani said, her eyes lit with admiration. "They came in perfectly! Right behind their targets, zero deflection shots, getting the relative velocity as low as possible!"

"But they still only have a short firing window before those rocks pull away." Geary watched shots going out from the spider-wolf ships, willing them to hit even though he knew hits or misses had happened over ten minutes ago.

"One, two, four, seven," Lieutenant Yuon called out as the systems reported kinetic projectiles knocked off of their trajectories by hits from the spider-wolf weapons. "Twelve, nineteen, twenty-six, thirty-eight."

Geary kept his eyes on the firing. Thirty-eight out of seventy-two rocks accounted for.

"Fifty-one," Lieutenant Yuon reported. The hits were coming faster now, as the spider-wolves perfected their positioning and aim, but the rocks were also pulling steadily farther away and were rapidly going out of effective range. "Sixty, Sixty-four, Sixty-eight, Sixty-nine."

"Come on!" Geary burst out. "Three more!"

"Seventy... seventy-one."

The six spider-wolf ships were pumping out shots as fast as they could fire, but it was obvious that their accuracy had fallen off dramatically as the range had increased. The bridge was silent again, every eye locked on the symbol showing the last bombardment projectile still on course for the inhabited planet.

"Damn," Desjani muttered.

"They've still got a chance," Geary said.

The spider-wolf barrage stopped abruptly and he felt sick inside. So close to complete success. But the spider-wolves had obviously given up—

A single burst of fire erupted from the spider-wolf ships, every weapon letting loose at once, all aimed at the point where the kinetic projectile raced ahead of them.

"Seventy-two," Lieutenant Yuon said in a shaky voice.

Desjani laughed, looked at Geary like she very badly wanted to kiss him, but settled for making a fist and punching his shoulder. "Thank you ancestors and thank you spider-wolves!"

"Madam Emissary," Geary said, feeling weak with relief, "and General Charban. Please send the spider-wolves our deepest, most sincere thanks."

Unlike the others on the bridge, Rione had a worried expression. "What if the enigmas fire more bombardment rounds?"

"The spider-wolves are even better positioned for intercepts now," Geary said. "They'd have even better shots at the next set of rocks. We still have to worry about what those enigma ships might attack, but no bombardments will get through to that planet as long as the spider-wolves stay between the enigmas and the planet."

The fleet's sensors had continued to track the paths of the seventy-two enigma bombardment projectiles, but those tracks no longer bore threat symbols as the rocks tumbled away on paths that would pass clear of the inhabited planet.

"Score one for diplomacy," Charban said.

Desjani, still elated, smiled at the comment. "General, I'd like to think of it as a great return on the investment of one case of duct tape."

"Captain, some of those enigma ships are making major vector changes," Lieutenant Castries warned.

Everyone's eyes went back to their displays. "Well done keeping an eye on things while your superiors were being complacent," Desjani told Castries. "Twelve of them."

"The twelve that fired the bombardment at the planet," Lieutenant Yuon confirmed.

The twelve enigma warships were diving far below the plane of the star system and turning back toward the welter of Alliance warships that were pursuing them and the other enigma ships. "A suicide run?" Geary speculated. "Are they going to try to get through to the auxiliaries or assault transports again?"

To his surprise, General Charban answered. "Only those twelve are making such a major change, Admiral. We learned while we were going through enigma territory that they are not a united species. This force of theirs must have been made up of contingents from different enigma nations. I suggest that what we're seeing is what's left of one of those contingents deciding that they have already gone far beyond the demands of duty to any agreement to attack the humans. They tried to bombard the inhabited planet here, and that failed. They're going home."

"That's possible," Desjani conceded. "They sure as hell threw off their immediate pursuers with that move." The Alliance warships chasing those enigmas, surprised by the radical course change of their prey and traveling at exceedingly high velocity, were having trouble bending their own vectors far enough to manage intercepts before the twelve enigmas got past on their way back toward the jump point. "Admiral, if some of the destroyers and heavy cruisers are detached from the main body, they can move to nail those guys."

Geary watched the twelve enigma warships breaking past their immediate pursuers, the last in line getting caught by Alliance fire and breaking apart. The other eleven continued on, outracing and outmaneuvering the human warships.

His gaze went to the rest of the battlefield, where disabled enigma warships were self-destructing, their surviving crews still on board, in an effort to keep the secrets of the enigma race. Only nineteen other enigma ships were left, five of those aiming for the inoperable battleship and the docks at the gas giant, and the other fourteen for the hypernet gate. He thought of the bear-cows fighting to the death and suiciding to avoid capture. "No."

"No?" Desjani questioned. "Captain Armus can detach more than enough cruisers and destroyers to get those enigmas and still have plenty of ships available to protect his high-value units if some of them try to ram again."

"No," Geary repeated. "There's been enough. General, send another broadcast of our negotiation offer to those eleven enigma ships. Add in a statement that we've shown what will happen if they keep fighting us, then reemphasize that we are willing to agree to leave them alone if they leave us alone."

"Yes, Admiral," Charban said.

Desjani sighed, then nodded to Geary. "I guess we've killed enough of them. If a few get home to tell the enigmas what happened to the rest, it might make them think twice before trying anything like this again."

"That's the idea," Geary said, but she gave him a look that told him that she knew it was far from his only reason for avoiding more bloodshed.

He watched the movements of ships on his display, feeling immensely tired now, knowing that if nothing changed, it would be hours or even days before anything else happened. But if any of the nineteen enigma warships still heading for targets made radical changes in their vectors, it might be only minutes before action occurred.

And warnings were popping up on his display about the fuel-cell levels on the destroyers in the pursuit force, with here and there a light cruiser also showing low reserves. The light cruisers and destroyers couldn't catch the enigmas as long as the enemy kept charging away from them, but those ships could run their fuel-cell reserves down to dangerously low levels in their futile chase. "All units in the pursuit force, this is Admiral Geary. Immediate execute reduce velocity to point one five light speed. Continue tracking enigma warships and engage them if the opportunity presents itself."

Desjani had that unhappy look again.

"We can't catch them," he told her.

"I know that."

"The Syndics might knock them back toward us."

She brightened a little. "Yeah. They might. Even Boyens might be able to handle fourteen enigma ships when he has a battleship and twenty other Syndic warships under his control."

Geary nodded, thinking that they should have heard from Boyens by now if he had sent a message once he saw Geary's fleet. But Boyens, it seemed, was keeping tight-lipped for the moment.

The battle hadn't ended, and neither had the chase; but the ships of the pursuit force relaxed their combat status, giving their crews a chance to rest and to eat decent meals. Far back toward the jump point they had used from Pele, the main-body formation came stolidly onward, not reacting as the eleven fleeing enigma ships en route to the jump point raced past well out of range of the main-body warships. Those enigmas had had enough, just as Charban had guessed.

After several hours, another message came in from the inhabited planet, once again showing Iceni and Drakon. Both were doing a very good job of trying not to look like people who had just had death sentences unexpectedly commuted. "We are in your debt again, Admiral Geary. I don't know the nature of your allies, but we owe them an immense debt as well."

"Wait until she gets a look at them," Desjani commented.

"My warships," Iceni continued, "will engage the enigmas heading for my battleship. I cannot control the actions of the flotilla near the hypernet gate. Do not trust that the flotilla there will act in our interest, Admiral. CEO Boyens, their commander, is known to you. If you make your orders clear to him, he may hesitate to act contrary to them. It is essential that Boyens understands that he is not in control of this star system and does not dictate what will happen here.

"For the people, Iceni, out."

"She didn't let that General Drakon talk this time," Desjani observed.

"Maybe he didn't have anything to say," Geary said.

"That doesn't often stop people from talking." Desjani grinned. "Though he did look like the type who doesn't run his mouth. Did you notice that Iceni called her units warships instead of mobile forces? And that she said 'my' battleship?"

"Yes. We'll see what Lieutenant Iger and Emissary Rione make of that." He considered his options. "Iceni clearly wants me to tell Boyens what to do."

"She wants Boyens to know that you're the big dog in this star system," Desjani agreed. "That serves us and her, doesn't it?"

"Not if it puts us in the middle between her and Boyens." He thought a little longer, then tapped his comm controls. "CEO Boyens, this is Admiral Geary. The small group of enigma warships headed for the gas giant will be engaged by the forces in that region. The remaining fourteen enigma warships heading toward you must be halted before they can damage the hypernet gate by weapons fire or ramming. My ships will continue their pursuit and attack any enigma vessel whenever opportunity offers. To the honor of our ancestors, Geary, out."

Whatever Boyens thought of events and the messages being sent him, he still didn't send any messages back to Geary, and his flotilla remained in the same orbit near the hypernet gate. On the other hand, Kommodor Marphissa sent Geary several updates, advising him of her planned vector for her flotilla to intercept the five enigma warships short of the gas giant, then providing new information when adjustments were required. Geary responded with a suggestion on employment of the two heavy cruisers at the gas giant, trying to phrase his words so that they didn't come across as orders but still strongly urged action. "She knows her stuff," Geary commented, "but the Kommodor seems to lack experience."

"Experience in how *we* fight," Desjani said. "Look how she keeps updating you. That's Syndic-style command and control. But she's not dependent on being told what to do. Her maneuvering solutions are technically good even if they're not things of beauty."

"You've just been spoiled by the spider-wolves." Another thing he had never expected to be saying to anyone.

"Damn right." Desjani twisted her mouth in a wry grin. "We're going to watch the Syndics, the former Syndics, that is, fight somebody else. I've never had the chance to do that. But I have to warn you, based on what she's doing against these enigmas, that Kommodor wouldn't be able to handle Boyens's flotilla with what she's got."

"But you still think it would be a mistake for me to try to teach them anything."

"Yes. Yes. Yes. Is my opinion clear?"

"It is," Geary said. Until he could find good arguments against her points, he couldn't debate Desjani on the matter.

It took six more hours before Kommodor Marphissa's flotilla rushed into contact with the enigmas, the two heavy cruisers, six light cruisers, and twelve Hunter-Killers splitting just before the intercept so they could hit all of the spread-out enigma ships. Two of the five enigma ships were knocked out, and a third hit badly enough that it lost maneuvering control, spinning off its track at an angle to its former course.

The flotilla partially re-formed, leaving three of the light cruisers to go after the damaged enigma ship, the rest curving around in an up-and-over loop to chase the two remaining enigmas heading for the gas giant. Geary watched with mixed anger and frustration as those two enigma ships finally launched bombardment projectiles at the orbital docks and the battleship, then themselves whipped down and around to avoid an intercept by the last two heavy cruisers as they came on from the area of the space docks.

"Thirty-five minutes until that Syndic bombardment hits the orbital facility and the—" Lieutenant Castries paused. "Um, they're moving."

Geary squinted at his display. The battleship had lit off its main propulsion at partial power but remained fastened to the orbital dock. "He's going to rip it apart. The dock can't take that kind of stress."

But as they watched, the battleship's propulsion kept straining without tearing the ship and part of the dock loose from the larger structure. "Captain Smythe's ships are almost a light-hour behind us," Geary said. "Do we have any engineers here who can talk to us about what we're seeing?"

"Engineering," Desjani ordered that watch-stander, "I need anyone with structural stress experience in large orbiting structures to contact the bridge right away."

It was perhaps no surprise that within a minute, the robust figure of Master Chief Gioninni appeared. "Yes, Captain?"

"You've worked on large orbiting structures, Master Chief?"

"I've worked on everything, Captain. What do you need?"

She pointed to the displays. "Can they do that?"

Gioninni squinted at the battleship stubbornly pulling at the vastly more-massive orbital dock. "They are doing it, Captain. Shouldn't be able to, though." The master chief's face twisted as he concentrated. "You know what they must have done, Captain? They must have figured out where the stress would concentrate on that structure when the battleship started yanking on it, and they jury-rigged heavy-duty reinforcement for those places and areas."

"They could do that?" Desjani questioned.

"They got the stuff they need, Captain. That's an orbital shipyard. Not a big, fantastolous one like the shipyards we trashed at Sancere, but it is a shipyard. That means they have the industrial equipment and the materials they'd need to do that kind of thing. All they needed was enough time."

"The bombardment was only launched about ten minutes ago," Geary said.

"Yes, sir, Admiral. But they haven't ripped off a piece of that orbital dock where that battleship is tied up and pulling at it, so they must have figured out what they might have to do and gotten started a while ago."

"Thanks, Master Chief," Desjani said.

Gioninni saluted smartly, then his image vanished.

"The enigmas showed up here about a day ago," Geary said, "so the Syndics, the former Syndics, on that orbital shipyard had only about a day to realize they might have to move that dockyard and get the work done. Somebody showed some very good forethought and initiative."

"Nice in an Alliance officer," Desjani replied. "Not so nice in a Syndic. Lieutenant Castries, can they get that thing moved enough to evade those rocks?"

"It's just barely started moving," Castries said. "Our systems are having to estimate its mass, and estimate how much thrust the battleship is putting out. There's a high degree of uncertainty, Captain."

"It sounds like the answer is 'maybe,'" Geary said.

"Yes, Admiral. It's 'maybe' calculated out to several decimal points, though."

"Captain," Lieutenant Yuon offered, "the enigma bombardment is centered on the points where the orbiting structure and the battleship would have been if neither could move. We use looser patterns to make sure some of the rocks get hits, but the enigmas employed a tight pattern. That would ensure the destruction of the battleship and the dock if they didn't move. But it also means they don't have to move as far to get clear of the rocks."

"Fifteen minutes to impact if they don't," Castries added.

At first there was some excitement as the two surviving enigmas from this small group tried to evade not only Kommodor Marphissa's flotilla but also the human warships still in pursuit. The enigmas made it past the Syndics, but one of them got boxed in by some of Geary's ships and blown apart. The other ran for the jump point at maximum acceleration, leaving its pursuers once more too far behind to catch it.

That left the ongoing drama of the incoming bombardment. Geary was used to watching ships move at thousands of kilometers per second. Now he watched as the battleship strained to move the far more massive shipyard only a couple of kilometers within the next fifteen minutes. It felt like the old joke about watching paint dry, except in this case an awful amount of destruction was hurtling down on the structure while the space dock built up speed meter by painful meter as the minutes dragged by at a snail's pace.

"They might make it," Castries reported with five minutes to go. "It's going to be close."

It was. The rocks plummeted past the shipyard and battleship without causing any damage, skipped over the upper ranges of the gas giant's atmosphere, then continued onward, their paths scattered by the interaction with the gas giant.

"Estimated range of the nearest miss was five hundred meters," Lieutenant Yuon reported. "Plus or minus one hundred meters."

"Somebody's ancestors were looking out for them," Desjani said. "Remember this incident, Lieutenant. When you employ rocks against an object in space, it doesn't matter whether you miss by a hundred kilometers or by a meter. It's still a miss and doesn't bother the target at all."

The new battleship had shut off its main propulsion, and now the far-weaker attitude jets on the orbital facility were firing to very gradually brake its motion and settle it back into a fixed orbit that would be slightly farther out from the gas giant, but not by any distance that would matter to anything but rocks aiming for where that facility had once been.

That left the fourteen enigma warships still heading for the hypernet gate, but an hour and a half after the bombardment missed the orbital dockyard, those enigmas saw that event, and it was apparently the last straw. Once again, the enigma ships spun about in maneuvers no human ship could match. Geary's forces caught one anyway, then, more by luck than design, managed to hit a second hard enough to cause it to self-destruct. "If they keep going like bats out of hell," Desjani said, "no one else has a chance to get the rest unless you cut loose some of Armus's ships."

"No." Geary felt not just a tiredness over the deaths this day but also a nagging worry that the fleeing enigmas might still choose to ram any pursuer that got too close. Losing another ship or ships to rake in a few more enigma warships didn't seem like a worthwhile risk given how badly the enigmas had been beaten here.

Near the hypernet gate, CEO Boyens's flotilla had still not moved.

Desjani saw Geary's glower directed at that force. "I guess Boyens thought it would be smart to avoid risking getting any scratches on his ships," she commented.

"Maybe that was smart in the short term," Geary replied, "but it seriously ticked me off in the long term even though I expected something like that. He's going to have to deal with me now. I know the people running this star system used to be Syndic CEOs, too, but they sent their ships out to fight while he watched to see what would happen."

"I can't wait to hear his first message to us," Desjani said. "And I'm looking forward to hearing your reply, too. Oh, congratulations."

"For what?" For a moment, he truly didn't understand what she was referring to.

"Uh, victory? Saved the star system? I do recommend you detach some of Armus's heavy cruisers and destroyers to shadow those surviving enigmas just in case they get ideas before they reach the jump point, but I believe that even the living stars wouldn't think me presumptuous to offer you congratulations at this point."

"Thanks, Tanya." He couldn't feel triumphant right now. All Geary felt was exhaustion as he watched the surviving enigmas flee.

19

"Midway continues to recognize its obligations under the treaties made with the Syndicate government on Prime," President Iceni was saying. "However, since we are now an independent star system, there will be a need to renegotiate agreements. I assure you that we seek agreements that will mutually benefit us and the Alliance and do not anticipate any problems reaching such agreements. For the people, Iceni, out."

He should let Rione deal with this, but there were still fleet matters to address. Geary straightened his uniform and tapped the reply command. "This is Admiral Geary. I will leave negotiations on such matters to the two emissaries of the Alliance government we have with us. They will be contacting you soon for that purpose. Of immediate concern, my auxiliaries are very low on raw materials. I would like your agreement for them to mine some of the asteroids in this star system for such materials so that we can begin to repair the battle damage suffered here."

The damage hadn't all been suffered here, of course, but he figured it didn't hurt to toss in a not-so-subtle reminder that his fleet had suffered damage and losses defending those he was now asking a favor of.

"Please pass on to Kommodor Marphissa," Geary continued, "my personal appreciation for the efforts of her and her ships in working with us for the defense of this star system. They fought well." He had been trying hard to think of Marphissa as someone other than a Syndic, and someone other than a Syndic would have received such a thanks from him. "To the honor of our ancestors, Geary, out."

Another message now. "Captain Smythe, I am anticipating a positive reply to our request for access to raw materials here. Prepare for mining operations and head your ships toward the asteroids you want to dig in."

For some unknown reason, the spider-wolf ships had been following his auxiliaries around since the battle, occasionally engaging in intricate maneuvering with themselves or even among the human ships. The fleet's personnel had begun referring to those movements as dances. Their purpose or meaning for the spider-wolves remained a mystery, but at least for the humans, the dances were benefiting morale. Since the spider-wolves had managed the impossible feat of deflecting a kinetic bombardment aimed at a human planet, they had become welcome visitors rather than objects of puzzlement and worry.

No one seemed to be using the term "Bub" anymore. Instead, Geary heard repeated references to "the Dancers." The tone of voice in such cases was always admiring or approving. He had been able to discourage but not eliminate the use of Bub to describe the spider-wolves, but now the spider-wolves' own actions had earned them the respectful name of Dancers.

Geary slumped back as he finished his message to Smythe, wishing that he could have grabbed a little more sleep before his responsibilities had called him back to the bridge.

"No rest for the weary?" Rione asked.

"Apparently not. Now what?"

"Our currently favorite Syndic CEO has finally decided to do us the kindness of communicating with us."

"That's just wonderful." Geary sat up straighter, blinking away fatigue. "How bad is it?"

"I haven't seen it yet. It's addressed to you. But it ought to be good," Rione remarked.

CEO Boyens looked much like he had when they had last seen him as they released their high-ranking prisoner with the war over. Then he had been appropriately solemn, but now Boyens smiled in the practiced, polished, and perceptibly insincere manner that must be part of the Syndicate Worlds' CEO-training pipeline. Then, as if realizing that his audience could read that gesture for what it was, Boyens tried to shift the smile to something approximating sincerity.

"Why do I feel like he's trying to pick me up in a bar?" Desjani asked.

"Is that what it looks like?" Geary said.

"Sort of. It never worked on me when I was buzzed, so it sure as hell isn't going to work when I'm sober. Are you trying to claim that nobody's ever hit on you in a bar?"

"I don't think I should answer that." He fell silent as Boyens began to speak in earnest tones.

"Admiral Geary, I am immensely grateful for your assistance in once again defending this star system against aggression by the enigma race. On behalf of the government of the Syndicate Worlds, I offer my thanks to you."

"Thanks to *you*," Desjani muttered. "Not to the Alliance or to this fleet, to *you*."

He might have missed that significant distinction if Tanya hadn't pointed it out, so now Geary listened even more critically as Boyens went on.

"Admiral, now that you've completed your work here, I will be happy to detach one of my mobile forces' units to escort you through Syndicate Worlds' space and back to Alliance space. I am certain that you cannot wait to return home."

Desjani laughed softly. "Don't let the door hit you on the way out, our friends and allies. I'd rather deal with the Kicks."

"Naturally," Boyens continued, "you'll want to proceed home via Prime in order to update the peace treaty to reflect current realities and share any information that would be of interest to the entire human race. If some of the ships with you are ambassadors of some sort, they will, of course, want to stop at Prime on their way to Alliance space. I have some business to conclude here, then will follow you, eager to learn everything that your explorations have contributed to human knowledge of the universe. For the people, Boyens, out."

That was simply too outrageous. Geary managed to keep his voice level as he hit the reply command. "Thank you for your offer," he began without any polite preamble. "The Alliance fleet is always prepared to repel aggression." Let Boyens, and his superiors at Prime, read anything they wanted into that. "However, our work here is not yet entirely complete. We have some discussions under way with local authorities." That would give Boyens something else to think about. "Just as your forces did not play any role in the defense of this star system, we will also not require any of your forces to assist in our movements. As you may have noticed, we are already ourselves escorting other ships to Alliance space and will choose our own path back. Our guests have expressed the wish to be escorted directly to Alliance authorities, and we will be honoring their wishes."

Rione stepped into the image beside Geary as smoothly as if the move had been practiced beforehand. "As you are aware, CEO Boyens, the peace treaty does not restrict the exact route we must use when traveling to and from the Midway Star System. Nor does it restrict our time here. As Emissary of the Alliance, I thank you for your offer of assistance and wish you a pleasant return journey to Prime. To the honor of our ancestors, Rione, out."

As the reply cut off, she turned an apologetic face to Geary. "You were done speaking to him, weren't you?"

"I certainly was."

One hour later, they received a message in which a gracious Iceni granted Geary free access to asteroids in the star system for mining, asking only that the Alliance auxiliaries coordinate their activity with the local "space-resource-extraction authorities."

Less than an hour after that, another message from the planet came in marked eyes only, private, for Admiral Geary. He went down to his stateroom to view it, wondering what this could concern.

The message was from General Drakon, this time sitting alone, looking ahead and speaking without any pretense. "I am asking a personal favor, Admiral Geary. I understand that you have no reason to grant that to a former enemy. However, the favor is not for me, but for one of my subordinates. Colonel Rogero is one of my most highly trusted and highly regarded officers. He has asked me to see if the attached message can be delivered to one of your subordinate officers. In light of his loyal service to me and as one professional to another, I am requesting that you forward the message to its intended recipient. In case any question arises, President Iceni is aware of this communication and the contents of the attached message and has no objections to either. I will answer any questions you have regarding this matter if you communicate them to me."

Drakon paused, his eyes looking outward as if he could actually see Geary. "I'm glad we never met in battle during the war, Admiral. I'm not at all sure I would have survived that experience, though I would have given you the fight of your life before it was over. For the people, Drakon, out."

Geary replayed that last part again, listening intently. General Drakon didn't put the enthusiastic lilt to the "for the people" phrase that Kommodor Marphissa had, but there was nonetheless something more than an automatic use of a meaningless phrase there. Geary thought he sensed a defiance, a determination, as if Drakon was actually willing to defend the ideals behind that saying, ideals long since forgotten by the Syndicate Worlds' government, if they had ever held any real substance at all to most Syndic leaders.

He turned back to the attachment. A message from one of the former Syndic officers to one of Geary's officers? He knew who it would be addressed to before he looked at it. Captain Bradamont.

There were difficult things he had to do as an officer, as a fleet commander, but reading a personal message between two people felt like one of the most unpleasant obligations he faced. Wincing inwardly, Geary opened the attachment, knowing that the fleet's firewalls and security software would have already checked it for dangerous content.

Colonel Rogero wore a uniform similar to General Drakon's. He seemed as straightforward as his general though speaking steadily as if reciting from a script or prepared speech. "For Captain Bradamont, commanding officer of the Alliance battle cruiser *Dragon*, this is Colonel Rogero, Midway ground forces. Much has happened in recent months."

Rogero provided a careful rundown of those events, giving details about activity not only here at Midway but also in some of the surrounding star systems. There had been fighting in many places, revolts and Syndic attempts to suppress rebellion. Midway had gotten heavily involved in those nearby star systems, plainly aiming for a leading role in… what? A small personal empire for Iceni and Drakon? Or, at the other extreme, a small alliance of free star systems? That last seemed very unlikely, but if it were true…

If only he knew more about Iceni and Drakon.

Rogero must have known that this message would be seen by people other than Bradamont. Drakon and Iceni must have known that, too. This was, then, not just a personal accommodation for Rogero but also a means to pass information to Geary under the cover of that.

Which also meant that Rogero's and Bradamont's personal feelings for each other were still being used by those in authority over them. Perhaps, to former Syndic CEOs like Drakon and Iceni, that was a matter of no consequence. But Geary felt a little unclean despite his own lack of involvement.

Colonel Rogero paused, his carefully controlled manner cracking. "Captain Bradamont... I must inform you that... my feelings will never change. That is why I must ask you to forget me, because it is impossible and can only harm you. I am now free of the forces that sought to use our feelings for their own purposes. I hope that, with the end of the war, you are free as well. But, if not, you may inform those people that I will provide no more reports. You can no longer serve them as a source of information. You have acted as a patriot and noble person at all times, and I will freely offer a detailed, official statement to anyone who questions your role over the last several years.

"Farewell, Captain Bradamont."

Geary sat back, one hand rubbing his forehead lightly. What Rogero had said confirmed what Bradamont had told him and what Lieutenant Iger had partially confirmed as well. As far as Geary knew, though, Iger wasn't aware that Bradamont was the officer who had been working for Alliance intelligence under the code name White Witch as part of a highly classified program. Once Iger saw this message, that particular rabbit would be out of the hat for certain.

"Captain Bradamont, I need to speak with you privately as soon as possible."

Her image appeared to him within minutes, standing at

attention. *Dragon* was close enough to *Dauntless* that only a little more than a light-second's delay affected their communications, a lag too small to notice.

"Captain Bradamont," Geary began, feeling awkward. "This is both a personal and a professional matter. Please sit down."

Bradamont sat stiffly, watching him warily. "Does this pertain to the matter we discussed some time ago?"

"Everything surrounding White Witch, yes." Geary offered her his comm pad, putting it on the arm of her seat and activating the message. "This message is for you, even though parts of it were also clearly intended for other people here."

She listened while he tried not to watch her reaction. Finally, Bradamont reached as if to turn off the pad, forgetting that her virtual presence couldn't do that, then withdrew her arm, her expression now revealing nothing. "Thank you, Admiral."

He shut it off. "Is there anything you want to tell me?"

"I've already informed you of the circumstances, Admiral."

"Do you have any wishes in this matter? At the very least, I can ensure that a reply is sent, in whatever form you choose."

"A reply." Bradamont shook her head. "What can I say? He's right. It must end. It has ended. Neither of us can be used anymore. The contents of that message will alert the fleet's intelligence personnel as to who I must be. I'll have to live with that. I've lived with worse things. I must live without him."

"I'm sorry."

"I know you are, Admiral. I don't know why this had to happen. I didn't ask for it. I know that you can understand."

"Is there anything I can do?"

Bradamont's smile was bitter. "Not even Black Jack can solve this matter, Admiral. Why the hell——" Bradamont stopped speaking. "Pardon me, sir."

"Forget it. I'm going to wait awhile before I forward this attachment to intelligence or show it to anyone else. If you want to talk, call me."

"Yes, Admiral." Bradamont came to attention again. "Thank you."

Barely half an hour later his hatch alert chimed. "Come in."

Rione entered, walking in as if she owned the place, went to a seat, and dropped into it. "I had a thought that I wished to share," she began.

He watched her warily, wondering why Rione seemed so casually cheerful. She hadn't acted that way since she had rejoined the fleet at the start of this mission. "And what would that be?"

"Wouldn't it be of great benefit to the Alliance to have an officer assigned to duty here long term? In this star system? What do you call it, a liaison officer?"

Now what was Rione up to? "A liaison officer. Left here."

"Right." Rione paused as if thinking. "Of course, that officer would have to be relatively senior given the importance of the assignment, and given the suspicions between our people and those here, it would be *very* helpful if she already had some sort of *liaison* among them."

"Liaison?"

"A personal relationship. Perhaps with one of their officers. I know that's a crazy idea, but——"

"How the hell did you break into my conferencing software this time?" Geary demanded.

"In any event," Rione continued, as if he hadn't spoken, "you'd have to find someone willing to accept official orders to remain here. Someone who knows the Syndics well enough to spot some of their tricks because even though these Syndics have changed their spots, they still doubtless play the same games."

"Official orders?" Was she actually helping?

"The Alliance needs someone to keep an eye on things," Rione said, studying her fingernails as she spoke. "Someone who can offer guidance to these people on proper military and governmental relationships. Someone who can perhaps suggest democratic reforms." She cocked her head sideways as if a thought had just occurred to her.

"Perhaps even a little advice on how to fight battles if the defenders of this star system needed it."

"You're suggesting the perfect solution to both my problem for offering support to this star system, and to Captain Bradamont's personal problem. Why?"

Rione frowned in thought. "It could be my inner compassionate nature asserting itself."

"It doesn't do that very often," Geary observed. "Especially not lately."

"Then maybe my inner bitch, which doesn't differ too much from my outer bitch, wants to ruin the plans of certain parties back in Alliance space." Rione met his eyes. "A fleet officer who communicated with the enemy after she was liberated from being a Syndic prisoner of war? Who passed information to the enemy? To an enemy officer for whom she had personal feelings? Think of the possibilities if a leak of that information was threatened."

Geary leaned toward her, his voice hardening as he spoke. "If you're aware of that much, then you also know that those communications were at the orders of military intelligence to pass false information to the Syndics."

"Yes, Admiral, I know that, too. I also know that people can be blackmailed, especially if the matter involved is classified so that those who actually know extenuating information aren't allowed to speak."

He sat back, wondering that he could still be shocked. "Someone is blackmailing Bradamont? You know that?"

"Yes. I do know," Rione replied in a low voice, her eyes on her fingernails again. "Or, rather, someone is prepared to blackmail her. It's all ready to go. Hints have been dropped to Bradamont, vague warnings of what might happen if certain things became widely known."

That explained some of the stress he had seen in Bradamont. "Why?"

"To force her to spy again, this time against someone other than the Syndics, someone who might occupy this very stateroom, and perhaps even to force her into actions that she would not otherwise ever agree to."

Geary had to pause awhile to absorb that, then to fight down the anger that arose inside him at the thought of such tactics. "Captain Bradamont was given command of *Dragon* before I was found."

Rione raised one eyebrow toward him. "Do you think that you're the only possible target of such spying and sabotage? The virtue of such a weapon put into place is that it can be employed against whatever target is deemed necessary. If you had never been found, and if Admiral Bloch had lived, he would have been the target."

"And what would have happened to the weapon?"

"Weapons, by their nature," Rione said, "are expendable." Her tone of voice, flat and hard, made it clear what she thought of such an approach.

"If I judge Bradamont right, she wouldn't give in to that blackmail," Geary said.

"And you'd lose a battle cruiser commander."

"One way or the other." Recalled by the government, ordered relieved of command by fleet staff until the "allegations" were investigated, charges leaked to the media so that her name was dragged through the mud, perhaps even driven to an "honorable" suicide by the contempt and anger of her fellow officers. "You're not just helping Captain Bradamont's love life. You're saving her life and her honor."

"Don't be ridiculous," Rione said. "I'm protecting the Alliance and my own interests. Any collateral impact on this Bradamont person is purely coincidental."

"Why didn't you tell me about this before?"

"For whatever reason, those involved didn't try to employ her before you left Varandal. Once we left Alliance space, there couldn't have been any attempt to blackmail her into cooperation without my knowledge."

That was important information. "Some of these people are within the fleet?"

"I don't know for certain. I do know that I haven't heard from them. You... have guessed that I'm being blackmailed to do certain things, and that I'm doing them only to the extent I must and not in any way that will actually threaten you or the Alliance. Draw your own conclusions. If this Bradamont had received the blackmail threat while we were outside of Alliance space, I would have known, and you would have heard about it then. Contrary to popular belief, there are methods that I will not countenance."

He couldn't help smiling at her. "And, contrary to popular belief, you do have a heart."

"That is a lie, Admiral. I would thank you not to spread it though I doubt anyone would believe you if you tried." Rione stood up. "If my husband recovers, it will be thanks to you. Do you think me so cold that I would not be aware of the debt I owe you for that? Call Bradamont, offer her the position. I guarantee you that both of the Emissaries of the Alliance government will approve of the posting of a liaison officer here, which truly is in the interests of the Alliance."

She left without saying anything else, the hatch sealing in her wake.

Geary thought about it for another five minutes, then reached for his comm panel. "Captain Bradamont. I must speak with you privately again." He would make the offer, and if she accepted, everyone would win. Everyone except those who sought to use blackmail, and they never deserved to win.

It took a while, but this time Boyens responded to their message. His smile was still present and not quite sincere-looking, but also definitely strained. "I am very sorry to have to remind Admiral Geary and the representatives of the Alliance government that the treaty between your government and the government of the Syndicate Worlds authorizes *your* ships to travel to and from Midway Star System. It does not authorize or allow the movement of ships belonging to other governments or… species. There is an alien warship with you. That is not an Alliance vessel, and it is not covered by the treaty. In light of my responsibilities as a citizen of the Syndicate Worlds, I must insist that you bring any craft belonging to anyone other than the Alliance to Prime, where my government can decide on the appropriate disposition of those craft.

"My flotilla will remain in place near the hypernet gate. It would be a tragedy if something should happen to that gate as a result of negligence or aggression.

"For the people, Boyens, out."

"Does he actually think we'd hand over the spider-wolf delegation and the bear-cow superbattleship to the Syndicate Worlds?" Charban asked with astonishment.

"It's called diplomacy," Rione said. "He's making an outrageous demand hoping that we will compromise with a deal that still grants the Syndicate Worlds something. And, as I thought, he is trying to hold the hypernet gate here hostage to our giving in to his demands. Admiral, I am not a specialist in space law, but am I correct in assuming that the bear-cow superbattleship is now the property of the Alliance?"

"You are correct," Geary said. "We captured it by force of arms. It is ours. We've got a crew aboard it. And she has a name. *Invincible*."

"And is *Invincible* different from the other ships of this fleet in any way other than construction?"

"No. I give orders, and the officer in command of *Invincible*, Admiral Lagemann, obeys those orders. *Invincible* was part of our formation during the battle, taking damage alongside the other ships."

"Excellent," Rione said. "And the ships of the spider-wolves are not ours. In no way are they ours. If I may, Admiral, I will be happy to send an official reply to CEO Boyens and the Syndicate Worlds' government regarding the latest proposition we have received."

"Feel free," Geary said. "I'm afraid my own diplomatic skills aren't up to the task of answering that message in the appropriate manner."

Rione sounded completely professional and looked completely immovable as she sent the reply. "Unfortunately, CEO Boyens, we are not in a position to comply with your request regarding the six ships that are accompanying us back to Alliance space. The inhabitants of those craft are not under our control, and we cannot compel them on your behalf or anyone else's. They have expressed the wish to remain with our fleet, and we have been more than happy to accede to that request. However"—and here Rione smiled so coldly that Geary felt a chill—"we have promised to defend them. If anyone else should attempt to compel them or force them to take any actions, we will be forced by our commitments and our honor to defend them to the limits of our abilities, taking *any* action necessary to ensure they remain safe.

"As for the craft you refer to as an 'alien warship,' I must inform you that this warship is in fact a vessel of this fleet, named the *Invincible*, crewed by members of the Alliance military forces and responding to commands by Admiral Geary. It is not legally different in any way from any other warship in this fleet. Naturally, any demand that we *surrender* an Alliance warship to control of the Syndicate Worlds' government is beyond absurd, contrary to the peace treaty governing your actions and ours, and cannot be taken seriously."

"We are grateful that you are concerned for the physical security of the hypernet gate here. Especially since the authorities in this star system have granted the Alliance partial ownership of that gate. Since it is now partially Alliance property, any damage inflicted upon it would constitute an attack on the Alliance, bringing on a state of war between the Alliance and whichever government owned the warships that launched such an attack.

"I once again wish you a pleasant journey back to Prime. Please do not linger in this star system on our account, as we would find it difficult to leave if you remained here. To the honor of our ancestors, Rione, out."

Geary stared at Rione. "They gave us part of the hypernet gate? Iceni and Drakon?"

"I suggested it," Rione said with more than a trace of smugness, "pointing out the benefits that would have for them as well as us, and they have already agreed."

"I'm glad you're on our side, Emissary Rione."

"Iceni and Drakon have definitely been expanding their influence outside this star system," Lieutenant Iger reported. "There have even been offensive operations despite their limited military capability. If that capability grows, they may actually attempt to expand their control by conquest of neighboring star systems."

"But Syndic authority in those neighboring star systems is either going or gone," Geary said. "There has been major fighting in some of them. This star system appears to be the most stable in the region. Have you found evidence that repressive Syndic practices are being used by the new regime at Midway?"

Iger made a frustrated gesture. "It's hard to tell, Admiral. Almost everything we know has to be drawn from the sources we can tap remotely, like news-media broadcasts, and those things are controllable. A dictatorial regime can ensure that nothing gets reported unless they want it to be reported. That said, there is a lot more media activity than normal for a Syndic-controlled star system. Since the last time we were here, there are many more media organizations and individuals reporting on events and offering opinions. That argues for a loosening of controls over society. But that could also be camouflage, a smoke screen of apparently independent voices to produce the impression of a freer society."

"Have you found out anything more about the records of either Iceni or Drakon?"

"Just fragmentary mentions in our database, Admiral. Drakon has been a front-line ground-forces officer, so we have a number of appearances of his name in intercepted communications, but the last of those was a few years ago. After that, there is no mention of him among forces fighting us, so the assessment in our files was that he had either died or committed some political offense and been internally exiled or imprisoned in a Syndic labor camp."

Iger's words reminded Geary of something. "Boyens told us that he had been internally exiled to the flotilla guarding Midway. He said Midway was where people in disfavor were sent because it was so far from any opportunity to influence events elsewhere or regain favor with Syndicate rulers."

"Yes, sir. That may well be why Drakon is here, but if so, we don't know why he was exiled."

"And Iceni?"

"Nothing except two citations of her while she was commanding Syndicate Worlds' flotillas. She seems to have spent most of her time in other kinds of assignments, though."

"But she was also sent to Midway." Geary nodded as much to himself as to Lieutenant Iger, thinking of how Iceni had refused evacuation during the first enigma attack, instead staying among those of her subordinates and the civil population who couldn't be withdrawn before the attack. With so little known of her, he had to regard that act of unSyndic-like concern for those working for her as a sign of Iceni's nature. "Has Captain Bradamont been briefed on everything as I directed?"

"Yes, sir," Iger replied, his discomfort clear. "Admiral, if Captain Bradamont was involved in compartmented intelligence activity under the White Witch code name…" He trailed off, searching for the right words.

"I know about that," Geary said. "Since she has served as a source before this, intelligence surely won't object to her in a post where she can report on what is actually happening in this star system."

"That… is true, sir, but I do feel obligated to warn you that the intelligence staff at fleet headquarters may not agree with your decision."

"Thank you, Lieutenant. I'm sure if they disapprove, they'll let me know." They couldn't do that until the fleet returned to Alliance space, of course, and not until various reports had made their way to various authorities.

Having covered all of his bases internally, and having done what checking he could on the nature of Iceni, Drakon, and their regime here, it was time to bring up two critical matters with the rulers of Midway.

Geary composed himself, then activated the message transmission.

"President Iceni, General Drakon, I have two matters I need to place before you," Geary said in his most formal voice. He was seated at the nicest desk *Dauntless* offered, wearing his best uniform, his appearance having been approved by Tanya Desjani only after she had inspected him as carefully as if he were a new recruit and she a boot-camp drill instructor.

"First of all, President Iceni, I have to inform you that while in space controlled by the enigma race, we were able to locate and free some humans who had been kept prisoner by the enigmas, apparently for study. All of them, except those born in captivity, originated from Syndicate Worlds' colonies or ships. All have been checked as thoroughly as possible, and no signs of biological or other contamination or threat has been found." It had been hard to make the decision to tell Iceni and Drakon about those people, but in the end he could not justify keeping from their homes people who had been denied that comfort by imprisonment for too long.

Geary took a deep breath. "It is important for me to emphasize that none of them know anything about the enigmas. They were sealed inside an asteroid and never even saw any of their captors. They can tell no one anything about the enigmas. They have all been impacted mentally, physically, and emotionally by their long imprisonment.

Given their condition, I intend taking the majority of them back to Alliance space, where I can arrange care and transport back to their home star systems elsewhere in the Syndicate Worlds. However, three of the prisoners say they or their parents came from Taroa, and fifteen others say they came from this star system. Those eighteen wish to return home now. We want to accommodate those wishes, but I desire first to know whatever else you can tell me about conditions at Taroa, and second to know your intentions toward the fifteen who come from Midway. I feel an obligation to see that they are treated well now that they have been freed."

He paused. "The second matter concerns formalizing our relationship with the new government of Midway. I am proposing to assign a senior Alliance officer here to represent the Alliance, to make plain our commitment to your star system, and to render whatever advice or assistance you might ask for in matters of defense and in your transition to a freer form of government. The officer whom I propose to assign here is Captain Bradamont, who has been serving as commanding officer of the battle cruiser *Dragon*. She is an excellent officer, and because she was at one point a prisoner of war, she has had some prior contact with Syndicate Worlds' officers and can work with them. Captain Bradamont has already agreed to this official posting, but I require your consent for such an assignment, which I think will be to the benefit of everyone involved. The emissaries of the Alliance government accompanying this fleet have already approved the posting of Captain Bradamont here, so all we require is the acceptance of your government.

"I await your reply on both of these matters. To the honor of our ancestors, Geary, out."

He didn't often wish that he were present when a message was received at the other end, but this time he did think it would be interesting to watch the reactions of Iceni and Drakon.

As for how Colonel Rogero might react…

By the time they heard back from CEO Boyens again, the Alliance auxiliaries were busy mining raw materials off several large asteroids and converting the raw materials into new fuel cells and parts almost as fast as they could be dumped into the bunkers. The Alliance fleet was concentrated into a single formation, swinging in orbit about the star Midway, as everyone once again focused on repairs as a result of battle damage or systems simply wearing out as they exceeded their designed life spans.

Geary had been going over the reports on his battleships. He hadn't lost any battleships, but the line between "lost" and "beat to hell" seemed to be growing thinner and thinner. Some of his battleships were so badly hit that they were barely combat capable, and a few others shouldn't really be risked in combat again until they could get major repair work in a fleet dock.

And then there was *Invincible*, which though very hard to kill, certainly deserved the term "threat magnet." Until he got that former bear-cow superbattleship back to Alliance space it would attract every possible attacker, all eager to find out what bear-cow technology might be learned from the ship. He had a nasty suspicion that the Syndic government itself might try something with their now-very-limited resources, given the unparalleled value of *Invincible* to anyone who could get their hands on her.

The spider-wolves seemed more than capable of looking out for themselves, but accidents could happen, and an encounter with a drifting mine or similar hazard might be very hard to explain when conversations were still limited to simple concepts. And from experience and the reports about star systems near Midway, some of the people in Syndic space who were inheriting pieces of the former Syndic military as the Syndicate Worlds fell apart were far from trustworthy or predictable in what they might do. A group of fanatics might try a surprise attack, especially since Geary couldn't keep the spider-wolf ships safely nestled within a screen of his own warships. The spider-wolves, the Dancers, went where they wanted to go.

All of which meant that Geary wasn't in a particularly receptive mood when the latest message from Boyens came in.

CEO Boyens didn't seem to be in a particularly receptive mood, either. He was openly glaring now, not trying to hide his unhappiness, not bothering with false gestures of camaraderie. "I am unfortunately constrained by the peace treaty that exists between the Syndicate Worlds and the Alliance, though it seems only the Syndicate Worlds is truly interested in honoring the letter and spirit of that treaty. Therefore, I cannot take the actions I wish to take to defend the Syndicate Worlds and its citizens from the overbearing arrogance of a foreign military force."

Geary had asked Desjani to view this one with him and the emissaries, and she seemed about to collapse from mirth. "Oh, feel free to try to defend it against us. *Please* try."

"Your journey home may not be as smooth as you anticipate," Boyens continued. "Since you have declined my offers of assistance, I won't bother providing any information I may have access to that might smooth your trip. However, I will pass on one item that I think you will find of great interest."

Boyens paused, plainly enjoying the anticipation he expected his audience to feel when they viewed this message. "You will doubtless be overjoyed to learn that one of your comrades, an officer, did not die as you thought during one of the battles in the Syndicate Worlds' home star system."

Michael? Is my grandnephew still alive? Did he survive the destruction of Repulse? Geary didn't know whether his heart had truly stopped for a moment or if he had imagined feeling such a thing.

He felt pressure and looked down to see that Tanya had reached across and tightly gripped one of his hands, her expression anxious.

And then CEO Boyens, who might have guessed the sort of hopes his statement had raised, smiled. "Yes, more than one officer who was thought to have died in that battle still lives and is being sent home to the Alliance as we speak. Their ship left Prime before my flotilla came here."

Wait a minute…

"Why would he be telling us good news?" Desjani muttered, her grip tightening on Geary's hand as she voiced his own dawning suspicion.

Rione was by his other side, her face harsh. "More than *one* officer?"

"Do you know who he means?" Geary asked.

"I wish you an interesting journey back to Alliance space," Boyens said. "And I guarantee you will find interesting things happening in the Alliance upon your return. For the people, Boyens, out."

Desjani uttered a curse under her breath.

"The new Executive Council of the Syndicate Worlds," Rione said, her voice hard, "is interfering in Alliance space. Just like the old Executive Council before the war began."

"What are they doing?" Geary asked.

"Your guess is as good as mine. Senator Navarro provided me with some of his suspicions before we left. He suspected Syndic meddling in Alliance politics, economic sabotage, and stirring up dissent wherever possible. Navarro had no proof, but in his willingness to bait you, CEO Boyens has given us the clearest confirmation about what the remnants of the Syndicate Worlds are up to. The Syndics have lost the war, but they don't intend to let the Alliance enjoy the peace."

"Which officer survived?" Geary asked again.

"Perhaps the one you hope for," Rione answered obliquely, "but there have been rumors that some of the executions we saw were faked."

"Bloch?" Desjani demanded, shocked into speaking to Rione. "Admiral Bloch?"

"I have no more idea of the answer than you do. But it was someone that Boyens expected to cause trouble for us. Perhaps he's just baiting us, trying to create as much anxiety in us as possible. Admiral, you know how shaky the Alliance is in the aftermath of the war. The war broke the Syndics, and it nearly broke us. There are those who for their own reasons would not hesitate to add a small push as the Alliance teeters on the edge of the abyss. How quickly can we get home?"

"I suspect not as fast as we thought," Geary said. Was Admiral Bloch really still alive? There had been Alliance senators who had backed Bloch in the past, either through believing he was right or out of personal ambition. Or was Boyens just playing on their worst fears? "We can't leave here without necessary repairs or we might lose more ships on the way home. And once we start back, Boyens implied that some roadblocks have been thrown up."

"They want *Invincible*," Desjani said. "They might want it badly enough to try something while we're on our way back. And we need to make sure the Dancers don't suffer any 'accidents' while they're in space within Syndic reach."

A playing board that already had too many players, many of them hidden, had just acquired more pieces, which might upset a lot of strategies and possibly the Alliance itself.

AUTHOR'S NOTE

There have been a few changes around here.

CAPTAIN TANYA DESJANI

Way back in the twentieth century (the late 1960s to be exact), I lived for a few years on Midway Island in the center of the Pacific Ocean. In those days satellite TV was, well, science fiction. The only TV we had on the island came from a single local station that broadcast old programs for a few hours a day. Even white sand beaches, a beautiful lagoon protected by a coral reef, and the antics of the gooney birds wear thin at times. When that happened, I could read, and most of what I read in those days was history.

But there was another diversion available at the base movie theater. On Saturdays and Sundays, it would show matinees consisting of a one-hour TV show like *Mission: Impossible* or *The Big Valley*, and a one-hour episode of *Star Trek* (the original series, of course). While the rest of the world watched Kirk, Spock, and McCoy on their small

TV sets, I got to see their adventures on the big screen.

When I started writing I found that those influences showed up in my stories. History offered many ideas, and the original *Star Trek* had shown me how SF could be exciting, thought-provoking, and fun. It had also impressed upon me how important the characters were. The spaceships were cool, but the stories wouldn't have been the same without people in them whose actions mattered and who tried their best even against seemingly impossible odds.

A lot of other things went into the Lost Fleet series. At its core lie those basic influences, but when a writer creates characters they can start influencing the story, telling you what they would and wouldn't do, telling you they would make a different decision than you had originally planned. As I've told Black Jack's story, he has surprised me more than once. He has found friends and allies, overcome a wide variety of enemies, and developed a very close relationship with a certain battle cruiser captain. When the opportunity arose to take him to new places and face new challenges, I was glad to carry on Geary's story in the Beyond the Frontier series.

While I wrote about Black Jack Geary, I also wrote about his opponents, and foremost among those foes has been the Syndicate Worlds. In every challenge that he's faced, Geary has done his best to hold to his duty, to simple truths, and to real honor grounded in how he acts. Against that, the Syndics have followed practices opposed to all that Geary believes in. Those characters could have been simple: people who were evil because they were evil. But that would have shortchanged the story because no enemy is monolithic, no foe is unvarying from person to person, with every man and woman marching in lockstep. The people of the Syndicate Worlds are human. Some are committed to the system that gives them power or have vested all of their faith in believing that only this system can maintain order. Others see the flaws in the system and work against it. Yet others have been turned against the system by the injustices they see or personally experience.

Many readers asked to know more about the Syndics, so I wanted to show this other side of the Lost Fleet saga. What about the Syndics who had believed their system was the best, until it failed spectacularly, with the Alliance triumphant? What about those who had long ago stopped believing in that system but saw no alternative while war still raged? The Syndicate empire is falling apart, the central government trying to hold on to as many star systems as it can while revolt and rebellion break out. And if revolution succeeds, what replaces the old way of doing things?

When the Alliance fleet returns to Midway near the end of *Invincible*, it discovers that the Syndicate Worlds is no longer in control. There has been fighting on the inhabited world and in space, and the two leaders of the star system now call themselves president and general. *The Lost Stars: Tarnished Knight* tells the story of the revolt at Midway. CEOs Gwen Iceni and Artur Drakon have had enough of the Syndic way of doing things, but it's the only way they know. They can't trust each other, they can't trust *anyone*, because that is how politics and everything else works in the Syndicate Worlds. But Iceni and Drakon need each other as they fight to not only defend their own star system but also carry the battle to neighboring star systems wracked by internal fighting and Syndic counterattacks. Two people who have long since ceased trusting in anything have to find something to believe in. If they can live long enough.

It has been great to see how well the Lost Fleet saga has been received by readers. There is no better reward for a writer than for people to want to read the stories he creates. In turn, I want to offer more to readers, more stories about more parts of the Lost Fleet universe. The Lost Stars series takes us to a part of that universe where a lot is happening, where new characters face tremendous challenges and the shadow of Black Jack looms large.

The Lost Stars: Tarnished Knight is coming October 2012 from Titan Books.

ACKNOWLEDGMENTS

I remain indebted to my agent, Joshua Bilmes, for his ever-inspired suggestions and assistance, and to my editor, Anne Sowards, for her support and editing. I've been well looked after by Katherine Sherbo and Brady McReynolds at the Berkley Publishing Group as well. Thanks also to Catherine Asaro, Robert Chase, J. G. (Huck) Huckenpohler, Simcha Kuritzky, Michael LaViolette, Aly Parsons, Bud Sparhawk, and Constance A. Warner for their suggestions, comments, and recommendations. Thanks also to Charles Petit and to "the remoras" (a. k. a. Alex and Daniel) for an important suggestion regarding the most essential achievement of human technology.

ABOUT THE AUTHOR

John G. Hemry is a retired US Navy officer and the author, under the pen name Jack Campbell, of the *New York Times* national bestselling *Lost Fleet* series (*Dauntless, Fearless, Courageous, Valiant, Relentless,* and *Victorious*) and the follow-on series *Beyond the Frontier.* Next up is the second new follow-on series *The Lost Stars,* set on a former enemy world in *The Lost Fleet* universe. Under his own name, John is also the author of the *JAG in Space* series and the recently reissued *Stark's War* series. His short fiction has appeared in places as varied as the last Chicks in Chainmail anthology (*Turn the Other Chick*) and *Analog* magazine (which published his Nebula Award-nominated story 'Small Moments in Time' as well as most recently 'Betty Knox and Dictionary Jones in the Mystery of the Missing Teenage Anachronisms' in the March 2011 issue). His humorous short story 'As You Know Bob' was selected for *Year's Best SF 13*. John's nonfiction has appeared in *Analog* and *Artemis* magazines as well as BenBella books on *Charmed*, *Star Wars*, and *Superman*, and in the *Legion of Superheroes* anthology *Teenagers from the Future*. John had the opportunity to live on Midway Island for a while during the 1960s, then later attended the US Naval Academy. He served in a variety of jobs including gunnery officer and navigator on a destroyer, with an amphibious squadron, and at the Navy's anti-terrorism center. After retiring from the US Navy and settling in Maryland, John began writing. He lives with his long-suffering wife (the incomparable S) and three great kids. His daughter and two sons are diagnosed on the autistic spectrum.

STARK'S WAR

by Jack Campbell (writing as John G. Hemry)

STARK'S WAR
STARK'S COMMAND
STARK'S CRUSADE

The USA reigns over Earth as the last surviving superpower. To build a
society free of American influence, foreign countries have inhabited the
moon. Under orders from the US military, Sergeant Ethan Stark and his
squadron must engage in a brutal battle to wrest control of Earth's satellite.
Up against a desperate enemy in an airless atmosphere, ensuring his team's
survival means choosing which orders to obey and which to ignore.

"High caliber military science fiction ... non-stop action
and likable characters." – *Midwest Book Review*

"A gripping tale of military science fiction, in the tradition of
Heinlein's *Starship Troopers* and Haldeman's *Forever War*. It serves as
both a cautionary fable and a science fiction adventure, doing dual
purpose and succeeding on both levels." – *Absolute Magnitude*

"Hemry has a solid sense of military thinking and lunar fighting
... I really liked this series." – *Philadelphia Weekly Press*

JAG IN SPACE

by Jack Campbell (writing as John G. Hemry):

A JUST DETERMINATION
BURDEN OF PROOF
RULE OF EVIDENCE
AGAINST ALL ENEMIES

Equipped with the latest weaponry, and carrying more than two hundred sailors, the orbiting warship, *USS Michaelson*, is armored against the hazards of space and the threats posed in the vast nothing between planets. But who will protect her from the threats within?

He is Ensign Paul Sinclair, assigned to the *USS Michaelson* as the ship's lone legal officer—a designation that carries grave consequences as he soon learns that the struggle for justice among the stars is a never-ending fight…

"First-rate military SF…Hemry's series continues to offer outstanding suspense, realism and characterization." – *Booklist*

"The legal aspects are brilliantly intertwined within a fantastic military science fiction drama." – *Midwest Book Review*

"Hemry's decision to wed courtroom drama to military SF has captured lightning in a bottle. He builds the story's suspense expertly." – SF Reviews

FOR MORE FANTASTIC FICTION FROM TITAN BOOKS
CHECK OUT OUR WEBSITE: WWW.TITANBOOKS.COM

NOVELS BASED ON BESTSELLING VIDEO GAMES

BioShock: Rapture by John Shirley

Crysis: Legion by Peter Watts

Darksiders: The Abomination Vault by Ari Marmell

Dead Space: Martyr by B. K. Evenson
Dead Space: Catalyst by B. K. Evenson (July 2012)

Deus Ex: The Icarus Effect by James Swallow

Dragon Age: The Stolen Throne by David Gaider
Dragon Age: The Calling by David Gaider
Dragon Age: Asunder by David Gaider

God of War by Matthew Stover and Robert E. Vardeman

An Elder Scrolls Novel: The Infernal City by Greg Keyes
An Elder Scrolls Novel: Lord of Souls by Greg Keyes

Homefront: The Voice of Freedom
by John Milius and Raymond Benson

RuneScape: Betrayal at Falador by T.S. Church
RuneScape: Return to Canifis by T.S. Church
RuneScape: Legacy of Blood by T.S. Church (June 2012)

Star Wars: The Force Unleashed by Sean Williams
Star Wars: The Force Unleashed II by Sean Williams
Star Wars: The Old Republic: Fatal Alliance by Sean Williams
Star Wars: The Old Republic: Deceived by Paul S. Kemp
Star Wars: The Old Republic: Revan by Drew Karpyshyn

Uncharted: The Fourth Labyrinth by Christopher Golden

WWW.TITANBOOKS.COM

MORE FANTASTIC FICTION FROM TITAN BOOKS

NOVELS BASED ON HIT TV SHOWS AND MOVIES

Angel of Vengeance: The Story Which Inspired the TV Show "Moonlight"
by Trevor O. Munson

The Cabin in the Woods: The Official Movie Novelization by Tim Lebbon

The Dark Knight Rises: The Official Movie Novelization by Greg Cox

Spartacus: Swords and Ashes by J.M. Clements
Spartacus: Morituri by Paul Kearney (August 2012)

Supernatural: Heart of the Dragon by Keith R.A. DeCandido
Supernatural: The Unholy Cause by Joe Schreiber
Supernatural: War of the Sons by Rebecca Dessertine & David Reed
Supernatural: One Year Gone by Rebecca Dessertine
Supernatural: Coyote's Kiss by Christa Faust
Supernatural: Night Terror by John Passarella
Supernatural: Rite of Passage by John Passarella (August 2012)

Transformers: Dark of the Moon by Peter David
Transformers: Exodus by Alex Irvine
Transformers: Exiles by Alex Irvine

WWW.TITANBOOKS.COM